LORDS AND LEMURS

LORDS
AND LEMURS

Mad Scientists,
Kings with Spears, and
the Survival of
Diversity in Madagascar

ALISON JOLLY

HOUGHTON MIFFLIN COMPANY
BOSTON • NEW YORK
2004

Visit our Web site: www.houghtonmifflinbooks.com.

Library of Congress Cataloging-in-Publication Data
is available.
ISBN-13: 978-0-618-36751-1
ISBN-10: 0-618-36751-9

Printed in the United States of America

Book design by Victoria Hartman

MP 10 9 8 7 6 5 4 3 2 1

Contents

ᧄᖳᖳᖳᧄ

Acknowledgments

I thank the people, animals, and plants of Berenty, with a few exceptions for zebu-flies and the lover-of-men liana. I thank the de Heaulme family for their care of land, lemurs, people, and visiting scientists. I thank everyone who told me their lives, most especially the Tandroy who explained their pride in their traditions, and invited me to share. I thank the book's readers, particularly Harry Foster, editor exemplary, Sarah Hrdy, a primatologist who understands people, John Parry, enthusiast of nature reserves for human wonder, as well as two anonymous reviewers. I thank all Berenty volunteers for their help and enthusiasm, whether students or Earthwatchers. Earthwatch, Wildlife Trust, Sigma Xi, and the National Science Foundation funded parts of the Berenty work.

I thank our children. Margaretta inspires me with her knowledge of the art of life-writing. Susie makes me realize how much I omit of the warp of women's lives (let alone those who call themselves queer) while I tell the woof of men's politics. (Of course it is vice versa for the lemurs, where politics are female.) Arthur urges me to sharpen both the adventures and the wit. Richard B. throws life-lines to pull me out of the toothed vortex of the computer when it threatens to chew me into a parcel of screaming electrons.

I thank my husband Richard for everything.

A Note on Malagasy Names

Malagasy has phonetic spelling. Most vowels are pronounced as they are in French: *a* as in alms, *e* as in fête, *i* like the *ee* in feet. However, *o* is like the *oo* in moose, and *ao* is pronounced *o* as in boat. The last syllable of a name is almost silent to Western ears. The stress is on the penult or antepenult.

Lahivano (La-i-VAN'), Leader-of-Men
Rasamimanana (Ras'-mi-MAN-an'), Everyone-Shares-Riches
Rehomaha (Re-oo-MA'), Abandoned
Rekanoky (Re-ka-NOOK') (Rekanoky declines to offer a translation)
Tsiaketraky (Tsi-a-KE-trak'), Cannot-Be-Thrown-to-Earth
Tsiminono (Tsi-mi-NOON'), Never-Suckled
Valiotaky (Va-li-OO-tak'), Troubled-by-Others'-Talk (a child whose
    parents are quarreling)

Names of people from the plateau begin with Ra (Sir, Madame) or Andriana (Lord, Lady). Tandroy names often skip the prefixes. French colonial law demanded that everyone have a first name taken from the calendar of saints, but many people now use just one name. Three of the women I interviewed gave me only their French name. I give two names in the text for any speaker who still uses two.

Customs change, of course. In this generation, Philibert Tsimamandro (Tsi-ma-MANDR'), the Tandroy anthropologist, has kept his father's surname in the Western manner. His father's personal name, however, was Tsimamandro (The Unexpected). The father's mother was a very lazy woman who sometimes slept as late as six A.M. before beginning her day's work, so the grandfather thought it an unexpected surprise when she gave birth to a fine healthy son.

Manichaean divisions into good against bad
are simply wrong.

— Roland Ramahatra

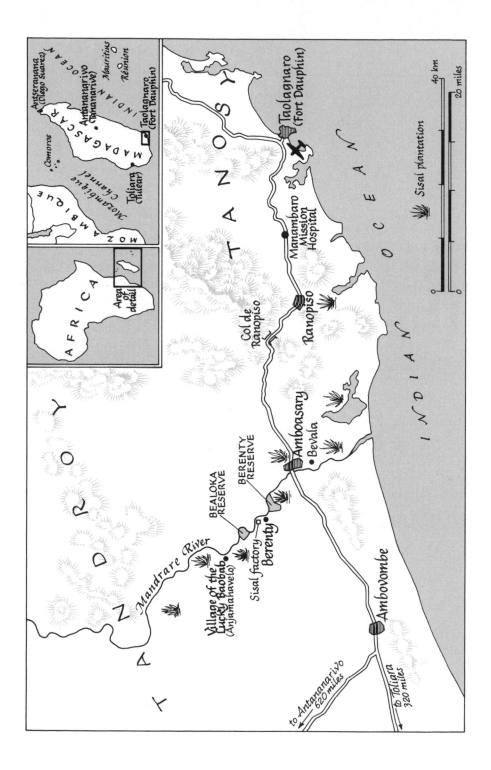

Antseranana (Diego Suarez)
INDIAN OCEAN
Mauritius
Réunion
Antananarivo (Tananarive)
MADAGASCAR
Taolagnaro, (Fort Dauphin)
Comoros
Mozambique Channel
Toliara (Tuléar)

AFRICA
Area of detail

ANOSY
Taolagnaro (Fort Dauphin)
Manambaro Mission Hospital
Col de Ranopiso
Ranopiso
INDIAN OCEAN
Sisal plantation

ANDROY
Amboasary
Bevala
BERENTY RESERVE
BEALOKA RESERVE
Berenty
Sisal factory
Mandrare River
Village of the Lucky Baobab (Anjamahavelo)
Ambovombe
to Antananarivo 620 miles
to Toliara 320 miles

40 km
20 miles
0
0

1

Lemurs Just Behind Their Houses

Madagascar is sometimes called the Island at the End of the Earth. Even within Madagascar there is an especially far-off place, the extreme south: extreme in its distance, extreme in its parching climate, extreme in the violent reputation of its people.

If ever you visit Madagascar, you may well come here. Among its spiny deserts lies a nature reserve called Berenty — a tiny place, but in its own way a microcosm of the world. At Berenty, tourists in Tilley hats and Gucci knapsacks stay side by side with people who are well off if they own a second shirt. The tourists do not even need to lock their bungalow doors. They had better shut the windows, though, or they may find a troop of ringtailed lemurs inside foraging for Coke and bananas. If twenty lemurs promenade toward your living room television screen, and the sunlight haloes black-and-white ringed tails like swaying upraised question marks, that is Berenty. If you see a group of white sifaka leap between trees in aerial ballet or bounce over the ground with flailing arms, that is Berenty. In fact, it is likely to be Berenty's parking lot, while the cameraman ties himself in knots to frame out the human side of the story.

Most visitors to Berenty spend a fascinated hour in the Museum of Androy. They stand on tiptoe to stare into the roof of a tiny house that once belonged to a woman of the Tandroy tribe, the People of the Thorns. They gawk at photos of a chieftain's funeral. They sometimes giggle at sacred talismans made of cow's horns and crocodile teeth. Meanwhile, in villages not five miles away, people live in just such houses, conjure with just such talismans. When a clan elder dies, zebu cattle stampede through the village amid gunfire and dancing and merrymaking and sex, all the way to the grand climax, when young men spear a whole herd of zebu to send their ancestor fittingly into the afterlife.

I do know a lot about ringtailed lemurs. As for people, all I can tell you is what they chose to tell me. Many of the tales told here come from single witnesses: stories, not history. The stories pass through slavery and colonialism, nationalism, socialism, and the neocolonialism of the World Bank. I make few judgments about these isms, except to quote Dr. Roland Ramahatra as he stood at his father's bedside: "Manichean divisions into good against bad are simply wrong." Berenty's real history is childbirth and marriage and bitter imprisonment. There are spear fights and stink fights and tombs adorned with the skulls of sacrificed cattle. You meet He-Who-Cannot-Be-Thrown-to-Earth and He-Who-Never-Suckled, Robin the English slave boy, Alison the American, and Hanta with her degree from Moscow. And, of course, Frightful Fan and Cream Puff.

Above all you meet a family tenacious in luxury and in disaster: the Lords of the Helm, feudal leaders who keep their pact with the Tandroy in a globalizing world.

The first time I saw Berenty, everyone else came in their own airplane. I turned up in my Land Rover unannounced. I had bucketed over five hundred miles of so-called road in less than a week, with no illusions that there would be a telephone. I'd already explored forest lands in many parts of the island continent and would not have gone to Berenty at all — except that so many people told me, "You must visit the de Heaulme family. They have lemurs just behind their houses."

Lemurs in the backyard sounded grim. Miserable captives with cords around their waists, I supposed. Still, they might be worth a detour on the way to discovering a wild paradise where I might finally settle to study the private lives of lemurs, the animals that most resemble our own ancestors of fifty million years ago. I was twenty-five years old, with a brand-new Ph.D. and a Sputnik-era research grant to swell my pride. I thought I knew everything, or at least enough to take on the whole of Madagascar.

"What's that strange name?" I asked my friends. "De Heaulme? An *H* that separates the two words, then *e-a-u*, like *eau* for water? Rhymes with Stockholm? Got it. Okay, when I reach the extreme south I'll go have a look-see."

I headed south along with Preston Boggess, a Yale undergraduate who was helping me look for a site for my lemur study. We traveled from peak-roofed brick towns surrounded by rice paddies to high, windswept plains studded with monolithic granite mountains, to hardscrabble villages of mud huts, and, finally, to tiny plank dwellings where a man could stand straight only beneath the ridgepole and must bend double to crawl out the door — houses scarcely distinguishable from chicken coops to my naive eyes. All along the way, herds of humped, long-horned zebu blocked the corrugated track, and dogs, chickens, and guinea fowl lay in the road taking dust baths.

The Land Rover reached a dropoff. The road dipped to the wide plain of the Mandrare River. Below lay sisal. Endless geometrical rows of spear-tipped leaves marched down to the river, which glinted like a basking snake in a valley beaten colorless by the heat of noon. Forty kilometers beyond, the land rose to a line of blue mountains, their summits capped with a whipped-cream froth of cloud. On the side toward me the cloud sheared off as though cut by a knife where it met the clear air of the desert. Over all arched a sky so blindingly blue that I wondered how people ever thought red the loudest hue. There is no color to outshout Berenty's sky.

Then, at the sisal plantation's hub, there were whitewashed split-rail fences! And whitewashed stones around flower beds of aloes and pink Madagascar periwinkles. The track was graded and swept as no road had been for the past five hundred miles. The houses were neatly squared cement, painted white, with torrents of magenta or salmon-

orange bougainvillea at the corners. The first house I came to had a
kind of carport, but instead of a car it held a single-engine Cessna 172,
green and white, call sign FOBSO. Had I somehow stumbled into
Texas?

Jean de Heaulme opened the door. He was ten years older than I,
with smooth black hair and round cheeks and merry eyes. I explained
that I was a scientist, an American lemur-watcher who had heard that
at Berenty they had lemurs behind the houses, and I introduced Preston, my assistant.

Jean told his wife, Aline, that there would be two more guests for
lunch. It seemed they were having a party. Friends would soon arrive
from Fort Dauphin, over the mountains. I protested haltingly that
we hadn't come to visit, only to see animals. My French was fluent
enough: I had spent a happy junior year in Paris and had even passed
my own father's survey course in French literature at Cornell. What
made me stammer was my first sight of Aline. She is one of those
women who would stay elegantly groomed in the midst of a cyclone.
She had already practiced on more real cyclones than most. I looked at
her trim black curls and white strap sandals, all too conscious that my
khakis did nobody credit. My field boots seemed to grow to the size of
dugout canoes.

My protests were cut short by the noise of motors. Two little planes
taxied down the grass strip beside the road; two couples got out. It became clear that we would all settle down to leisurely drinks and a four-
course meal awash with good wine. I can still remember the main dish:
a whole *capitaine* fish caught in the sea off Fort Dauphin at dawn,
poached within the hour, flown to Berenty in the Cessna, then piped
with a geometry of homemade mayonnaise and nestled among radish
roses.

It was a long day. We went with the other visitors to see the sisal-
processing factory. Then somehow it was dark, too late to look for lemurs or to return to Amboasary town. (American Lutheran missionaries had loaned Preston and me an empty house there.) Jean and Aline
sent us off to dine with his father and uncle.

The uncle, Alain, already frail and white-haired, was always deferential to his older brother. Everyone else deferred to him, too. Monsieur Henry de Heaulme was terrifying.

I still do not know why. Monsieur de Heaulme was a square, stocky man, then about sixty, his face like his son's image set in granite. It fell in straight-hewn lines, with a straight-line mouth and cleft chin. He chose phrases and ideas with absolute precision, a necessity, since every pronouncement would be taken as law. He never, or never that I heard, raised his voice. He addressed persons of every degree with the same slow-spoken courtesy and interest. Any primatologist knows, though, that to decipher a dominance hierarchy, you don't watch for aggression in the dominants. You look for signs of fear in the subordinates. When Monsieur de Heaulme entered a room, like the statue in the final act of *Don Giovanni,* strong men summoned all their courage to speak and timid ones wanted to hide under the table.

In the morning, finally, it was time to visit the forest. I understood now that Berenty estate held a real forest, a nature reserve with lemurs living in it, and that we would need a guide. I laced up my boots and tucked in my trousers and hung my telephoto lenses about me. As we came to the door, Jean said, "Oh — would you mind taking our daughter, Bénédicte, along? She adores the woods."

Bénédicte looked up at Preston and me, her knuckle in her mouth. She was three years old, dressed in the bottom half of a turquoise bikini. What kind of forest was suitable for a naked child? The guide, clearly a friend, swung her up on his shoulders and we set off.

A path led into woods like none I had seen in Madagascar. By now I knew the somber mysteries of tropical rainforest. I had sweltered among the shadeless thorns of the spiny desert. But in this woodland, rough-barked tamarinds, which Malagasy call *kily,* spread their horizontal branches like huge old oak trees. Under the desert sun they cast emerald shade, as if it were June in the Forest of Fontainebleau. Above them towered emergent acacias called *benono,* the many-nippled, for the thorn bases that stud their gray trunks. The ground in the shadows held a brown carpet of leaf litter and fallen, crackling kily pods. At intervals the sun poured down into little grassy glades lined with curtains of glossy liana leaves that swung from the tree crowns. Kilys grow in single file along many Malagasy riverbanks. Berenty forest lies cradled between the Mandrare and one of its old arms: two square kilometers of well-watered river land. This is the woodland of fairy tales, where lovelorn prince meets enchanted princess.

In the more robust Malagasy version, Berenty means Many Eels, or the Great Eel. When the old river arm flooded after cyclones, people say, it left fat marbled eels stranded on the forest floor. In those days female river eels were two meters long and broad to match (the males are smaller). The females grow for twenty-five or thirty years until a trigger in their brains tells them to begin a one-way journey to the middle of the Indian Ocean to spawn. Not so romantic as enchanted princesses, but better eating.

The guide took us off the path to a part of the forest that squeaked and chattered. We looked up at trees hung with bats — bats with red-gold fur and large-eyed faces like those of fox cubs: Malagasy flying foxes. The guide clapped his hands, while Bénédicte squealed and pulled his hair with excitement. A thousand bats whirled into the air. The sun shone through the membranes of their four-foot wingspan, as large as any bats' in the world.

I didn't really want to upset the bats, and I couldn't bear sharing the forest. I murmured that I would drop back to look for lemurs.

The lemurs found me. Staring lemon eyes in a black, heart-shaped face set in a square, white-furred head: a white sifaka clung vertically to a vertical trunk, its tail rolled up like a watch spring. Then, without warning, it leaped. It seemed to double in size. Its hind legs, longer than head and body together, propelled it backward into space in a curve as taut as ballet. It did not jump away, but toward me! It turned in midair to land with both hind feet first, then folded up and clung vertically to another trunk, still watching me. Another followed across the same gap, and another, until a troop of five converged in a half-circle less than fifteen feet away — maddeningly inside the range of my telephoto lens.

"Hey, who's watching who?" I asked severely. (I have never gotten over talking to animals.) One answered with a growl remarkably like a snore. "Shi-fack!" it told me. "Shi-FAKH!" it said even louder, the first syllable bubbling in its throat, the second a click like an amplified hiccup. Soon all five were mobbing me the way birds mob a cat, less than a single spring away. At that point, say the Malagasy, sifaka may leap on you and slash you viciously; when these placid vegetarians fight among themselves, red blood stains their white fur. But this was just a chorus of dubious swearing. The sifaka turned to go.

Now their way was blocked. A troop of twenty-odd ringtailed lemurs had approached from behind. Their tails dangled like long fuzzy caterpillars; their pointed, raccoonlike face masks caught the dappled forest light. They too joined the mobbing, yapping in synchrony like so many ill-mannered little terriers.

In any other forest I would be lucky to see the tail tip of a lemur disappear at speed. The national reserves of Madagascar at that time had so little protection that lemurs treated all humans as hunters. As they should do — I had nightmares of habituating a study troop, only to have somebody serve it up as stew. But the Berenty lemurs had not been hunted in the twenty-five years since the de Heaulmes had set up the forest as a reserve — or even longer, for lemurs are *fady* — taboo — to the local Tandroy people. I sat, enchanted, in the woods for half an hour, being sworn at by sifaka and yapped at by ringtails, unwilling to move. I just waited, like the desert Arabs who would not leave the waterfall, waiting for it to decide to come to an end. Preston and Bénédicte and the guide finally hauled me away.

By the time we came out of the woods, my study plan was clear. Somehow I would find the courage to ask that granite man for permission to spend a year in his forest. Then I would rent the missionaries' empty house in Amboasary town so that I would not be wholly dependent on the de Heaulme family or under their feet.

In my crumpled khakis, all hot with excitement, I barged in on Monsieur de Heaulme in his office at the sisal plant and poured out my hopes. It took him only a few seconds to agree. They had no housing on the estate for me, but I would be free to spend as much time as I pleased in the forest reserve for the coming year.

Driving back toward town through the sisal rows, my head spinning, I understood a little of what had happened, who this family was.

No, not Texas. The de Heaulme family were aristocrats who had never actually noticed the French Revolution. They thought it normal to have a naturalist in their game park, as they might have a librarian in their library or an archaeologist assembling their museum. All I had to do was drive my Land Rover straight into the eighteenth century, park under a kily tree, and start work.

Of course it nearly did not happen. Preston and I walked into the unused house where the Lutheran mission had said we could camp for a few nights. Another visitor had arrived in our absence — a pastor from an upcountry station who had never heard of us. He was now out behind the house, conferring with his catechist in shocked tones. His prim black suitcase stood in the exact center of the main room, with a black Bible lying on top. Even the suitcase seemed to be gathering up its skirts in horror, staying as far from every wall as possible. We had left in a hurry the previous morning, leaving beds unmade, Preston's cigarette butts in unwashed Nestlé milk tins, and the sink full of empty beer bottles. Fortunately it was beds, not bed. I had no romantic interest in a mere undergraduate (nor he in me). I had someone else to wait for, in any case.

Oh, and we'd left a five-foot boa constrictor in the screened food cabinet. We'd brought the snake back two days before to photograph. There seemed no place else to keep it. The owner of the black suitcase must know all too well that Malagasy sorcerers consider boas the familiars of *kokolampo,* pagan forest spirits, so our snake was not an appropriate pet in a mission home.

In the end, the whole American Lutheran assembly held a meeting and prayed for me. They decided that if they rented me their house, I might be saved.

2

Meow! Sifaka! Pig-Grunt-Grunt-Grunt-Grunt

Lemurs and Lemur-Watchers, 90,000,000 B.C.–2000 A.D.

⌒〰〰〰⌒

"Disney is coming!" Jean de Heaulme beamed. "A team of journalists arrive this afternoon at Berenty! Well, not actually Disney, but people from magazines and television, to publicize the French-language release of the Disney movie *Dinosaur.* It seems, Alison, that the film is about a baby dinosaur adopted by a family of lemurs! The journalists want to reveal that real lemurs still exist on Madagascar. Will you join us for dinner, and then help show them around?"

That was on a day in October of 2000. I am forty years older and a whole lot fatter than when I first saw Berenty. I still manage all-day troop follows, though that does not say too much for my stamina: ringtails travel little more than a kilometer a day, mostly around and around in a small home range. There are well over a thousand lemurs per square kilometer in the forest: tiny nocturnal mouse lemurs and lepilemurs, diurnal ringtails and sifaka, and the bumptious interlopers called red-fronted browns (of whom more later). Berenty is extraordinary. Most of my friends who study primates have to charge after their animals up steep mountain slopes or wade through truly horrible swamps. Most nature reserves are by definition on land that nobody is insane enough to farm. Tiny though it is — only two square kilometers, or four if you count the adjacent, more degraded forest — Berenty

is one of the few bits of prime, fertile, sea-level land that have been retained for nature. In all of the vast reaches of Madagascar, with its
scores of more impressive and more important reserves, Berenty is still
the *easiest* place to study wild lemurs. It is much the easiest place to
film them.

I cried when I left Berenty in 1964. I never expected to see it again. I
patted goodbye to the rough bark of the most ancient kily tree by the
river, the long view of river and mountain shimmering through my
tears. It wasn't just that I planned to go away, to live happily ever after
in countries far from Madagascar; I knew that Berenty — that any nature reserve — is a social construct. The forest was there because of the
power and magnanimity of the owners. Also because of the self-re-
straint, and imposed restraint, of the local people, who did not eat its
lemurs and who pastured their zebu cattle in other forests, not this one.
In the postcolonial changes to come, how could the forest survive?

In the year 2000 Berenty and its lemurs still flourished because the
de Heaulme family are still here. And vice versa. Forest and family
saved each other.

It happened against all odds. Most French colonials fled Madagascar in discouragement and fear. Many of the Malagasy elite left for the
greener pastures of Paris. The Tandroy tribe of the Mandrare River valley, around Berenty, are not exactly Madagascar's elite. They don't have
the choice to leave the country, though many seek work in other parts
of the island to eke out their meager living. In the forty years that I've
known Madagascar, it has plummeted to become one of the poorest
countries of the world. The Tandroy count among the materially poorest people of Madagascar.

This book is the tale of the forest, the family, and the Tandroy. They
are the heroes. They are flawed heroes, colonials and tribal lords alike.
Even lemurs are no way as sweet as they look. But they have managed
to coexist in the face of wars and revolts and the indifference or malev-
olence of the outside world. They have survived the terrible years when
the rains fail. The extreme south of Madagascar has always been a place
where people die.

Foreign visitors rarely see any problems, as we sop up roast beef gravy with good French bread or crack the claws of fresh-caught sea crabs. Berenty's original sisal factory has flung out wings and veranda, grown a bar and a courtyard kitchen, and turned into a restaurant that seats a hundred people. On that October night in 2000, Jean de Heaulme placed himself at the midpoint of a long table laid with white cloths for the whole Disney crew: photographers, journalists, producer, sound man, and a couple of promoters, plus the scientists currently in residence. Tourists at the other tables nudged each other and whispered, "That's the *owner.* That must be *Monsieur-de*-how-do-you-pronounce-it! Quick, pass the guidebook!" The kitchen staff outdid themselves to offer a fitting meal for Monsieur's guests: creamy leek quiche, Malagasy stew of beef and peppery daisy greens over mountains of rice, ultra-French *oeufs à la neige* with its white meringue, drizzled caramel, and custard redolent of Madagascar vanilla.

On the wall behind Monsieur, an enormous black-and-white photomural showed the Tandroy Dance Troupe of Berenty in 1960 performing for Madagascar's independence celebrations. The men wear loincloths, tiny straw hats, silver bracelets, and beautiful muscles. They dance with spears in their hands. Kneeling women beat with their palms on traditional drums. The mural is a testament to the people who greeted the family when they first came to settle here. Carved wooden Tandroy house panels ring the restaurant walls. In the corners stand spindly eight-foot-tall figures that Giacometti might be proud to claim. They were not stolen from tombs but commissioned by the de Heaulmes from a traditional tomb sculptor.

By the turn of the millennium Jean de Heaulme had come to look very much the way I remembered his redoubtable father, but he somehow never acquired his father's granite mien. There was still a twinkle in Jean's eye. He poured out the wine for his guests, a delightedly genial host.

"When did I myself arrive here?" he answered the journalists' questions. "I was born in Tananarive. I came to Fort Dauphin when I was six months old, in the sidecar of my father's Harley-Davidson. Yes, indeed: my father drove a Harley-Davidson motorcycle from Tananarive to Fort Dauphin in 1928, and my mother rode in the sidecar holding me! You can imagine what it was like. There was a road, but it was not so easy to be sure where the road was!

"My father made the reserve, the lemur reserve beside the river. He said, 'This forest is too beautiful ever to be destroyed. We must never cut it; nobody must cut it.' So he set aside Berenty Reserve simply because it was beautiful. In the same way, he was all too aware that the life of the people would change. He said, 'I ask about their history and their customs. Their lives will change — *we* are changing them, as we plant sisal and they work on the sisal. However, this country was so fantastic — *formidable* — when I first arrived, that I want to leave some witness of how it was.'

"That is what my father thought. That is also why I created the Museum of Androy, which you will see tomorrow, to show local weaving and sorcery and funeral ceremonies. The museum used to be my own home, with my Cessna airplane in the garage, but that room now holds a traditional Tandroy house. The museum's name is Arambelo. 'Arambelo' is the benediction a Tandroy father gives his son before the son emigrates to look for work outside the region of Androy. The father mixes a bit of ash from the hearth fire with a little of his own saliva and touches it to the son's forehead, heart, and shoulders, to keep him safe and make him return. I urge you to go and see the museum, even if you have no time to meet Tandroy people."

The TV crew's mission was lemurs, lemurs, lemurs. They knew better than to develop an interest in people. They had to offer up a video-magazine clip of what viewers expect to see about Madagascar. *Cute* lemurs, *baby* lemurs, with a few scientists as talking heads to provide a story line. The producer's chief goal at dinner was to identify available talent.

It did not take him long to fix on Dina, Takayō, and Erica. It's a fact of life that three beautiful female students, Malagasy, Japanese, and English, will attract the attention of a French film crew.

By half past five the next morning the crew had Erica out tying fluorescent pink flagging tape onto a sapling. "This is a scent-post," she explained. "Males gouge the bark with their wrist spurs. You can see the scars on the bark. Males and females also do handstands to press their genitals on the trunk at nose height for ringtails of the next troop to smell when they pass by. When males challenge each other directly, though, they stink-fight. They draw their tail through their wrist glands, then shake it forward over their head to make sure the scent gets up their enemy's nose." Then she had to say all that again and tie the ribbon again. By take ten, even Erica's flashing smile began to pale.

At long last she was allowed to find her troop and walk beside them as they promenaded. Long before, lemurs used to mob me. Now they fed and ranged casually in front of the cameras. Berenty lemurs know all about life in front of Big Brother. Males gouged saplings; mothers with upside-down babies clutching their belly fur did handstands to mark the trail, exactly as Erica had promised. An immigrant male with a deeply slashed left ear turned up and tried to stink-fight the resident males. They displayed back at him, quivering scented tails like outraged feather dusters, the contestants facing each other like two halves of a heraldic design.

Erica and Dina were following a recently divided troop to see how the two new daughter troops would partition their former range. At noon the crew found Dina sitting where dappled sun flecks filtered through to the bronze fallen leaves of the forest floor and reflected upward to the golden brown curve of Dina's cheeks. Her lemurs slept beside her. There is nothing so relaxed as a hot, siesta-ing ringtailed lemur, on a liana with tail and all four legs adangle or frankly spread-eagled on the forest floor. At most they opened one amber eye or shifted over to groom their closest friend's baby, scraping the fur with lower teeth shaped just like the teeth of a comb. Dina had learned the trick of not disturbing them. When she wanted to move on the leaf litter, she told them serenely, "Don't worry, it's only me." The soft voice reassured them this was no predator rustling leaves, just their human troop-mate.

Takayō posed with her own adjacent troop. American and Malagasy scientists have been comparing troops and species, but the Japanese team is following one hundred and fifty individual lemurs. Takayō, fizzing with excitement like a small firecracker, instructed the French-men that each animal has a distinct personality. She pointed out the group's lead female, who had pale yellowish eyes and was carrying her tiny infant. (That female later starred as Jezebel of the West Side Gang in the BBC's *Gangland Lemurs*.) The cameraman panned from Jezebel to Takayō's notebook of portrait photos, each one annotated in careful Japanese characters. He framed his shot rather carefully to avoid show-ing the equally explicit photos of each animal's backside and genitalia.

To be fair, the French team also filmed matronly Anne Millhollen. The frontier between Erica's lemurs and Takayō's lies within five me-ters of the same troops' boundaries during Anne's first study at Berenty in 1975. Some boundaries even date from when I watched their fore-mothers in 1963. Dina's troop was being exiled from that range, so it had to move away and poach range from the neighbors. The bound-aries seem to be fixed by a kind of tradition. The tradition depends not only on lemur memory but on constantly renewed scent-posts, which seem to hold as permanent a record as Anne's old maps — backed up by recurrent challenges to rival female gangs. To the television people the point of scientists is to give them the answers quickly — after we have hung around for twenty-five years puzzling the answers out.

Then, of course, that film team went away. Goodbye Takayō, Dina, Erica, Anne! We will send you copies of the tape! We'll tell all of France that real lemurs are more adorable than *anything* Disney could make up!

No television crew can afford to ask about local Berenty people. They generally don't even want to hear that behind those sugar-sweet black-and-white ringtail face masks, under the soft, soft fur, ringtailed lemur life is a perpetual soap opera. Worse. It's a life-and-death thriller about which bitch will keep the inheritance.

Frightful Fan was annoyed. She was chronically annoyed. She spun on one heel, her sun-bleached, reddish-ringed tail rippling behind her, her bare thighs pumping as she accelerated into a chase. Jessica looked up. She dropped a scrap of manioc right out of her mouth. She squeaked a submissive spat call and sprang aside, her baby clinging to her back. She wasn't quick enough. One of Fan's upper canines raked Jessica's thigh, slicing through fur and skin into red muscle. Jessica scooted, limping, off among the spiny trees of Berenty's botanical garden. Fan spun around to see if Jessica's younger sister was within chasing range. She ignored the manioc scraps scattered near the Berenty guardian's hut. She was much too busy being spiteful. Jessica's sister was at a safe distance, so Fan displaced her anger with a token lunge at the troop's alpha male, who cowered in turn (but then, all ringtail males cower away from females). This was in 1994, as Fan rose to be the dominant female of her half of the A-Team.

I don't want you to think that Fan is unique or even that her character has something to do with living in the front part of Berenty Reserve, among guardians' huts and tourist bungalows. I think of edgy Caffeine, way out in the dry scrub, and Aunt Agatha, harridan of my first troop in the rich gallery forest, and of many other quick-tempered females. Nor are all dominant female ringtails aggressive: there was calm Diva; there is still Shadow of the splendid coat. It seems to be a matter of temperament, not environment. Still, as nasty characters go, Fan wins hands down.

Fan's mother, Fish, was the third-ranked female of the A-Team back in 1990, when Fan was born. Fish was the tough girl of the gang. Mid-ranked females are sometimes the most aggressive within the troop, as though they are throwing their weight around while they eye their route to the top spot. Fish's low gray brow, dividing her white forehead into two wings like a fishtail, seemed to give her a built-in scowl. Her baby, though, was as cute and cuddly as any ringtailed infant. Fan's head was a little Ping-Pong ball painted with black and white clown makeup around her unfocused baby eyes. Her minute tail was a dashed line drawn in soft black pencil where it curled over Fish's waist. Fan clung to Fish's belly fur and nursed nearly nonstop for the first two weeks. Then she began to scramble onto Fish's back, where she could balance her growing weight and take a good look at the troop's shenanigans.

When they rested, mother and daughter groomed. They remained best friends and grooming partners all their lives. The upper canines of a ringtailed lemur are as sharp as any switchblade, honed on the almost equally sharp premolars below. Their lower canines and incisors lie side by side like the teeth of a comb. The tools of both extreme aggression and extreme care and trust lie right at the front of their mouths. As infant Fan grew, she picked up the rhythm of grooming, so her head and her mother's moved simultaneously like reciprocating pistons to comb each other's soft, soft fur.

By 1992 Fan was a truculent two-year-old. She was adult in size but a year away from bearing her own first child. She tested her growing femininity (femininity for a ringtail reads like virility for a human) in the A-Team civil war. Perhaps "civil war" is a strong term for the fission of a troop of just nine adult females and their daughters, but it was not a minor tiff in a sewing circle.

Diva was the A-Team's original alpha. Her wide-peaked white forehead seemed like a diadem of absolute power. She rarely chased anybody; the others simply got out of her way. (I couldn't help thinking of the way people treated Monsieur Henry de Heaulme.) Diva's daughter, "Pretty-Pretty-Baby-Cover-Girl Jessica," inherited the same wide peak over a thinner, more aquiline face. Jessica was a delicate beauty who clung to the side of her dominant mother. Young Fan cuddled and groomed her own scowling mother. When Fish attacked someone, Fan was likely to be right beside her. In 1992 they did not dare to attack Diva or Jessica. Instead, they concentrated on splitting up the troop.

A subordinate group of the A-Team traveled behind Diva, Fish, and friends. They were always the last to enter a feeding tree, taking the leavings from the table of Diva's gang. Diva herself rarely came into personal conflict with the second lot. Diva may well have been the sister of the oldest female in the group, from a time only the two of them could hark back to. (I am not claiming they actually remembered — just that an old amity seems to have formed their relationship.) The rest of Diva's gang, however, took every opportunity to sideline the subordinates. Fish badgered them through three successive birth seasons, while the subordinate group put up with the harassment. Targeted females rarely, if ever, *choose* to leave a ringtail group. They will take almost any treatment rather than stake their own claim to independence. It wasn't till the drought year of 1992 that the lead half of the A-team physically drove the subordinate half away.

For several weeks the exiles ran all over the front part of the reserve, across the ranges of at least five other neighboring troops. They could feed only when nobody saw them. If another group met them on its home ground, it chased them out at speed. They gave way without any attempt at a challenge. Their worst enemies were their own cousins in Diva's gang. One of the pursuers caught up with Sly, the alpha female of the exiles, and nearly took off her right ear, slashing the scalp to the bone so the torn flap hung down at half-mast. Fortunately, ringtailed lemurs simply "zip up wounds like Terminator." In three days the wound was no longer red, though Sly's ear stuck out to the side ever after.

I remember a bunch of Swiss tourists cooing, "Ach, du *schöne!* Sie hat ein *kind!*" (Oh, you *cutie!* She has a *baby!*), without even registering Sly's awful ear. In the midst of the fighting, three females in Sly's group and four in Diva's managed to give birth. They went into battle with their infants on their backs.

I watched lovely Shadow bear her first child, while the subordinate troop lay on the forest floor only twenty meters from their pursuers. The chasing had gone on right up to the time the exhausted troops called a halt for siesta. Sly's troop was so scared they curled up to sleep in a tight line, all tails wrapped around. Shadow moved all of a meter away, straining in silence, then licked the newborn for half an hour to clean it. When the troop woke and began to move, she was not quite finished, but she still had to follow, meowing her contact calls. A ringtail simply cannot lose its troop for fear of predators — or of other ringtails.

When Shadow meowed, her friend Blotch came back to nose the mother and newborn, her own two-day-old infant clinging to her breast. The two mothers cuddled each other and licked the tiny faces of each other's infants.

"One of your students is behind the bungalows. She wants you. It seems she is crying."

It was a week later. Monsieur Rakotomalala, the plantation manager, found me at breakfast in the restaurant to tell me. I had visions of a Princeton student sprawled on a broken leg, of an emergency medical evacuation to America. Surely no one had attacked the girl or raped her! Not in safe Berenty! Not at breakfast time anyway. Oh, what would I tell her parents? The sun was already hot on me at seven A.M. as I galloped toward the bougainvillea-fringed tourist quarters.

Laura Hood stood all alone on open ground. She stared apparently at her feet. Tears streamed down her cheeks.

"It's still peeping," she wailed. "It won't die. Blotch just went off and left it, and the male bit it — and I saw it born. Oh, I wish it would die!"

The nine-day-old infant lay on the sand on its left side. Its tiny black hands and feet opened and closed. The right side of its abdomen was slashed open diagonally from kidney to groin. A loop of intestine hung redly from the wound. The infant raised its head and began to beep — a sound more like a digital watch in distress than an animal. Laura shuddered.

I hugged her. "Tell me exactly what happened while I think what to do."

"It came off Blotch when their troop was fighting and grappling with Diva's. I didn't see how it came off when the females were fighting, but afterward the two lots just stood and faced off against each other. Blotch could have picked it up. She had plenty of time. Then Diva's females charged again, and her group ran right away. I know the baby was all right then, because it was moving perfectly well. It began to peep loudly, and all the Diva females came over to nose it. None of them picked it up. Then the females left — and Geek came up and grabbed the infant. He acted as though he was fighting it — almost as though it was fighting back — shaking it and pulling at it. Then he just slashed it open with a canine and ran away."

"Who do you call Geek?" I asked so she wouldn't start crying again.

"Oh, the male that's always so timid and cowering and carries his ears flattened down. He just looks like a geek. He's an immigrant male."

It didn't seem the moment to mention that "geek" originally meant a man who bit the heads off live chickens in circus freak shows. I said, "You know that Michael Pereira will be just delighted — or anyway torn between delight and jealousy that it was you who saw the infanticide."

"I know," said Laura in a small voice.

The infant struggled again and lifted its head to peep its piercing distress call. "We can't let it suffer — I'll just have to do it." I held my fingers over the soft little nose, closing the nostrils and crying mouth. It did not take long.

I do not understand why so many people who love animals actually want to be vets.

Laura suddenly turned back into a competent Princetonian, blond bobbed hair under white golfing hat. "I don't usually cry over things." she said. "This isn't like me at all."

"What you need to do is go and write it all down — every detail that you can remember, before Michael starts to jog your memory with his own ideas. You've just turned into hot property in the war between the professors — and if you think male lemurs are dangerous, just wait till the next symposium."

Laura went off to write. I kept silent with difficulty. Even when Michael Pereira came to lunch, brimming with news of the latest aggression in his own lemur troop, I managed to keep from telling him that his pet theory of infanticide had just been spectacularly confirmed. It was Laura's news to tell. Instead, I looked at him, an eager man in his thirties, long and lean and hungry like Cassius. His black hair and beard rippled down to his shoulders, as though he were about to play a Shakespearean role or perhaps a pageant of Vasco da Gama. Besides the hair he wore red and white sneakers, cutoff jeans, a sleeveless undershirt, and a hat from a paint-and-wallpaper store in Durham, North Carolina. This was the man whose observations showed how female ringtailed lemurs maneuver for advantage over their troop-mates day by day and who had construed females' attacks on immigrant males as defense against infanticide, long before Laura saw it happen.

Geek's infanticide has been the only fully observed killing by an immigrant male ringtail at Berenty, though there have been other, rare attacks by males. A quarrel among the academics continues over whether infanticide has been evolved for the male lemurs' advantage or not.

What came the next day was a much more common occurrence,

one that is much more easily understood as behavior evolved to dispose of rivals: a female simply arranged for someone else's infant to die.

This time it was Sly's. Baby ringtails are tough. The tiny newborn was only ten hours old, but it was wriggling and peeping, the umbilical cord still attached. New infants normally cling firmly to their mother's belly as she leaps through the trees. Sly's infant lay alone on its back on the ground, clutching at the only thing it could find — its own tail.

The two troops had confronted each other for the fourth time in a day. Ringtails move so quickly that I can never see whether one female actually pulls the infant off another, but in the jerky motions of battle, a baby sometimes falls. Females from the opposing troop charge at the mother. Sometimes it seems that they are simply battling an enemy, but sometimes it is clear that they are deliberately keeping a mother from retrieving her infant. When her infant fell, Sly recoiled from the fight — and Fish let Sly's baby crawl onto her beside her own infant. Fish then ran off with Diva and her own gang. The baby hung on for twenty minutes, long enough to be carried hundreds of meters away from any region the subordinate group had been allowed to enter since the troop split. Young Fan came over to groom this temporary foster sibling, but then Fish grew annoyed and scraped the baby off. Fish's semimaternal response condemned Sly's baby to death as surely as Geek's canines had condemned Blotch's. Sly couldn't even hear it crying from where it lay on the sand.

Laura and I bent over the minute scrap of a creature. "I don't care," I decided. "I am not going to kill another infant. We have sometimes returned fallen infants before, outside of the study troops. Let's score that this one died once already and still give Sly the chance to have it back." I scooped it up onto a clean check-sheet on my clipboard, hoping that would smell less human than sweaty hands.

We carried the infant quickly to where Sly's troop was recuperating from the fight and laid it on the ground. It peeped again and again. Both Blotch and Sly descended to the call: any female is likely to come to any crying infant. Usually the real mother dashes straight to her offspring and hovers above it so it can grab her fur, even if she does not scoop it up with a hand. But Sly stood well back. She stuck out her nose to sniff the peeping baby as though she had never smelled it before, though she'd had ten hours to learn its scent since its birth at dawn. Blotch did the same. To look at them, you couldn't have told which was the real mother, if either was.

They leaped away, leaving the infant lying there. It cried again. Sly sat two meters off, looking back and listening. Her troop moved deeper into the forest, starting the last trek of the day toward their sleeping site. Sly meowed her contact call at her departing troopmates, who chorused back their beckoning meows. She followed them into the shadows.

An hour later Michael Pereira turned up at my bungalow. "I've been telling the students all along to expect less maternal behavior," he said. "These females are fighting for their lives, so it may be worth their giving up this season's reproduction to save energy for fighting."

"You are getting like Cassandra. Your predictions come true too often!"

"Are you sure the baby was healthy? It didn't just drop off because it couldn't cling? She really just abandoned it?"

"Sly was a targeted subordinate even before she conceived this baby. She has been thrown out of her troop while pregnant, been chased by every troop she comes across for a whole month, and had her ear half ripped off three days before parturition. If stress does anything to a mother's behavior, it should hit Sly. But the infant itself looks fine."

I held out my Malagasy straw hat, where I'd crumpled up a nest of soft Kleenex for the baby. It had dozed off in the dark, but now it woke and grabbed for its tail and beeped with undiminished vigor, though it had had no milk for two hours. Michael hung up his weighing scale and gently picked up the infant. "Oh, God, Alison. It's purring at me."

Not many people have heard a ringtail purr, a tiny, gentle sound that it makes when it is happy, curled up against another lemur's fur. Wild ones, even such tame wild ones as ours at Berenty, are rarely confident enough to relax and purr when a human is near enough to hear. In the warmth of Michael's hand, the newborn thought it had finally found succor. But we could not save it.

The next day the subordinates changed their tactics. Or, rather, they developed a tactic — the only innovation I have seen in ringtail behavior. Almost always when troops confront each other, the actual aggression is carried out by only a couple of animals. Now, suddenly, Sly and all her friends presented a united front. At first they continued to lose battles. Two days later Fish and Fan swaggered over as usual. Dust flew as lemurs spun over each other or broke to face new opponents. (Bites are rare: parries and feints, grapples and breaks follow too quickly for them often to deliver a slash like the one on Sly's skull.) The combatants paused and stared at each other. Sly's females sprang on top of a bungalow. Their faces glared out from the thatched roof like five little gargoyles with sharp canines, Sly's ear still at half-mast. Fish climbed a flamboyant bush to glare back as Shadow launched herself from the roof. Fish and Fan backed off — literally. They didn't dare turn for fear of being jumped from behind. At a safe distance they promenaded away down the path at a stately pace that fooled no one.

Shadow led the group into a flowering eucalyptus grove that had been off bounds to them since the troop split a month before. They gobbled and gobbled. The grove was loud with bees. White-stamened flowers dusted lemur noses with pollen like powder puffs, and the conical ivory bud caps pattered on the ground. The one surviving infant, Shadow's son, the baby I saw born, peered out upside-down from the safety of his mother's belly. The new troop had earned their reward. All around them the air smelled of honey.

Males approached Shadow's all-female gang submissively, as males do. No males committed to the new troop until it was clear that they would survive. Shadow led what we began to call the "Together Troop" into victories that gave them the best of their former range, beginning with the eucalyptus grove. Four males then joined them permanently, including Geek, the killer. Males are subordinate to adult females. They never, ever claim rights to food or space. If a male wishes to impress a female he runs his ringed tail through the spurs on his arms and twitches it over his back to waft his scent forward. Other males take this as a threat and respond in kind. A female, though, looks away, clearly bored. If the male persists she cuffs him over the nose.

The inhibition of the ringtail males seems to contradict everything we teach in freshman biology. The standard story biologists tell is that males evolve to compete with each other. They grow weapons, and their brains are tuned to aggression. Their power over females is just a byproduct. In humans, of course, men on average outweigh and out-muscle women, so it's no wonder we usually think that male dominance is natural. Not *right,* of course, and certainly not inevitable in any given situation, but natural.

Ringtail females choose to mate either with dominants or with winners of jump fights, serious battles in which a whole group of males leap in the air at each other and slash downward with their razor-edged canines. This sort of fighting should select for the genes of the biggest, meanest, longest-toothed males — but the males remain totally deferent to females. I keep thinking I will wake up some morning with a good explanation for the males' behavior, but I haven't yet — and I was the first scientist to notice ringtail female dominance, forty years ago.

At least our studies at Berenty make it clear why the females must be aggressive to survive. They are fighting for long-term ownership of resources.

Diva's gang had made a huge miscalculation by throwing out the subordinates. The Together Troop claimed the best of the range, starting off tree by tree in the eucalyptus grove. Diva plummeted from power. Worn, battered, skulking on the troop's periphery, she died in 1994. Fan grabbed the top spot while Diva's daughter, Jessica, stayed at the bottom.

Fan's group felt the pinch of reduced range and aggressive neighbors. The Together Troop under Shadow consolidated its position year by year and raised more and more daughters to compete. Every day Shadow's troop challenged Fan's at the edge of the eucalyptus grove. Over the years their aggression became formalized. Two small saplings, just two meters apart, served as goalposts, scent-marked by the two sides. Females and males stood on their hands and rubbed their genitalia at lemur nose height. Males gouged their wrist spurs into the bark until the two little trees were ringed with scars. The troops still charged each other and leaped smartly aside, but I have seen Fan saunter alone over to where Shadow was feeding and all but look at her watch to say, "It's match time," waiting for the Together Troop to follow her back to the tournament ground.

Frightful Fan became the angriest lemur in the reserve. She kept having sons rather than daughters, so her main ally was her younger sister Finch, distinguished by her protruding "psycho eyes." Everyone else in the troop got chased, especially Jessica.

Pretty-Pretty-Baby-Cover-Girl Jessica was slender and lovely when she was the princess hiding behind the power of her mother. But after Diva died, Jessica grew thin and stringy. Her aquiline white brow shrank to a narrow streak; her fur molted in patches from her thighs. Just as the Together Troop had endured three years of second-rank status, so Jessica accepted the bottom slot for three long birth seasons. In 1994, when Fan actually slashed her, she managed to raise a daughter who inherited Diva's wide brow and superb coat of fur.

In 1997, Frightful Fan made the decisive move of splitting the troop yet again. She did not move Jessica a mere meter or so away; she chased her for hundreds of meters, galloping at top speed down the long perspective of the road next to the de Heaulme airstrip. Whenever Jessica and her little group — her daughter, her niece, and their young — approached within eyeshot, Fan left her own troop to give chase. Tracy Dubovick, a student who returned to Berenty two years in a row to keep tabs on the A-Team, happened to be a rugby player. To play rugby you have to be very, very solid or very, very fast. Tracy was fast. Even Tracy had plenty of workout running after Fan. Jessica's group had to run even faster to get away from Fan. Tourists and restaurant waiters looked on amazed at apparent track meets between gaggles of ringtailed lemurs and a blond student sprinting down the road clutching a clipboard and check-sheets.

It was apparently cheaper for Fan to exile her own cousins, running flat out, her thighs molting fur, her tail bleached red, her stress hormones through the roof, rather than try to enlarge her troop's range and feed the cousins, too. Unlike the Together Troop's, Jessica's story did not turn to triumph. Her family never gained a range of their own. One by one they died or disappeared.

Fan's mother, Fish, had failed to eliminate her competitors in the

Together Troop, who fought back until Fish held only the smallest piece of the original A-Team range. Frightful Fan held on to that small range for her own family, even though it meant she had to wipe out all that remained of the proud lineage of Diva.

This is a soap opera. There is no end. In 1999 psycho-eyed Finch displaced Fan as dominant. Fan is still there, but wholly subdued. She won't be exiled herself as long as her sister Finch is in charge. Fan could live to be as old as fifteen, still raising babies for as long as her strength lasts. Lemurs, like most nonhuman primates, have no menopause. In the end we may find her skeleton curled up in the crotch of a kily tree, all but the smallest bones intact, picked clean and white by the great black housekeeper ants, the undertakers of the forest.

As for the Together Troop, at its peak in 2000 it numbered thirty-three animals, including ten males jockeying for acceptance by this phenomenally successful gang. When they streamed into the forest in the evening, the whole of the main path would fill with lemurs, the late sun gleaming through the spires of thirty-three backlit ringed tails. Togetherness paid off.

When Androy exploded, continents moved. The lemurs' inheritance goes back for forty or fifty million years — or possibly even twice as long. The Disney film's claim that lemurs lived here alongside dinosaurs could actually be right, though they didn't gabble in Disneyfied voices.

Some eighty-eight million years ago a plume of magma and hot gas welled up from the earth's lower depths just about underneath present-day Berenty. It bulged the overlying rock into a giant geological blood blister. The rivers of both Madagascar and southern India flowed away from the mountain that strained upward above the force heaving from below. Up till that time, peninsular India still clung to the side of Madagascar. They may even have had land bridges south to Antarctica. Together, they were remnants of the great southern continent of Gondwanaland. (Africa had split away long before.) When the mountain-blister of Androy finally burst, the explosion kick-started the final rift of the continents. After that, Madagascar was all alone.

It wasn't just a single explosion but perhaps eight million years of volcanic venting. I picture titanothere dinosaurs of the time as a phlegmatic lot, who raised their snakelike necks in bemusement rather than terror when the red-hot basalt began to flow. Those that were not deep-fried resumed their chewing. Dinosaurs still had twenty million years to keep on chewing before the meteorite (or whatever it was) eventually finished them off.

When the magma plume vented its fury, the center of the blister sagged downward to form the Androy basin, floored with a plug of basalt one hundred kilometers in diameter. Only the eastern and northern sides of the surrounding mound remain today, but any map of Madagascar shows a semicircle of mountain ranges two thousand meters high between Fort Dauphin and Berenty, too geometrically perfect to be the result of anything but a focused cataclysm. From Berenty on a clear day you see the rim as granite mountains embracing half the horizon. The granite itself is far older than the volcano. It dates from the dawn of life. The Androy plume was just one of the pressures that upthrust, squeezed, shaped, heated, and congealed that ancient granite over eons of time until it oozed out deposits of slow-forming minerals: mica in transparent sheets, black grains of titanium oxide, radioactive thorianite, sapphires as blue as Berenty's sky.

All that geological history matters to people (and lemurs) today. The trade winds reach eastern Madagascar at the pretty port of Fort Dauphin (Taolagnaro in Malagasy), which is set about with palms and pandanus and orchids under the wet sea wind. The trades drop their moisture on the coast and on the high rainforest of the encircling mountain rim. Inland the wind arrives in the Androy basin as a parching blast that cracks your lips and evaporates your eyeballs. What rain there is filters downward through sandy soil that is fit to grow only the succulent fingers and twisted stems of the spiny forest. Cattle can live, but field crops all too often die. The minerals of the granite mountains tempt young men to leave their desert homes to dig for sapphires in handmade pits like human ant lions. In recent decades people have mined mica and then thorianite; they hope that in the future it will be titanium.

When Androy exploded, among the dinosaurs roamed little hairy mammals. Maybe they were lemurs. There is a riproaring argument over where lemurs began. (The social life of professors is all about thoroughly satisfying arguments.) We know for sure that there were lemurs in the north fifty and forty million years ago. All over the north: their fossils lie in Paris and China and Wyoming. They were startlingly like the lemurs of today, some with upright, leaping bodies like Berenty's white sifaka. But where did they come from? How did they get to Madagascar?

Perhaps they evolved in the north where we find their fossils. If so, some of them then worked their way south to Africa. A few drifted out to sea toward Madagascar on rafts of tangled vegetation, clinging with all four hands to the wave-washed twigs. Perhaps it was only one, curled up inside a hollow log, grooming her pregnant belly with her tooth-comb, a furry little Eve some forty million years before Eden. Perhaps a whole group of them chose a tree next to the water for their winter hibernation and woke up in a whole new land.

But maybe the lemurs began long, long, before on Madagascar itself! Or, rather, on the linked landmass of Madagascar-India-Antarctica. It is a big leap back in time from the fifty-million-year-old northern fossils to the eighty-eight-million-year-old eruption of the Androy volcano. Still, modern molecular evidence keeps pushing the timeframe earlier and earlier, into an unseen Volume I of evolution, with the known lemur fossils not appearing until Volume II. According to that scenario, Malagasy lemurs today are living where they always have lived. A single branch of them traveled north with India as their cruise ship. When India collided with Asia, that branch escaped over the future Himalayas, to evolve into monkeys, and apes, and us.

Whatever their origin, lemurs flourished on their island home. Madagascar is a thousand miles long, the distance from London to Naples, Italy, or from New York to Orlando, Florida. It has evergreen rainforest in the wet east, deciduous forest full of bloated baobabs in the west, spiny forest in the south. The lemurs radiated into a kaleidoscope of species. About forty kinds remain today, from tiny mouse lemurs up to animals the size of small dogs: the singing indri and the dancing sifaka. There were once at least fifteen more species, all larger than today's survivors. Some hung from branches like huge sloths. One that was as big as a gorilla shambled along the ground. The biggest Madagascar animals, though, were the flightless *Aepyornis,* the ostrich-like elephant birds, three meters tall and a ton in weight.

Monkeys and apes never reached Madagascar. The first alien primates that the lemurs met were humans. Madagascar was one of the very last habitable places that our parvenu species invaded, sometime around 500 A.D. Indonesians of a great pre-Hindu seafaring empire colonized the high central plateau; Africans settled all around the coast. They found in Madagascar an untouched world.

Malagasy legends and the Arabian tale of Sinbad's roc — and many, many fossils — still testify to the elephant birds, to tortoises the size of a baby's bathtub, floppy-eared dwarf hippos and giant lemurs. Perhaps the last giant lemur lived near Lipomamy Pool, between Berenty and Fort Dauphin. In 1661 Sieur Etienne de Flacourt, governor of the first French colony at Fort Dauphin, recorded:

> Tretretretre or tratratratra, it is an animal as large as a two-year-old calf, with a round head and a man's face, the front legs are like a monkey's and the hind legs also. It has frizzy fur, a short tail, and ears like those of a man . . . One was seen close by the pool of Lipomami, in which region it has its haunts. It is a very solitary animal, the people of the country fear it greatly, and flee from it as it flees from them.

"Tretretretre" with Malagasy pronunciation might be a sound used toward ground predators, like the sifaka's "shifakh!" alarm. I suspect its name was what the human hunters heard as the frightened tretretretre watched them coming with their spears.

Chantal woke up wondering if she'd gone deaf. Jean de Heaulme's sister waited for the usual thunder of feet on the roof of the two-story plantation house that she and her husband, Georges Dupray, had built when he became Berenty's manager. Every morning her red-fronted brown lemurs served as her alarm clock. She had brought them to Berenty as pets from a forest in western Madagascar, orphans of mothers trapped for meat. They are a subspecies of the so-called browns, which are actually gray, fox-red, and carrot-orange. The little orphans had long since found a hole in their cage. They usually slept on top of the cage's chicken wire, popping back inside for meals. The rest of the time they climbed in trees overhanging the plantation house, taking shortcuts across the corrugated iron roof. On that peculiar morning though, Chantal heard no dawn hammering of hands and feet, no throaty GRUNT-grunt-grunt-grunt-grunt, as though her pets were a troop of flying orange piglets.

And no bird song. No cawing crows or whistling kites. No twittery warble of the magpie robin or bell-toned *tou-lou-lou-lou-lou* of the toulou bird. No pure note from the hook-billed vanga, like an extraterrestrial radio frequency beamed directly into your head. Chantal actually rustled a sheet to make sure she could still hear.

She pulled on shirt and trousers, ran a brush through her close-cropped hair, and went out to explore. The brown lemurs had indeed disappeared, along with all other signs of life. Even the leaves hung immobile in air like glue.

At last the radio began its morning broadcast. January 25, 1975. A massive cyclone was building in the Indian Ocean. By midmorning it flattened matchstick coastal villages. It flicked the iron roof off the Fort Dauphin airport like a tiddlywink. In the afternoon it roared across the mountains and pounced on Berenty.

For three days the wind blew and the rain poured down. Tall acacias snapped or simply fell, their roots gouged out of the ground. Giant limbs tore off the tamarind trees. People huddled in cement buildings, while many traditional plank houses of Berenty village simply blew away. Carcasses of sheep and cattle rolled downstream in the muddy waters of the Mandrare.

When the sun returned, Georges and Chantal were far too busy patching up the village and the sisal factory to worry that their pets had definitively moved into the woods. In the western forests where they came from, brown lemurs live together with ringtails and white sifaka — why not at Berenty? They would probably all be fine.

Besides, Chantal couldn't catch them.

Twenty-five years later, we still do not know whether Berenty's wild brown lemurs are a boon or a disaster. There are more than two hundred of them, and the population is growing exponentially. Is this building an even richer biological community? As many as a dozen species of lemurs may coexist in other forests; isn't it a triumph to add one more to Berenty's resident mouse lemurs, lepilemurs, ringtails, and sifaka? Or are the browns dangerous intruders who crowd the ringtails out of their favorite feeding trees? Literally, I mean. The two species mostly ignore each other, but when push does come to shove, a brown can chase a ringtail right off the end of a branch. The ringtail drops with hands and feet windmilling in the air until it grabs a new hand-hold on the way down. Also, the browns are leaf-eaters who strip the tamarinds of their new leaves. Does their feeding pressure contribute to the drying out of the shady forest?

Good or bad, the browns are here to stay. Nobody else will have them. Over the years the de Heaulmes added another half-dozen or so — orphans rescued this time from the Fort Dauphin market. These animals came from the eastern rainforest. They are a different race from Chantal's western browns. The western subspecies is *rufus:* males with gray bodies and bright orange topknots, females with fox-red fur and white clown eyebrows. The eastern Fort Dauphin subspecies, *collaris,* has a chocolate coat. Females are gray-headed; the males have orange muttonchop whiskers instead of a crest. The two parent stocks have different chromosome numbers, so they shouldn't even be able to produce viable offspring, but nobody told the lemurs.

No zoo would want them now — not even a few, and certainly not two hundred. Purist conservationists and good zoos do everything they can to keep wild races separate and to sterilize zoo-born mixed animals. Meanwhile, field biologists have become fascinated by such mixes. We seek out natural hybrid zones to study as creative hotbeds of evolution. My guess is that if Berenty survives intact for another twenty-five years, there will simply be another fascinating subspecies. I think of a gorgeous animal named Lion, who sported a complete sunburst of orange fur — both the *rufus* crest and the *collaris* cheek whiskers — with the lugubrious expression of the Cowardly Lion in the *Wizard of Oz.*

My problem is that I don't really appreciate any of the brown races. It takes a lemur-watcher about two days to figure out whether she is a brown person or a ringtail person, just the way there are cat people and

dog people. Ringtails have highly ritualized etiquette. Their squeak series called a "spat" runs the entire gamut from a twittered "So sorry!" to
the deep "I abase myself before you!" Brown lemurs have no equivalent
submission call. Their similar call is undifferentiated aggression, more
like "Scram!" Ringtails stink-fight with arched tails and scent-mark in-
cised saplings. Browns rub their pungent backsides on each other, especially males on females. Ringtails have fairly strict segregation by sex
and total female dominance. With the browns, dominance is a matter
of individual bullying, not gender. Browns often sit in male-female
couples within their troops, which on principle I approve of, but I
draw the line at a male throwing a female out of a tree when he gets annoyed. The browns range all over the map. If a banyan fig comes into
fruit, every single brown troop in the reserve converges on it, while the
ringtail troops are stuck in their own backyards. Ringtails and sifaka
are property holders. Browns act like squatters. This is not because
Berenty's browns are newcomers: they behave much the same way in
any forest. They don't even care if it is day or night, and run around at
any hour they please. No sense of order at all. I once wrote a song for
the browns to the tune of the "Marseillaise," starting "Comrades, take
over the forest!" and ending, "And piss on the researchers!" Which they
do, and shit, too.

What browns need is a scientist who loves them — somebody
young, left-wing, egalitarian. Somebody who turns away from the formal ringtails, looks over at the browns, and shouts, "Freedom!" At
Berenty this person is Susan Pinkus. Susan first arrived at Berenty as an
undergraduate in 1993, and she returns every year or two. How likely is
it that two only daughters of elderly professors of literature, one from
Ithaca, New York, and one from Vancouver, British Columbia, would
both reach one small reserve in the south of Madagascar? Well, if both
professors thought appropriate bedtime books for their little girls were
Rudyard Kiplings and Rider Haggards, a destination like Berenty becomes almost inevitable. No wonder Susan and I wound up here! I
guess I have to forgive her preferring brown lemurs over ringtails.

I asked Susan, "Tell me about just one individual, for my book on
Berenty."

"It's got to be Cream Puff. She has mismatched eyes — one lemony yellow and one orange. There is a postcard of her on sale in the cafeteria. Jan Jekielek named her in 'ninety-five when he was collecting DNA samples so he could study the hybridization. He offered the browns a smidgen of banana with one hand and pulled a couple of hairs, with the roots, out of their tails with the other for the DNA. Cream Puff just stood there holding on to Jan's leg. Most of the females look up at you beseechingly. Cream Puff was looking up angrily, because there were no more bananas coming. She was *not* beseeching. Jan said, 'I think I have a name for this one.'

"I have this picture of her from 'ninety-three: a Naturaliste troop member standing on the steps of our student house, refusing to get out of the doorway so I could walk through. It has mismatched eyes. And a huge baby. Cream Puff has *enormous* babies. Maybe someone else in the reserve occasionally beats her, but she always has the first baby in her troop, and it's always twice as large as everyone else's baby. She's as ferocious with other lemurs as she is with people. She has a wide, beautiful, dark gray face and pale orange muttonchops from the collared lemur side. There aren't that many females with beards. Her body is very red from the red-fronted lemur background. There is also something about her posture. I think of her as having a bit of a stoop, to look down on other lemurs, but that's not quite what it is morphologically. Even backlit with no color, her silhouette is enough to tell me it's Cream Puff. Cream Puff looks like one of Charlie's Angels — a big, take-charge woman with beautiful red hair."

Two mornings after Susan's praise of her favorite lemur, Takayō came running to find me. "Cream Puff has caught an infant ringtail!" I dashed to join the circle of students and professors under a little yellow-blossomed cassia tree in front of Naturaliste House, the lodging that the de Heaulmes built for students. Cream Puff sat on a branch, perhaps ten feet up, ignoring the telephotos and camcorders below. She was holding something in one hand, upright like a carrot, and crunching on the top. When I arrived, the head was already gone. She ate steadily downward. Her own huge baby watched as she chewed. A brown eating an infant ringtail has been seen only once before, in just the same place. I wouldn't put it past Cream Puff to be a serial killer.

The ringtail infant's mother hovered in the distance, but she was no match for Cream Puff, not even trying to challenge her.

Cream Puff did not quite finish her meal. After ten minutes she fumbled the remaining hind leg. She jumped casually onto the white split-rail fence below the tree, scooped up the scrap, ate down to the toes, then dropped the last bit of tiny ringed tail. She sauntered off down the rail, sun on her red fur, tail swaying, her own baby on her belly, every inch the self-satisfied Charlie's Angel after a good breakfast. The ring of telephotos dissolved into the current mix of scientists staying at Naturaliste House.

An extraordinary number of the Science Tribe were there that morning in October 2000. That evening we assembled for Susan's Sabbath. Susan's mother died when Susan was fifteen. Every year she lights a candle on the anniversary of her mother's death. She announced that she would hold a memorial ceremony and that we should all come. It did take a bit of preparation. An orange and purple *lamba* (the cloth the local women wrap on for a skirt) cloaked the big lab-cum-dinner table. Sprays of salmon-orange bougainvillea dressed up an empty beer bottle. Candles stood in beer bottles, too. (We all have candles. The plantation generator goes off at ten P.M., so the usual late-night scene at Naturaliste is young faces of all colors lit by an eerie mix of warm candle glow and the pallid gray of laptop screens.) We brought in wine from the restaurant and French bread, but it had gone rock-hard, so we made do with dried apricots and almonds. Susan said that traditionally we each needed a swallow of wine and a lump of bread the size of an olive, but that California almonds would do just fine.

The Sabbath evening, she explained, is a happy ceremony for Jewish people, a family gathering where everyone ends up singing. Her memorial would not be sad. We were not meeting in grief for the newly dead but to light a candle that would burn for twenty-four hours in memory of all the good things in her mother's life. Oh, and this evening we would also honor the birthday of Erica's mother in London. On top of that, we would solemnize the death of an old beat-up male brown lemur in the study troop of Nicoletta from Pisa. You see what I

mean about informality. Someone who prefers brown lemurs to ringtails is likely to hold religious ceremonies with a flavor of radical femi-
nism.

Susan brought it off. She asked Rebecca Blumenfeld, a teenager
there with her mother, Kathryn (repeating Kathryn's forest survey of
1972), to help her sing the opening prayers. We all watched the lighting
of the memorial candle, with a further chant in memory of the dead.
Bit by bit, then, the singing spread. "Happy Birthday" for Erica's mum,
of course. Erica, half English and half Argentine, offered a sultry tango.
Dina and her classmate Tahiry crooned a Malagasy love duet. Nicoletta
warbled florid Italian. Dieter piped a Flemish children's ditty, plus
some amazing parrot whistles. Takayō trumpeted the Alma Mater of
her university on Japan's snowy Hokkaido Island (such a big voice
from such a small woman!), while her compatriot Ichino added tenor
on the choruses. George Williams from California mystified people
with Gilbert and Sullivan patter. (George himself is a dealer-in-magic-
and-spells, that is, the global-positioning system for computerized lemur ranging maps.) Sue Caless from Bolton in the north of England
started in on the Beatles, the world's one universal culture. Only Long
John Walker, Susan's henchman on the brown lemur census, refused to
sing. "And a good thing, too!" he declared.

Of the Berenty silverbacks who advise students, I was there, of
course, and Hanta Rasamimanana, the leader of the Malagasy team,
though Naoki Koyama was still on his way from Kyoto. As a bonus,
Peter Klopfer had come back to Berenty for the first time since men-
toring a flock of Berenty Ph.D.s in the 1970s. We clamored for Peter, as
the senior of us all, to perform. True to his own radical past, he belted
out the union ballad "Solidarity Forever," which of course Susan knew
too.

A great night in Naturaliste! Surely field biologists are all one global
tribe, across age and nationality, whatever we study (even if one study
species occasionally eats another). Solidarity Forever!

I started to giggle. I suddenly remembered Long John Walker asking the chief Berenty guide, "Doesn't it seem a bit odd to you, Andreas,
that people come here from all over the world just to follow lemurs
through the woods?"

Andreas paused, then answered in his dry, precise English, "No, John. *Not* 'a bit odd.' *Very* odd."

Andreas spoke for all the other tribes of Berenty. The people who built the plantation and who call it home, not a field site half a world from home, think that the Science Tribe is stark staring mad.

3

He Wanted the Whole Forest!

The de Heaulmes and the Tandroy, 1660–1940

✺

"Lahivano, drive to the Man-Stone!" Tsiaketraky simply took charge. He always does. Lahivano the chauffeur climbed behind the wheel without so much as a glance at me for confirmation. Tsiaketraky turned to me. "Madame, if you want to write a book about Berenty, there is only one place to begin. We must go to the standing stone. There I will speak of our history."

Soon, in a part of the forest called Ankoba, we reached a three-meter-tall slab of rough pink-red granite set on a concrete plinth marked BERENTY 1936–1996. At the time I did not actually know who Tsiaketraky was. His name means "He-Who-Cannot-Be-Thrown-to-Earth." He is nobleman, sisal commander, an elder so much respected that his title is Father-and-Mother. When Tsiaketraky stepped up onto the Man-Stone's base, though, all I saw was an archetypal Tandroy tribesman.

The Tandroy are a people of Madagascar's extreme south. Their home is the lunar landscape of the spiny forest. The *roy* itself is a mimosa, a thornbush with zigzag twigs and tiny leaves. Androy is the place of the *roy*, and Tandroy are the people of the place of the *roy*. To pile up confusion, both people and region are often called Antandroy, literally the place of the people of the place of the *roy*. It's simpler just to think of Tandroy as the People of the Thorns.

By tradition they are warriors and cattle thieves. Not so long ago their cattle rustling combined sport, test of manhood, and capitalism: the quick route to wealth. Many other Malagasy, especially the quieter, paler, plateau dwellers of Indonesian ancestry, openly fear the tall southerners. Throughout the island Tandroy work as security guards, as incongruous as if Americans sought out Comanches as bodyguards.

Tsiaketraky kept the erect carriage of a warrior despite his years. It was not the solid stance of a foot soldier weighed down by weapons and body armor, but the pantherlike poise of the spearman. His high cheekbones and the laughter wrinkles of his face were dark against the pink stone. Sunlight glittered off mica flecks in the granite, then gleamed in full splendor on the five gold teeth in Tsiaketraky's smile.

He flung out a hand as he began orating.

"Here, exactly here, Monsieur Henry de Heaulme and his brother, Alain, crossed the Mandrare River in the year 1936. Here stood the farm of Mahafaha, He-Who-Makes-Full, in the place called Ankoba, Where-There-Is-Fertile-Ground. Mahafaha became a friend of the de Heaulmes. He was the first Tandroy to grant them land. It was here, exactly here, beside the river, that Berenty estate began!

"Later, when Monsieur Jean de Heaulme was imprisoned, it seemed Berenty estate might fail and disappear. When Monsieur Jean returned from prison and made the plantation great again, it is here, exactly here, he raised the Man-stone to mark the first sixty years of Berenty!"

Jean de Heaulme remembers crossing the Mandrare in 1936, when he was nine years old. He knelt between his uncle Alain and his redoubtable father as Mahafaha the ferryman paddled the dugout pirogue. The Mandrare was three hundred meters wide and two or three meters deep, with a muscular current too strong for any swimmer, and five-meter-deep holes where people fished. The river was full of crocodiles bigger than any nine-year-old boy. A year never passed without some woman losing her arm or her life to the crocodiles as she washed clothes by the river. When one croc was killed, its stomach held a pair of gold earrings. The reptiles even bit the tongues out of drinking cattle. Little Jean did not trail his fingers in the water beside the canoe.

Henry and Alain strode up the alluvial clay bank to Mahafaha's hamlet, half a dozen huts beside the ferry crossing. Mahafaha's wives came out from their own houses and spread a clean rush-straw mat under a kily tree for the visitors to sit on. Elders crouched on the mat with the visitors, and children crowded around. Tier upon tier of faces — so many people in such a tiny village. Long-legged chickens strutted and scratched beneath the stilts of the granary hut. Perhaps a troop of ringtailed lemurs scampered among the kily branches, for lemurs are fady — taboo — to hunt, though Mahafaha had cut many of the surrounding trees for his farm, and lemurs would not venture to the ground anywhere near village dogs. One thing was missing. Among the babies who tried to crawl onto the mat, and the wide-eyed toddlers, and the teenagers at the back, there were almost no children of Jean's own age. In the great famine of 1931, many Tandroy children under five had died. That famine was caused by drought, but it was made far more lethal by an insect, a scientist, and French colonial policy — a story to tell you a little later on. Now, five years after the famine, this French family was proposing to come and live in Tandroy homeland.

Henry de Heaulme was an accomplished orator. He had spoken Malagasy since babyhood, taught by his nurse on Réunion Island. (She was a descendant of Malagasy slaves.) He already knew Androy and the Tandroy, having spent eight years there prospecting for mica. He chose flowery metaphors and pithy local proverbs to address his village audience, circling around the point with no impolite bluntness. At last he made his request. He asked for land.

A tall teenager listened from the edge of the circle: Mahafaha's grandson Jaona (say "Jonah") Tsiminono. Jaona was lucky to be alive at all. His mother died at his birth. Tsiminono means "He-Who-Never-Suckled." Such a child is raised on *habobo,* which is yogurt made from zebu milk, and by the kindness of other nursing women. Jaona lived and thrived, lucky again to be old enough to survive the famine of '31. The six-foot-tall seventeen-year-old was already famous for strength in the *ringa,* the Tandroy wrestling in which boys and men try to fling each other to the ground (one hold is to grab the sides of your opponent's loincloth), while kneeling girls beat out frenetic rhythms on the tom-toms.

"Monsieur de Heaulme asked my grandfather Mahafaha for land," old Jaona remembers today. He laughs out loud. "My grandfather said, 'Of course! You may take whatever you need.' We all thought he wanted a cornfield! Just a half-hectare to cut and burn like anybody else. Later he asked for more, and more. It was a long, long time before we understood he wanted the whole forest!"

Tsiaketraky gestured to me to move to the shade, under a massive tamarind tree — perhaps the same one where Mahafaha's wives had spread out mats for the de Heaulmes sixty-odd years ago. He settled himself on the dry leaves to continue talking. I was not the only listener. If Berenty's Science Tribe is a mixed collection, that is nothing compared to the diversity of the other people. Tsiketraky's audience embraced four tribes, two nations, and two species.

As Tsiaketraky talked, Rekanoky, chief of the forest guardians, hunkered down nearby, planting the butt of his spear upright in the earth. The forest guards' badge of office is the traditional Tandroy weapon: a rosewood shaft about five feet long with steel ferrule and a leaf-shaped blade that looks thoroughly ornamental. It is no ornament. If you test the edge of Rekanoky's spear with your thumb, you'll likely carry the scar for life.

Lahivano the driver joined us too. He has lived here for forty years, but he is a Tanosy from the east coast, near Fort Dauphin. His squarer stature and round bullet head mark him as subtly different from the high-cheeked Tandroy. Benoît Damy, who translated for me, hails from yet another part of the coast. He is a burly, smiling man who traded life as a high school language teacher for the better-paying job of multilingual tourist guide. Guiding pays well enough that he was wearing a snazzy white windbreaker and Yves St. Laurent sunglasses, both resplendent against his chocolate face. In contrast, my lemur-watching colleague Hanta Rasamimanana is an olive-skinned, Indonesian-featured Merina of the high plateau. She wore a hugging-orangutan T-shirt she'd picked up at the International Primatological Congress in Bali, where everyone mistook her for a Balinese. Long John Walker circled the group with his camcorder — every inch (lots of inches) the pale-faced, blue-jeaned Man from Michigan.

To top it off, a troop of ringtailed lemurs arrived on cue in the low stems behind us. They approached to within a couple of meters, peering and clicking dubiously. A baby, perhaps ten days old, clung slightly askew on its mother's neck, while she weaved her head to figure out why we were here. Four Malagasy tribes, two nationalities, two species and about as many social ranks as individuals (you already know that ringtailed lemurs have social distinctions), all under one kily tree.

Tsiaketraky explained that Mahafaha, the de Heaulmes' first friend, was not the actual king. He was just a local headman hired by the French to ferry people across the Mandrare. Eventually he moved away and let Monsieur de Heaulme take his whole farm. The real king and ancestor of the region lived just across the river. He was Tsiongakarivo, which means "Even-a-Thousand-Men-Cannot-Lift-Him-Up." He and his descendants are members of the Andriamagnary, the royal clan and ruling class of the Tandroy tribe. (The de Heaulme genealogy is in printed volumes; Tandroy genealogy is recited, in a special singsong voice.)

To show the importance of King A-Thousand-Cannot-Lift-Him, Tsiaketraky took a handful of dry kily leaves and held them out on his palm, his other hand poised above. His fingers, amazingly long, curled backward as he gestured. A silver bracelet as thick as my index finger shone on his arm. It was the old style, decorated with punched linear patterns and with slightly wider ends that met with no visible split.

As the leaves filtered down, he said that the king was so important that when he was taken to the cemetery, he was not buried in the earth when the body was fresh like an ordinary person. Instead he was placed above all the others, on a platform. When the evil fluids — the blood and snot and urine and rotting flesh — fell down from the corpse like falling leaves from a man's fingers, they fell onto the other bodies; no one could let such things fall on the king.

Monsieur Henry de Heaulme, recounted Tsiaketraky, became

blood brother to Tandroy kings and nobles. Jean de Heaulme doubts that his father actually went through the full ceremony, in which blood brothers cut each other's chest and mingle their blood or drink a few drops of the other's blood. They swear to die for each other if necessary and also to avoid incest with each other's many sisters. But Henry de Heaulme did something like it — something enough like it that every Malagasy tells me of the de Heaulme blood brotherhood with heads of all the local clans.

Monsieur de Heaulme observed Tandroy customs. He spoke at the traditional decision-making meetings called *kabary.* He also listened. He specifically asked what were the sanctions if a person committed a fault against society. People answered, "We make the wrongdoer pay — a chicken or sheep for a small fault, a zebu steer for a large one." He said, "Then if you come to work for me, I will do likewise. If you do wrong, I will fine you a part of your salary or dismiss you for a time. But I will never send you away to forced labor, as other Frenchmen do. And if you, meeting in council, find that I have transgressed your customs, I am also prepared to pay, even up to one or two zebu."

Alain and Henry did not pay for the land. Clan lands were inalienable, part of the limitless wealth of nature bequeathed by God and the Ancestors. They negotiated to clear the forest, though. The clans consulted with each other, their sorcerers, their spirits, and their Ancestors. Led by the queen of Rapily village, they agreed to cut the spiny forest in return for paid wages and for security against recurrent famine. Thousands of Tandroy had died in the famine of 1930–31. When Henry and Alain asked for land, the people had little choice but to accept further change.

In return for permission to cut the forest, the de Heaulme brothers offered zebu cattle to celebrate their compact. They were soon invited to funeral celebrations as family. Rekanoky, the forest guardian who squatted beside his spear, a wonderful old rogue with a checkered past, is one of the few who will openly say to me, "They took our land, and all they gave us was a few zebu for a party." But then he brightens up. "Anyway, Monsieur Jean de Heaulme has to come to my funeral."

Tsiaketraky, He-Who-Cannot-Be-Thrown-to-Earth, magisterially continued his explanation. "The old customs are being forgotten. People are turning Christian. Even I am now Christian. About five years ago I decided that I am old and must think about my funeral. If I am a Christian, my sons do not have to kill all my three hundred cattle, perhaps only twenty-five of them. I have a big herd — and also a bank account! So I converted. I am now treasurer of the church as well as president of my village, which insures an inheritance for my sons.

"But being Christian means that I can keep only one of my wives, Tsoloho, the youngest. I gave the others houses of their own.

"Of course Christianity does not mean we ignore the older spirits. Kokolampo, for instance, live in trees or boa constrictors or even in river mud. Kokolampo are not Ancestors, or wandering ghosts of the dead, or manlike devils. They come from nature. They can be male or female. Their chief attribute is curiosity. That means they know things, like why a person falls sick. The drummers drum, people dance, the healer goes into trance." Tsiaketraky, fists in the air, briefly mimed uncontrollable shivering. "Then the kokolampo will tell the healer in trance which medicines to gather in the forest, and what sacrifice to offer, to heal the sufferer. Whatever is asked, even if the sacrifice is very large, must then be accomplished.

"When Monsieur Jean de Heaulme was in prison, we freed him by releasing the kokolampo. Monsieur Jean was keeping boa constrictors in a cage in Berenty. I was one of the men who tried to release him by arguing with the police, but when that did not work, we made a sacrifice and let loose the snakes. The kokolampo were appeased. Within two weeks he was free!

"Later Monsieur Jean raised the Man-Stone to celebrate Berenty. He followed the rituals and accomplished everything correctly. He asked a descendant of King A-Thousand-Cannot-Lift-Him to cut the throats of five zebu, a feast for everyone on the estate. Four were killed at Berenty village. Over there is the skull of the one sacrificed here at the Man-Stone itself." (The skull's frontal bones, nailed to a tree, gazed back at us with empty eye sockets, the horns curved symmetrically above its head like a dancer's upraised arms: the most perfect animal for sacrifice.)

Tsiaketraky concluded, "I received my own name from a koko-lampo. A possessed woman dreamed. She came to my mother, who was pregnant, to tell her that the child she carried would be a son. The baby must be named Cannot-Be-Thrown-to-Earth."

He was not thrown down in the wrestling game of the ringa. Not thrown down in dignity when he became plantation commander with a thousand men at his command. He was not even downcast morally when things went wrong, when Berenty plantation closed and his employer was imprisoned. He was definitely not downcast as a man: he has had seven wives, fathered thirty children, and so far has thirty-two grandchildren!

Tsiaketraky grinned his golden smile, crinkling all the laughter lines of his face.

A de Heaulme ancestor survived the massacre of the pink girls. The family has its own history — a great deal of it. Heaulme itself means "helm," the helmet of a knight in armor. There is still a village of Heaulme near Paris, with the remains of an ancient chateau fort. "Henry," spelled with a *y* rather than an *i,* is not Anglicized. It is just medieval. However, the ancestor who first reached Fort Dauphin was no heroic knight. She was a heroine.

Fort Dauphin began in 1643 as a struggling French settlement on a windy peninsula beside a terrible port. Nowadays ship carcasses of all centuries lie in the blue crescent of the bay, piled like cars in a junkyard. The colonists originally tried a calmer site at the lagoon of Saint Luce, a little farther north, but so many died of malaria that they moved to the present town. There they might die of shipwreck, but at least onshore trade winds blew sickness away. They built a stockade looking out to sea on three sides. Inland lay a forest of "extremely large trees, always covered in greenery unless they are stripped by an old age of four or five hundred years, or by the lightning-bolts which often fall here, with terrible thunderclaps multiplied by the concavities of the mountains."

The local Tanosy name, Taolagnaro, ominously means "Bone-Place." The settlers renamed it Fort Dauphin not for the dolphins that leap in the bay, but for the dauphin, the crown prince of France. They did not know that by the time they reached harbor the five-year-old dauphin had already been crowned Louis XIV.

Sieur Etienne de Flacourt governed Fort Dauphin from 1648 to 1655. We know a great deal about the place, because he wrote a detailed book on the island-continent of Madagascar in 1658. He set forth geography and tribal kingdoms, plants and animals, even ringtailed lemurs and white sifaka and the giant lemur tretretretre. An enlarged edition appeared in 1661, but by that time its distinguished author had been blown up at sea by Barbary pirates.

After Flacourt, the colony degenerated quickly. About a hundred French lived in and around the fort, defended by a palisade of wooden posts and a few cannon. They spent their time bickering about who should lead them and scheming without much success to extort tribute from the locals. At that time, most of the Tanosy and Tandroy warriors were a head taller in stature than the Frenchmen, an indication of how much better nourished the southern Malagasy were than the immigrant French. Local rulers saw little reason to obey the puny white men.

Two great warlords dominated the region: Lord Manangue, king of the Mandrare River, and a Frenchman called La Case. Manangue was originally an ally of the French. With their guns, and a few of their soldiers, he conquered all of Androy. (Strictly, the area was not yet called by that name but by assorted clan names; Lord Manangue may have been the first leader to conquer westward.) Then, however, a zealous Catholic priest informed Manangue that he must become Christian. That meant renouncing all but one of his wives. Manangue refused, though he was willing to allow his children freedom to choose their religion. The priest tore the king's talisman from around his neck and threw it in the fire. Result: one poisoned priest, and an implacable Tandroy enemy of the French, who could fight them with their own tactics and their own guns.

The warrior La Case meanwhile became a white Tanosy, based on the seaward side of the mountains. La Case bested one local chief in single combat before their massed armies and then spared the man's life and lands, to general amazement. He married a beautiful and powerful Tanosy princess, who not only bore his children but fought beside him in battle. Between them they seized thousands of cattle and slaves from defeated enemies.

Over and over, Lord Manangue attacked French expeditionary forces and even the fort itself. Over and over, La Case came to the rescue of his compatriots. Jealous governors of the fort never wanted to reward him. He had gone native far too successfully. Eventually La Case died, leaving Fort Dauphin to its fate.

The colony staggered on until 1674. Then a ship sailed into harbor bearing the final spark that blew the fort apart. That spark was fifteen French girls, only fifteen to eighteen years old. They were called the "Daughters of the King." Inspired by Flacourt's great book, and by the expansionist minister Jean Baptiste Colbert, Louis XIV deemed it wise to send out orphan girls to marry settlers in his far-flung colonies — some to French Canada, some as far as the Indian Ocean.

The young women were assembled at the Hospice de la Salpêtrière, which still stands as a great hospital in Paris today. A few were indeed orphaned daughters of good families fallen on bad times, others were beggars and prostitutes. We know that one called Nicole Coulon came of humble stock, the sort of girl who might have been picked up for petty crimes. Another, sixteen-year-old Françoise Châtelain, was somehow special. Whether she had a more elegant background, or beauty, or sexiness, or just plain courage, Françoise was a survivor. I can't help imagining a young Scarlett O'Hara who would volunteer for any adventure to get herself out of the Salpêtrière.

A nun sailed with them as chaperone, and a priest went along to solemnize their future marriages. They were bound for the Île de Bourbon, present-day Réunion. The captain then delayed his ship's departure to load up a cargo of eau de vie to sell for his own profit, which meant they finally left France at the worst season of contrary winds. It took ten whole months to reach Fort Dauphin, where the captain meant to offload his firewater en route to Réunion.

But oh, that port! Fort Dauphin had already finished off a few pirate craft. Now the love-ship foundered on the harbor sand, its anchors dragging in a storm. The pink girls begged to stay where they were, to escape from the sea and the chaperone. Surely they could marry colonists in Fort Dauphin! And so a mass wedding was arranged for August 27, 1674. Nicole Coulon was betrothed to a carpenter; Françoise Châtelain to a ship's ensign rather higher in the social scale.

The newcomers were by no means the only women in the fort. Most settlers already had Tanosy wives. Those wives, along with other native servants, were called by the jovial nickname *marmites,* which means cooking pots: cauldrons black with woodsmoke from the fire. Any colonist who embarked on a solemn Catholic wedding with a French girl was expected to send his marmite wife back to her Tanosy kinfolk.

A second ship fortuitously sailed into the harbor. It could take passengers away on a route toward Africa, then India, and finally Réunion. Many decided to go. Now the marmites were not only furious but also afraid. They had thrown in their lot with the French. Who would protect them if the fort itself was abandoned?

They turned to the remaining power in the land. Lord Manangue was still king of the Mandrare River, and still bent on revenge.

The day of the wedding, August 27, the Tanosy wives returned with their menfolk, spears, and guns. They attacked in the midst of the ceremony, cutting Frenchmen's throats like sacrificed zebu. Seventy-five French were killed; just sixty-three escaped. The well of Fort Flacourt was filled to the brim with bodies. The survivors fled to the ship in the harbor. On September 9 the colonists spiked the cannon, capped the dreadful well, burned their stores and their fort, and sailed away.

In the end, twenty-one survivors of the massacre reached Réunion. Nicole Coulon arrived with her carpenter husband, who also helped Nicole's friend Françoise make the long journey. Françoise was otherwise alone. She had been widowed on her wedding day.

On Réunion, Françoise married a gentleman from Provence named Michel Esparon. He too was killed in a slave uprising only five years later, leaving her with two children. Her third husband, Jacques Carré de Talhoet, lived for eight years — and she now had three more offspring. Finally, when she was thirty-six years old, Françoise found a husband who lasted. Augustin Panon fathered five children, making ten in all. Panon outlived his redoubtable wife, who died in 1730 at the old age of seventy-one.

Her family became the grandest dynasty on Réunion. Françoise Châtelain Panon was the foremother of most of the island's aristocrats, including the de Heaulmes.

During the eighteenth and nineteenth centuries, while France had its Enlightenment philosophers, its Revolution and Napoleonic Empire, plantation owners on Réunion got on with farming. They also attempted to face down Britain over control of the Indian Ocean. For them, the American Revolution was just an excuse for French privateers to harass the British fleet.

In 1729 Jean Roland Boutsocq de Heaulme emigrated from the Ardennes in the north of France to seek his fortune overseas. He became an officer of the Grand Compagnie des Indes Orientales, which dominated French trade with India — Louis XIV's answer to Britain's East India Company. Boutsocq de Heaulme prospered. His family soon owned sugar plantations covering a large share of Réunion Island. Their family seat, La Basse Terre, was a palace. Its pillared façade was vaguely Indian, something like Brighton's Royal Pavilion, with a noble curved staircase leading upward into the pillars, its tower a visual center point for the twin volcanic peaks behind. The de Heaulmes were later overshadowed by still higher born settlers who emigrated just in time to avoid the guillotine. Réunionais genealogies read like a roll call of ancient French noble families: Panon Desbassayns, de Villèle, de Villentroy, de Châteauvieux, de Dieuleveult, de Heaulme.

Aristocrats married each other. Réunion is a very small island! In fact, it is only seventy kilometers in diameter — much of it a live volcano, which towers three kilometers tall. The habitable space is a miniskirt of coastal land around live and extinct volcanoes, with a ruffle of breaking seas.

The aristocrats found that Malagasy slaves substituted rather well for the grimy peasantry of France. Not all the nobles were reactionaries, though: a de Villentroy from Réunion was the first deputy to rise in the French Chamber of Deputies to demand an end to slavery. In France and Réunion slavery was outlawed in 1848, fifteen years before America's Emancipation Proclamation.

Some Réunionais, however, were ultra-royalists. One de Villèle was a minister for the last French king, in the restoration of 1830. He concocted a pompous family genealogy that went straight back to the year 1000. In his account the pink girl from the Fort Dauphin massacre becomes Françoise Châtelain de Cressy, a nobleman's daughter from Falaise in Normandy — a piece of wishful thinking.

Links with Madagascar continued through the centuries. After all, Réunion and Madagascar are comparatively close. Fort Dauphin became the major staging post for the export of slaves to the Réunion plantations. With the end of slavery, Madagascar sent indentured servants instead. When the French finally conquered Madagascar in 1895, they exiled the last Malagasy queen — but at first no farther than Réunion.

I shall tell the history of Madagascar's Merina people of the high plateau only from the vantage point of the extreme south. The Merina came from Indonesia perhaps a thousand years ago, about the same time as more African tribes arrived, like the Tandroy and the Tanosy of the outlying coastal regions. There was a king wearing the warrior's mother-of-pearl medallion on his forehead, who conquered and unified the plateau Merina around 1800. He established Antananarivo, the Place of the City of a Thousand, as his capital. His son, the Malagasy Napoleon, conquered most of Madagascar. He wore a scarlet British uniform of the era of Waterloo, invited British missionaries to teach technology, and acquired the services of one Sargeant Hastie to equip and drill his army, in return for banning the external slave trade. Internal slavery went right on. The paler people of the plateau owned people from the coast and even bought slaves from Africa. The racial divide in Madagascar is uneasily familiar to Americans. The majority of people actually spring from mixed ancestry, but the distrust between Malagasy *mainty,* blacks, and *fotsy,* whites, has grown out of a long, long history.

After the kings came a queen who rolled Christians off the cliff in front of her palace (sewn up alive in straw mats!) and another queen, and another, and a prime minister who specialized in marrying queens. What mattered to the south was that the Merina Napoleon had succeeded in conquering the Tanosy of Fort Dauphin as early as 1825. Merina governors took over the stone ramparts of the old French fort on its windy peninsula and extracted taxes from the people of the coast. Though the Merina launched several expeditions, they never conquered the Tandroy amid the thorns and thirst of their desert home. Tandroy were never slaves to other tribes.

The last Merina queen, Ranavalona III, was crowned in 1883 at the age of twenty-two. Her official portrait shows a sad-eyed young woman, slightly hyperthyroid, in Victorian crimson velvet, flowered satin, and ruffled lace, her hands daintily posed to display her golden rings and bracelets. At her coronation, Ranavalona III spoke to crowds massed in Antananarivo's valley of Mahamasina, the Sacred Stone. Dressed in a gown of white embroidered silk, shaded by gold-edged scarlet parasols, and surrounded by chanting women, massed soldiers, and four hundred schoolchildren, she vowed, "If anyone wishes to seize a part of this land, even if only the space covered by the width of a grain of rice, I will place myself before it, as if I were a man, to defend with you our common fatherland. Is it not so, O my people?" At which the crowd of thousands shouted back its approval, *"Eny!"* "Our mother!"

Twelve years later, on September 30, 1895, a French expeditionary force conquered Antananarivo. Right after the first two explosive shells fell into the palace garden, the white flag of surrender was hoisted up to flutter from the queen's palace. Apparently the Merina court was astonished by the attack. False reports of victories kept them from realizing that their army essentially never held back the French. In the whole French campaign, the invaders suffered only twenty dead and one hundred wounded in fighting — but lost six thousand to malaria and dysentery. Only after the palace and the army surrendered did a serious revolt break out. The Merina were accustomed to rule over "blacks" from the coast; they would not bend their pride in turn to become chattels of the "red" Frenchmen. General Joseph Gallieni, the new governor general, quelled the revolt by summary execution of prominent men, and by exiling the queen. She was carried in a *filanzana,* a sedan chair, on bearers' shoulders across the rippling plateau hills, then down over the rainforest escarpment, among orchids and frog-calls and the eerie song of the indri, Madagascar's largest lemur. Finally she reached the sea and a boat for Réunion.

The queen found haven in one of the elegant townhouses belonging to Madame de Villentroy, grandmother of Henry and Alain de Heaulme. Madame de Villentroy befriended her guest. She saw not a conquered enemy but a lonely and frightened woman. Two years later the French government decided that Ranavalona III was still a symbolic threat and moved her to faraway Algeria.

When the queen was forced to leave, she gave the filanzana she used on Réunion to her hostess and friend as a parting gift. A hundred years later the Bellier de Villentroy family returned it to the Malagasy embassy in France. A desperately uncomfortable conveyance. The queen, a good Victorian, must have sat ever upright: it gave me a crick in the back just to look at it. Still, I could see that the cushion was once ribbed golden velvet, with real embroidery braid brought all the way from Europe. The leather-sheathed carrying poles were still dark with the sweat of men who bore the last queen in the first years of her lifelong exile.

Five de Heaulme brothers sailed off to fight in World War I. It was the first time they saw France. Henry de Heaulme was born on June 23, 1899, the year the queen was packed off to Algiers; Alain was born December 10, 1900. They were two of the six daughters and six sons of Narcisse de Heaulme and Marie Bellier de Villentroy. The family lived in a lovely house with white verandas in the Réunionais town quarter called Le Chaudron, surrounded by the dark green tiered pinnacles of *Araucaria* trees. Theirs was a world where descendants of slaves brought up children of French aristocrats with a working knowledge of the Malagasy language. The de Heaulme family was deeply Catholic and conservative, filled with feudal pride and an archaic code of duty.

The sons were the eighth generation after the first Jean de Heaulme left France to live beside the Indian Ocean. When World War I began, it was inevitable that they would enlist for France.

Unbelievably, all five brothers survived the war. A troop carrier brought Henry and Alain back from the wide world of Europe to their minute island. En route, their ship stopped at Tamatave, Madagascar's chief port. Alain and Henry looked out at the green coastline stretching north and south as far as the eye could see — a single sandy beach a thousand kilometers long.

They left the ship. They rode the tiny narrow-gauge rail line that snakes up the rainforest escarpment beside a river of splashing waterfalls, following the route that Queen Ranavalona descended on her bearer's shoulders. They arrived in the capital city in the first flush of modernization. The French occupiers had "rationalized" the name of the capital from Antananarivo, "The Place of the City of a Thousand," to mere Tananarive, something more like "Thous-ville." Wide, colonnaded Avenue Gallieni was being laid out in a valley below a rosy hill town of gabled brick houses, overlooked by the French governor's mansion on its balconied hill. A photograph captured them there, still in uniform — Henry in officers' high boots, Alain in colonial baggy shorts. Alain is tall, broad-shouldered and bespectacled; Henry, shorter, holds his arms crossed, his cleft chin jutting forward. Henry shows already (though perhaps I see what I know) the obstinacy that builds empires.

The brothers resolved to escape from claustrophobic Réunion to this burgeoning new colony. The family tradition was that the eldest son inherited all the family estates. Younger sons were expected to go out and seek their fortune without much family backing. Even the eldest de Heaulme son was not so well off, for three successive cyclones had devastated the family sugar fields. When Henry and Alain returned to their parents, they announced their decision to leave Réunion and make their way in Madagascar.

Then their sister Marthe dropped her own bombshell. She had made a secret vow to God. If her brothers survived the war, she would become a nun and give her own life to the church. Her devout family had no choice but to agree. Aged eighteen, she sailed to Fort Dauphin to begin her novitiate. She became Soeur Gabrielle of the Daughters of Charity. That is the female arm of the order of Saint Vincent de Paul, the ex-convict saint who rose from a prison galley to devote himself to the poor of Paris. The Daughters of Charity are also called the Little Sisters of the Poor for the strictness of their vows to help the world's deprived peoples, to keep nothing for themselves. They formally renew those vows every year. The Daughters of Charity used to wear the *cornette,* a headdress the size of an unfurling pillowcase. Soeur Gabrielle sailed among the poor like a white-clad galleon surmounted by the starched white wings of her coif, carrying education, nursing, and famine relief to those in need.

The family speak of Soeur Gabrielle as a saint, always innocent, always believing the best of everyone. A saint, perhaps, but also a de Heaulme. With the family flair for organization, she eventually founded and headed three separate religious communities in the far south of Madagascar. She sounds to me like the most intimidating of the lot.

Henry and Alain tried to farm near Tananarive. Athletic, high-spirited Alain headed up a Boy Scout troop in his spare time. A photo shows him with a troop of boys of all races in Baden-Powell uniforms. He took his Scouts hiking and camping. One night on the bare plateau they slept in a grove of trees next to a cemetery. The cemetery rats carried bubonic plague. Most of the boys quickly died. Alain expected to die, too, but Doctors Girard and Robic of the Tananarive hospital had just developed an untested vaccine for plague. By family account, Alain became the first human being to try the vaccine and the first to owe it his life.

Bloody jaundice then struck the brothers three times running, with malaria on top. Their doctor told them to leave the plateau or expect to die. They gave up farming and went to work for an uncle, Pierre Bellier de Villentroy, who exported mica and graphite from Madagascar to the industrial world. He sent his nephews down to the drier, healthier southlands. Alain became manager of a mica mine at Ambihy, near Tsivory — a town nearly off the map even today. He organized his work force to dynamite out the slabs of layered, transparent rock, which was then a crucial insulator for the world's electrical industry. Henry, the entrepreneur of the pair, managed the shipping and exporting.

On December 28, 1926, Henry married the mica magnate's daughter, Marcelle Bellier de Villentroy. Vivacious rather than pretty, she was a cousin who shared all of Henry's own background. He had known her all his life. They never considered speaking to each other with the familiar *tu* used by almost every other French couple. In ancient aristocratic families, husband and wife used the formal *vous*. Henry did not address his charming, lively bride by her name, Marcelle, but always as "Madame." Their children (and grandchildren) ate with a nanny who taught them manners. On Sundays and holidays the family would dine together. Children must stay silent until the dessert course was served, when their father would announce that it was now their turn to speak. In the Villentroy and de Heaulme tradition, manners tempered love with continuing respect. The young couple understood each other.

Alain fell in love in his turn. On a trip back to Réunion he met a visiting American girl, an eighteen-year-old beauty from New Orleans who had come to meet her Indian Ocean relatives. She was as dashing and athletic as Alain himself. They went for early morning horseback rides across the island and danced into the night at Réunionais balls. Then Alain's parents formally forbade the romance. Perhaps it was because she laughed too loud, she rode astride in jodhpurs like a man, she was altogether their idea of a 1920s American flapper. Perhaps the reason was really the one they gave. There had been three generations in a row of Villentroy–de Heaulme marriages. Henry had married one first cousin. Alain, always second to his brother, was forbidden to marry yet another cousin. No question of liaison with Marie-Céleste Bellier de Villentroy of New Orleans. Her dark eyes and tumbling brown curls still look out from the photograph Alain kept on his dresser for the rest of his life.

Henry and his bride traveled south on a Harley-Davidson amid dying prickly pears. Madame Marcelle de Heaulme gave birth to her first son, Jean, in Tananarive on May 18, 1928. That clearly was not going to slow Henry down. He bought a big Harley-Davidson motorcycle, put his wife and six-month-old son into the sidecar, and set off on the five-hundred-mile trek south to Fort Dauphin. That was the route I took in 1963, which seemed adventurous enough even then. In 1928 there was a sort of track, but as Jean remarked later, it was frequently hard to see where it was. (The road had first been laid out six years before.) The great advantage of the motorcycle was that the couple could lift it out of mudholes themselves. Henry could ferry it across a river in a single dugout canoe, with a second trip for Madame and baby Jean and the sidecar.

They crossed the Androy region. In theory French troops had officially subdued Androy in 1903. The colonial government had confiscated twelve thousand firearms there, mostly ancient flintlocks. It seems that the Tandroy gave up only the worst of their weapons and hid the rest. The government in theory abolished slavery, cattle stealing, and clan warfare.

In fact, the final skirmish between Tandroy and their western neighbors, the Mahafaly tribe, occurred in 1932, well after Henry and Madame Marcelle arrived in Fort Dauphin. Cattle raiding continued as merrily as ever. The French built a string of forts along the roads, each manned by two or three French officers and a score of Senegalese troops. The forts were square two-story blockhouses, surrounded by open ground and a square stockade — an attempt to impose Cartesian discipline on reluctant people. The forts were linked by a telegraph line to signal emergencies. Nonetheless, it proved almost impossible to stop the Tandroy from turning that lifeline wire into bracelets.

The most dramatic change in Tandroy life, however, was not the presence of the soldiers, the freeing of the slaves, or the odd French custom of feeding people for several weeks in jail as a reward for stealing cattle. It was the death of the prickly pear. The wickedest thorns of all in the south were not native. They belonged to a Mexican cactus. Back in the eighteenth century, long after the debacle of the pink girls, the French had tried again to found a colony in Fort Dauphin. Its governor, Count de Modave, wrote to his friend Voltaire, "I shall hold the people under a yoke so light they will not even perceive it." Within a short time he was selling slaves like everyone else. The Tanosy got ready to massacre the French colony yet again. De Modave made a visit to Mauritius, where he saw a wonderful solution: *Opuntia,* the Mexican prickly pear. He imported the cactus to fortify the landward side of his fort. He miscalculated. Prickly pear did not do well in Fort Dauphin's wet coastal climate. The Tanosy overran the town.

Inland, though, desert-living Tandroy seized on prickly pear for their own purposes. They used it to protect cattle corrals and to serve as food for beasts and men. It thrived in the nonforest areas of Androy, growing into impenetrable thickets. Tandroy settlements lay behind narrow trails, hemmed in by ten-foot cactuses with six-inch spines. When the French soldiers came, they were forced to walk in single file on twisting paths. Then the troops would suddenly reach a barricade of cut, paddle-shaped leaves with thorns like rolls of World War I barbed wire. Tandroy warriors rose from behind every cactus, firing ancient muskets and stabbing downward with their spears. The local proverb announces: "The prickly pear and the Tandroy are brothers."

In 1923 or '24, somebody imported cochineal scale insects, the natural enemy of the prickly pear. It might even have been Raymond Decary, the French governor of Androy, who later had to cope with its effects. That first box of the insects must have seemed innocent enough, for it was sent to a research station in Tananarive where the insects might have been studied and contained. Instead, the cochineals were dumped out of a window onto a hedge of prickly pear. They began to demolish that hedge. They spread to more hedges around Tananarive. The French botanist Henri Perrier de la Bathie observed the effects. In 1925 he deliberately collected cochineals and sent them south. It was ostensibly just an experiment to clear prickly pear from the lands of a settler friend.

Did Perrier de la Bathie foresee the plague that would follow? Anthropologist Karen Middleton argues that he hoped for just such an outcome. His philosophy was right in line with the harshest colonial policy. Along with the governor-general, the high-handed Marcel Olivier, the botanist planned to contain, or even destroy, local agriculture in order to provide workers for the colonists' plantations.

Perrier de la Bathie's arguments were outrageously self-contradictory. First he claimed that the prickly pear was holding back the Tandroy and other desert tribes. Hidden among the thorns, their villages were so isolated, and their own nutrition and that of their cattle so miserable, that the sullen tribesmen could not imagine coming out of the thickets and going to work for wages. Simultaneously he argued that the area's soil was so rich, the cattle so numerous, Tandroy physical robustness so impressive, that if French settlers could free the lands of the noxious weed, then all those potential riches — and manpower — would be at the settlers' disposal.

What no one could have foreseen was the cochineals' success. Karen Middleton points out that each strain of prickly pear and its pests are exquisitely attuned to each other. At that time Australia and South Africa were investing enormous effort in cochineal breeding programs, trying to eradicate the prickly pears that had invaded their own pasturelands, with only mixed success. By pure chance, the boxful of cochineal insects introduced in 1924 exactly matched the monoculture of prickly pears that had spread through Madagascar's south from that single eighteenth-century introduction to Fort Dauphin.

Swarms of flying male insects blanketed the land. Their bodies were filled with the crimson pigment that we still use for red food coloring. When a swarm hit one of the few early cars, the driver would peer through a windscreen apparently drenched in blood or climb out to see his vehicle flayed and dripping red gore like some Stephen King nightmare. There is no record whether Henry and Madame Marcelle drove the Harley-Davidson through such a swarm in 1928. Certainly, all along their route, the barbed fortress walls of Androy were contorted, shriveling, covered with white blotches like pervasive mold, the shielding excreta of the cochineal. If Henry explored one of the furry white blotches with a thumb, the insect inside disintegrated into a crimson smear. The imported cochineal almost obliterated the imported, vulnerable strain of prickly pear.

In 1930–31 drought and famine struck. Governor Raymond Decary knew the importance of prickly pears in the local people's lives. He quoted that proverb "The Tandroy and the prickly pear are brothers," understanding that the plant provided food and water for man and beast and was the crucial last resort in famine. People could fill their stomachs with the watery fruit. They burned the thorns off piles of cut leaves that the cattle then chewed, spitting out wads of green fiber. The Tandroy had taken full advantage of the Mexican cactus, and their way of life collapsed when it was gone. In 1931 Governor Decary watched in horror as skeletal bodies staggered out of the villages — and as the strongest stole the final crumbs of food from the weakest. Decary demanded and got aid from his colonial government, but thousands of Tandroy died anyway, including much of the cohort of children under five.

Botanist Perrier de la Bathie and Governor-General Olivier saw instead their desired result. Destitute Tandroy began to migrate far from home to earn wages in the newly developing plantation economy of Madagascar.

Madame Marcelle de Heaulme did not share her husband's passion for rural Madagascar. When the couple reached Fort Dauphin, the seaport town their ancestor Françoise Chatelain had fled two hundred and fifty years earlier, Madame de Heaulme settled down firmly in the small French community to raise her growing family. They lived at first in a tiny thatched hut while she supervised the building of a house with memories of life in Réunion. The house, still used by the family, is modest by American standards, just two stories with verandas, set against a hillside, sheltered from the road. The flooring is patterned in great concentric hexagons of multicolored hardwood, copied from the Maison de Chaudron in Réunion, and the shielding trees are tall *Araucaria* pines, again like Madame's Creole home. She kept up the family traditions and contacts and was wholly sociable within the little European world of Fort Dauphin.

Henry, meanwhile, looked to the future, not the past — a de Heaulme trait — leaving history to the de Villentroy side of the family. He and Alain ranged over the countryside. They prospected for mica and kept an eye out for the right site for a plantation of their own.

What Henry and Alain wanted first on the far side of the Mandrare River was softwood for mica packing cases. The rainforest near Fort

Dauphin was all hardwoods, too precious, and much too difficult to work, to turn into shipping crates. Inland, though, grew the spiny forest, dominated by the twenty-foot thorned spires of *fantiolotse,* which look at first sight like candelabra cactuses. They are actually members of an endemic plant family, the Didiereaceae. Their trunks are real wood, a lightweight durable wood, not cactus pulp. They provide the planks for those little Tandroy houses, and they were perfect for the brothers' packing cases. As Jaona said, when Henry and Alain crossed the Mandrare to Berenty, they wanted the whole forest.

The death of the prickly pear meant that the Tandroy themselves faced a new future.

"I would let my head be cut off for Monsieur de Heaulme!" Rehomaha ("the Abandoned") introduced himself to me with those words, drawing his hand with a great flourish across his wrinkled throat. As a ten-year-old child, Rehomaha became one of the very first plantation workers. His father had died young, leaving wife and son abandoned and destitute. The orphan, summoning all his courage, went to terrifying Monsieur de Heaulme to ask for a job that a boy could do. Henry made him day guardian of the vegetable garden: squashlike *voazava,* watermelons, red beans, manioc, and sweet potatoes. An older teenager watched the garden at night. The guards were not armed heavies. Their sanction was that if somebody stole the crops, they would know and would tell. One night somebody did indeed steal the sweet potatoes right out of the ground — the older boy had fallen asleep.

Monsieur de Heaulme said that as a fine for the theft the equivalent of one hundred and fifty francs today would be deducted from the guards' wages. They would lose two and a half cents a month! The boys were miserable and angry. They went back to the garden, studied the thief's footprints, and set out to track him. They followed the trail into Berenty village. Berenty was turning into the factory town that it is today, with hundreds of huts built for migrant labor. The houses were no worse, but also no better, than traditional village dwellings. The Mandrare was the only running water; scraps of nearby forest were latrines. When one of the workers earned enough to buy cattle for his bride price, he generally left, and a new name would be stenciled on his hut.

Berenty had grown far larger than any normal village, but the boys carefully deciphered the maze of footprints. They tracked the thief right to one of the huts. Then they called for help. The stolen sweet potatoes were piled high inside the culprit's home! Monsieur de Heaulme restored the boys to full wages and fined the thief instead. Rehomaha grins in triumph at the memory, even today.

The boy Rehomaha is now a seventy-five-year-old man in a dust-colored dustcoat and rawhide sandals. We met in the tourists' cafeteria. He was a little afraid. He ordered but could not choke down an unfamiliar Coca-Cola. His lifetime of service with the plantation has left him still poor. He was the person who told me that Monsieur de Heaulme asked about the traditional sanctions against a person who transgressed: fines in cash or kind, not other punishments. The worst times of his life, Rehomaha said, were when he suffered just such sanctions. He was suspended from work twice: once for refusing to move to a second plantation with his work gang and once because he was accused of killing a lemur. He protested that he had never killed lemurs. The problem was that he had a little sweet potato crop down on the river's floodplain, so he was always going through the forest, and it was easy for jealous people to accuse him. Plantation "justice" was, on the whole, more swift than sure. Still, the plantation gave him a livelihood that he had no other way to earn.

On the polished table Rehomaha unknotted a bright purple bandanna to show me ancient treasures. The first exhibit was coins saved from the wages he had earned as an orphan boy. One coin was labeled "Bon pour 2 Francs, Chambre de Commerce de France, 1926." On the obverse an armed woman represented France with the motto, "Commerce et Industrie." In the colonies the French Chamber of Commerce minted money in more senses than one. Next he unwrapped a little bundle that looked like cocktail toothpicks, held with elaborate bark-fiber stitching instead of rubber bands. They were the original nails for the corners of mica packing cases. People who could not get daily work would whittle the nails and sell them to the de Heaulmes at so much per thousand. They were made of *katrafay,* the endemic bitter-juice tree, whose bark cures stomachache and worms. There are hardly any left now, for the wood is both tough and termite-resistant. Big katrafay trees have almost all been cut down for coffins; small ones turn into charcoal for Fort Dauphin.

Rehomaha's final treasure was treasure indeed: a very small school notebook with the names of the first 120 workers on the plantation, grouped by clan village. He remembered them all: not just names, but men and women with village homes. I was baffled, for Rehomaha is illiterate, and this was written without erasure in a school-formed hand. Rehomaha had dictated the list to his forty-year-old wife, Segonde, who had gone to the plantation school. The best record of the first labor force comes from Rehomaha and Segonde!

Ready to leave, he took down the half cigarette that had sat behind his ear throughout the interview and casually lighted it. Startled, my colleague Hanta asked him to do that again. The match was age-old flint, probably the gun flint from a flintlock rifle, struck on steel, with the sparks caught in his tinderbox, a dried inner stalk of sisal with a removable top and shredded fibers inside. It is all cheaper than buying matches.

As he rose to go, Rehomaha made sure that I wrote down his most important message. He leaned forward and declared again, "I would let my head be cut off for Monsieur de Heaulme. My life here has not been all happy. I was suspended once for not wishing to move my work crew far away, and another time because someone falsely accused me of killing a ringtailed lemur. But as simply as I say to you, yes, you can record my voice, yes, you can take my picture, if it was necessary I would let my head be cut off for Monsieur de Heaulme."

Jaona Tsiminono, the Never-Suckled, went to work to pay his head tax. The noble picture of the de Heaulmes negotiating with villagers and being kind to orphans can be painted instead in the stark light of postcolonial cynicism. The government authorized Frenchmen to seize people's land. The government also imposed a tax on all men over twenty-one. The amount was trivial, and the tax probably cost more to collect than it raised in revenue. Its purpose was to make men work for

the Frenchmen's coins. In societies that had always been based on sub-
sistence, on barter, and, very importantly, on gifts, both British and
French colonial governments enforced poll taxes to bring their subjects into the money economy. The alternative to "voluntary" employment was the hated *corvée:* forced labor on roads and other public
works. The corvée was SMOTIG, for Service de la Main d'Oeuvre des
Travaux d'Intérêt Générale, inaugurated in 1926 by Governor-General
Marcel Olivier. Later the International Labor Organization (ILO) in
Geneva condemned SMOTIG and compared it to Hitler's *Arbeits-
dienst.*

At the same time Madagascar inaugurated nature reserves before
any other African countries did. In 1927 Governor-General Olivier,
under the influence of the botanist Perrier de la Bathie (the one who
launched the cochineals), set up ten great wilderness tracts and soon
added two more. Ever since, conservationists (including me) have applauded their foresight. The reserves are magnificent areas of botanical
richness, what today we would call "hot spots." The areas set aside
were chosen not only for their scientific importance, but for their inac-
cessibility, in places not suited to agriculture — that is, to French agriculture. The people who might actually want to use the reserves and
who must be excluded were slash-and-burn farmers and roaming pas-
toralists. The administrators tried to fix titles of ownership to land,
with some parcels reserved for their scientific value and others assigned
to specific owners. The government believed that a necessary first step
toward civilization and economic progress was to move people out of
the apparently haphazard lifestyle of shifting cultivation and nomadic
cattle-herding and into the fixed use of land.

The constellation of saving land for nature, fixing land titles, and
promoting "economic progress" later recurred in a World Bank mission of 1989, which I'll tell about in Chapter 9. It is sobering to realize
that the nature reserves we now so much admire fit right in with Governor-General Olivier's arrogant colonial policies — and that there is
an all too clear continuity with modern conservation, again attempting
to protect land from some people for the benefit, or ideals, of other
people.

Settlers like the de Heaulmes gained official "concessions" of land.

There were, admittedly, rules for the concessions. Settlers must not displace villages or infringe on the sacred sites of tombs. During an initial three-year trial period, they had to show that they were developing the land: "putting it into value." The administration did not even remotely consider that what the local people did with their land might be valuable. The maze of little clearings that pockmarked the forest, the herds of scrawny cattle grazing the landscape, had zero value in colonial eyes.

Léon Cayla followed Olivier as governor-general of Madagascar. He ruled from 1930 to 1939, during the early years of Berenty plantation. Cayla was a big man, strongly built, athletic, energetic, decisive. He piloted his own light plane around the vast island, dropping in for tours of inspection of his domain. He confronted the general sagging of the world's economy with a determination that Madagascar's economy should grow. He borrowed funds for the colony at first, then managed to pump exports up to a surplus by 1934. Coffee exports more than quadrupled, from 8,000 tons to 40,000. Road length doubled, from 12,000 to 25,000 kilometers — not paved, of course. Mining of graphite and mica and the harvesting of vanilla and cloves expanded and grew ever more profitable. Cayla reconstructed the port of Tamatave after a cyclone. He built hospitals, opened higher primary education to Malagasy, and even launched a lycée for Malagasy girls. The lycée was named for Jules Ferry, the educator who proposed that France's mission was to bring the light of her civilization to benighted colonies.

In response to 1930s political unrest in Tananarive, Cayla put the two chief leaders, Ralaimongo and Ravoahangy, under house arrest. (As a student in Paris, Ralaimongo had been a roommate of Ho Chi Minh.) Three outspoken French Communists worked with the independence movement. Cayla unhesitatingly slapped them into prison. They greeted their eighteen-month sentence by singing the "Internationale" and got two more years added on. Cayla "imposed by his imperial countenance . . . by his presence, by an impression of justice, protection, and powerful friendship . . . He liked to appear in a plumed casque, among a flotilla of horsemen in red coats . . . He liked to please, he had pleased, and did not doubt that he would always please." Irreverent colonists nicknamed him Léon I.

The first hundred and twenty Berenty workers listed in Rehomaha's little notebook were at the opposite end of the social scale from Léon I. Some worked by choice in hopes of a better life, but most were just trying to pay their poll tax to escape the forced labor gangs.

Jaona Tsiminono the Never-Suckled, Mahafaha's grandson, was one of those first workers. Old Jaona still stands tall in his greasy black jacket, no shirt, shorts with more holes than a loincloth, and rectangular rawhide sandals. His skin remains glossy and taut over strong ribs and collar and the high Tandroy cheekbones. At eighty he still proclaims an athlete's build — and he still spends much of the day in the fields: his own fields, uphill from the vast plantation that took away his grandfather's farm.

Jaona mimed for me the work he used to do when he was young and strong, jogging with a heavy, heavy plank, destined for the mica packing cases, on his shoulder. At first the plantation had only one ox cart, in terrible shape. The men had to pull the cart themselves with its load of timber, because it was too rickety even for oxen to tow. They manhandled it down to the Mandrare, then carried the heavy planks on their shoulders across the river. They could do that for ten months of the year, while it was possible to wade. In the rains of December and January, they stopped — but not because the river was so deep or because the crocodiles came at high water. They stopped because they could not even reach the river. The fine alluvial clay of the banks makes a slurry called *fotaka* when it is wet. It is the consistency of chocolate mousse, and it swallows Land Rovers to the axle while their wheels spin futilely. People's feet skid so much in fotaka that a man carrying a plank just falls flat.

Later on Jaona became a *chef d'équipe,* a crew boss. His crew consisted of ten or twenty Tanosy men from Fort Dauphin. He said that they were a consignment of men assigned to the *corvée* because they had no money to pay their head tax. I have not been able to verify whether Berenty was one of the private plantations that benefited from the infamous SMOTIG, or whether these men were just local recruits needing money for the tax, but Jaona did say corvée. When the men arrived, they were given clothes and a blanket and were paid a wage.

Thus they started out happy. Soon they realized that clearing the forest was hard, hard work. They had to dig out deep-rooted kily trees. (Normally it is taboo to destroy kilys because their leaves give shade and their pods, like the prickly pear, are famine food.) They also chopped down *sasavy* and prickly *filofilo* (needle-needle). Worst of all was *tehalahy* vine, "the one who loves men" so much that once its hooked barbs catch you, it never lets you go. A couple of my friends have a theory that tehalahy is two-thirds of the way to carnivory. It has perfected seizing people and drawing blood; it has not quite managed to digest us yet.

The plantation managers couldn't force the men to work, but they had signed a contract. Some would pay another man — with a zebu or some lesser bribe — to take their place in the work gang. To the Europeans one worker was the same as another. Their only concern was to keep the numbers up. As long as the count was right, said Jaona, the bosses did not care.

Their wages, of course, were trivial. By outside-world norms, plantation wages were and are extreme exploitation. (Workers now receive Madagascar's official minimum wage, less than twenty-five dollars a month.) However, the vast majority of workers did (and still do) work on the plantation just four hours a day. For them the wages were an extra on top of the real life of caring for fields, cattle, and children. Even the full-time workers supplemented their income by bringing along six or eight dependents. The families went out to cultivate fields. If they had no nearby fields of their own, the de Heaulmes allocated them land on the plantation. Modern wage-earning dovetailed with traditional life rather than replacing it.

The de Heaulme brothers developed a good-cop/bad-cop act. Alain was the plantation manager. People called him *masiaka,* which means some blend of nasty, tough, and dangerous. In Madagascar, when you want to keep robbers away from your house you buy a barking dog and put up a sign with a picture and the words "Dog Masiaka!" The day-to-day running of a new plantation staffed by a tribe of warriors needed someone willing to be masiaka — or at least firm.

Henry was the manager, shipper, and exporter, the blood brother who orated using the local proverbs. His family stayed in Fort Dauphin. Madame Marcelle was not about to move to the wilds of Berenty and live among Tandroy. Henry summed up his wife's feelings in his nickname for Berenty: *La Terre des Milles Reproches,* the Land of a Thousand Recriminations.

The brothers pulled off a major coup when they bought a German steam engine and a sawmill. The government had built a railway from the high plateau to Manakara, a coastal town about two hundred miles north of Fort Dauphin. (The railway itself is an engineering feat. At one point the narrow-gauge track steps down the eastern rainforest escarpment by turning a complete circle under itself, like a spiral staircase.) When the track was finished, the machinery went up for sale. Henry bagged a giant machine saw and a steam engine to run it. The steam engine was essentially a boiler on wheels with a tall smokestack. It could either move under its own power or else run a big flywheel to power other machines like the big saw.

The only problem was that it was way up the coast. Henry went to Manakara, dismantled the engine, and loaded the parts onto a coastal steamer. In Fort Dauphin harbor, he unloaded it onto bobbing lighters, this time without shipwreck. Then the pieces were put on ox carts for the two-day trek inland. The oxen strained up to the mountain pass and pulled back desperately in their harnesses as the carts rolled down the inland side. At last Henry reassembled the machines in his new factory at Berenty. The saw has long since disappeared, but the steam engine stands outside the old factory, now the tourist restaurant. Under the Berenty sun it glows with red and black paint. The brass plate shines, proclaiming that it was built in 1928, the year Jean de Heaulme was born.

While the de Heaulme plantation grew, other groups established concessions elsewhere in the Mandrare Valley: the Confolent family, the Gallois family, a company-run plantation, and yet another noble family named de Guitaut. François and Aymar de Guitaut, with François's wife and two small children, reached Fort Dauphin in 1936. They all moved to a little house on stilts in Amboasary town, "so termite-ridden that when roaming pigs scratched their backs on it in the night, the whole house trembled." I remember Aymar and another brother, Arnaud, from a later time. They each drove a Deux Chevaux (2CV), the magnificent little Citroën car with a hiccup in its back axle. They remarked that when a Land Rover bogs down in the chocolate mousse fotaka, it takes a whole village to lift it out, but you can pick up a 2CV by yourself. Aymar did so with only one hand, having lost the other to a harvesting machine. I thought of him just the other day when I spooked some unfamiliar ringtails. The troop took off with their little juveniles absolutely airborne, hind legs splayed sideways and tails flat out behind. A vision rose in my mind of the de Guitaut brothers in their flotilla of 2CVs, the little cars speeding along the plantation roads so fast that they just grazed the highest points of the corrugated tracks, while Aymar simultaneously steered, shifted gears, and gesticulated to punctuate conversation with his all-purpose hand.

Grubbing up stones and tree stumps would not have been worth it just for wood for packing cases. The de Heaulmes, the de Guitauts, and the other settlers had bigger plans. When the forest was gone, people would need some long-term resource. A few entrepreneurs had tried planting sisal in other parts of Madagascar, but it did not do very well. Sisal needs a desert climate, but processing it requires a permanent water source to sluice down the leaves when they are crushed into fibers for rope and carpets. The de Heaulmes saw the Mandrare Valley as an ideal site. The Mandrare, flowing in a vast loop out of rainforest mountains to the north and east, is almost never dry. After clearing the spiny flora, the brothers would grow a desert-adapted crop beside the great river, providing work for the Tandroy and riches for themselves. The two men already knew the hazards of the business. In a brief experiment with sisal on Réunion, one of their own brothers had lost a hand in a crushing machine.

Sisal, like the prickly pear, is Mexican: an agave or century plant. It looks like a gigantic pineapple top with leaves one or two meters long. Each leaf is tipped with a hardened point that can pierce even a zebu hide, not to mention human skin. If sisal had a mentality, though, it would be most like a Triffid. Its motto is grow big and tough and spear the opposition.

Spirits live in the forest: lolo, hobgoblins. They haunt the darkly shaded riverbanks, under the tamarind trees. So do brigands — young men in the age-old game of cattle stealing — and murderers. In 1936, when the de Heaulmes arrived, most people went into the river forest only in daylight, on wide cattle droves that led from villages on higher ground down to the riverbank. In tamer parts of the world, little boys herd cattle, but in Androy, even when I first came, behind each zebu herd jogged a man with a spear. Traditional villages were set a couple of kilometers back on the valley bluffs, in sparse forest away from the tamarind trees' deep shade. When people build a village, they clear a sunlit hole in the dangerous woods to keep away the lolo — and, incidentally, the malarial mosquitoes that breed in leaf litter.

Yet Jaona the Never-Suckled and all the de Heaulme forest cutters were dismantling their home. The surrealist fingers of thorn-studded fantiolotse gave the planks for Tandroy houses. Baobabs and bitter elephant's-foot trees held water a thirsty man could drink. Underground tubers offered famine food. Fat, hedgehoggy tenrecs roasted crisp over cook-fires of wood from the forest. Medicines came from the forest, and poisons, which have their uses too. In the forest Tandroy made clearings to grow corn. In the forest — their forest — their cattle grazed.

When villagers agreed to cut the spiny forest, they knew they were embarking on a whole new way of life. Then the imposing Frenchman who knew all their proverbs made a wholly incomprehensible request. He wanted one forest not razed but saved. Saved for no use at all! The forest by the river, the gallery forest, he said, was too beautiful ever to be cut down, especially the part never cleared for farms, where there were still a few ringtailed lemurs and wild white sifaka. If he preserved it forever, would people keep their cattle out of it, as they did with the sacred forests around tombs? The village councils again considered. They agreed that they could spare the pasturage. Their zebu fed uphill in the spiny forest. However, a zebu needs to drink every two days. The villagers must have access to the river for their herds and also for the women with their water gourds. The de Heaulmes agreed.

Thus Berenty Reserve was created. In all, of the six thousand hectares of the de Heaulme concession, one thousand remain today as forest, including the main two-hundred-hectare patch by the river-side, and a one-hundred-hectare gallery forest called Bealoka, "Much Shade." The rest of the woods are spiny flora, including groves around traditional tombs, small tufted islands of vegetation amid the sisal. However, even the main riverside forest is split by a cattle drove, along which up to two hundred head of zebus, goats, and sheep run daily down to the river to drink. Women walk five kilometers down the trail carrying spherical brown gourds or bright plastic buckets on their heads. A second active cattle drove runs through Berenty village itself.

A third drove was in fact closed. Its hinterland became airstrip and plantation. Visitors to Berenty today walk into the forest reserve from the main gate, under a concrete portico painted with bats and sifaka, and then down to the river — a five-meter-wide swept path, overhung with huge kily trees, where lemurs come to greet them. Many tourists think it all too tame. They understand that this French family pre-served a lemur woodland in Madagascar, just as they might have a deer forest next to a château in France. But a grande allée leading down to the river? Too much! The de Heaulmes did not create the grande allée. It is the old central cattle drove, where their tractor driver, Toliha, as a boy helped herd his father's zebu to drink from the Mandrare River.

Is Berenty the end of the earth? Lived distances are a function of trans-port. In Madagascar you grow obsessed by transport. Paris to Antana-narivo: an overnight jet flight. From there an hour's flight to Fort Dau-phin. In the year 2000, given the state of the potholed road, it took two hours to drive the seventy kilometers from Fort Dauphin to Berenty.

When the de Heaulmes first settled, that journey took two days. When the plantation geared up to transport planks to Fort Dauphin, ox trains of twenty two-wheeled carts would cross the Mandrare River at its shallowest. The oxen climbed the rough track up to the Col de Ranopiso among three-cornered palm trees and rosy periwinkles (now used to treat childhood leukemia). The second day the carts rolled downhill and eastward toward the coast, past green paddy fields with rainforest mountains beside them until at last they came to Fort Dau-phin's blue bay.

Two days was far too slow for the de Heaulme brothers. Early French administrators had adopted the filanzana, the sedan chair, like the one that bore Queen Ranavalona III into exile. Governor Decary remarked that it had great advantages: "In a filanzana one can travel thirty kilometers a day without fatigue." Without the Frenchman being fatigued, that is. Alain de Heaulme improved on the filanzana: he built an *aeropousse.*

Jaona the Never-Suckled graduated from forest clearing to become a runner on the aeropousse team. He took me to see an old one still lying abandoned in a lumberyard. It had two long parallel poles like a filanzana, with a plain piece of plank for a seat between them, and another plank at an angle for the back, low enough that I think it would dig the rider in the kidneys at every jounce of the road — basically an unpadded version of the queen's gold velvet chair. Underneath was an ancient motorcycle wheel with an iron rim, spokes, and axle. The wheel still had black shreds of something attached. I thought at first it was bound in goat hair. No, the shreds were the fibrous remains of what had once been a Michelin rubber tire.

When Jaona seized the handles in front of the seat, the aeropousse started to tip sideways. I tried to hold its weight but couldn't. Lahivano the chauffeur caught the back end. For all his eighty years, Jaona set off at a fast pace, then mimed *de-dumpity-dumpity-dumpity.* The runners *jogged* all the way to Fort Dauphin; with two sets of runners spelling each other in relay, they made Fort Dauphin in a day! Jaona's shoulders and the knobby knees on his long thin legs bobbed up and down. He looked down and waved his knees. (Don't ask: he did.) "They are not what they used to be," he said. "My old knees feel the result of all that running with the aeropousse. Besides, I used to be a dancer. I helped found the dance troupe of Berenty, with all the Tandroy dances. I danced for Madagascar's independence! If you wish to know how it was, my picture as a young man dancing greets visitors to Berenty's museum!" It is Jaona whose muscles gleam in the photomural of dancers that hangs in the tourist restaurant and whose proud face and bare chest hung with necklaces greet visitors to the Arambelo Museum of Androy.

Alain built his aeropousse, but as always Henry was ahead: he had

Baghdad. Mica from the rainforest mountains was shipped out from Fort Dauphin to a New York firm called Alatari and Pitts. Archibald Alatari was an American of Greek-Lebanese extraction, who became a business partner of Henry's father-in-law, the mica magnate. Soon after the de Heaulme brothers arrived in Fort Dauphin, Alatari sent a Chevrolet truck to transport the mica. This was a colossal machine — the first-ever truck in the south of Madagascar — quickly nicknamed Baghdad.

One problem. The truck arrived in pieces in a series of shipping crates. Henry took the manual in one hand and a wrench in the other and put together his Chevrolet.

When it stood complete, there was a second problem. Henry had indeed piloted a Harley-Davidson half the length of Madagascar, but he had never driven a car. He climbed in, manual in hand, and headed west. The truck performed magnificently. It surmounted the mountain pass on the existing cart track, forded the Mandrare River (it must have been dry season), and carried right on to a little market town called Ambovombé, which had a restaurant run by an Indian. (Restaurants appeared early in French colonies.) Henry was hungry. He braked to a halt, climbed down from Baghdad's high cab, and ate lunch. Afterward he got back in for the return trip.

Problem number three: he did not know how to find reverse. Baghdad lurched forward and demolished the restaurant.

Back in Fort Dauphin, Henry cabled Alatari to admit he had a problem. He needed the price of a restaurant. Alatari cabled back the words on the sign posted in French bars: "Qui casse les verres, les paie." Whoever breaks glasses pays for them. Alatari then deducted a tenth of Henry's salary every month for two years.

Henry gritted his teeth, economized, and shipped out mica. Baby Jean became a toddler. By the time Jean's sister Huguette was born on May 23, 1932, the debt was paid. At Huguette's christening, another telegram arrived from Alatari. He was returning all the money he had deducted, saying, "This is for your daughter's dowry." Henry de Heaulme emerged, not with his daughter's dowry, but with forced savings that became the nest egg that allowed him to build a plantation at

Berenty. He also came away with a huge fondness for America — or at least for Americans like Archibald Alatari.

Sometime during those years he became simply Monsieur de Heaulme. He dropped the cumbersome second name of de Boutsocq. Instead, he took the mantle of a status well recognized among the Tandroy: as the oldest male, he was the spiritual head of his entire clan, a position he held by right as well as by character. Everyone called his younger brother Monsieur Alain. His sons, Jean and Jacques, became Monsieur Jean and Monsieur Jacqui. One would no more think of their titles as merely "M." than one would abbreviate the queen of England to "Q." Henry was, and now Jean is, *Monsieur de Heaulme,* to Malagasy and French alike, throughout Madagascar.

4

I Licked His Feet Very Heartily

The Tandroy and Their English Slave, 1703–1717

〰️

"For us, the only life is with our fields and our cattle. It's not Monsieur de Heaulme's low wages that keep us away. He could pay us a hundred francs [two cents] a day and it would be worth working. The problem is that paid work keeps us from our herds. A permanent job means living at Berenty village. I actually worked on the plantation for a while as a sisal guardian, but I left because my children were small . . . No, of course I did not leave to take care of my children. I left because the children were too small to take care of my cattle."

Kotomahasolo (Grandson-of-Son-Maker) sat on a woven mat under a tamarind tree in his family compound, just uphill from Berenty's sisal fields. Around his village perimeter rose ragged spires of spiny forest, wound through with cow paths. To me it was a degraded forest: too fragmented for sifaka or ringtails, tenrecs hunted out, just the blazing eyes of mouse lemurs and lepilemurs among the nighttime trees, and a few chameleons aiming their eyes in opposite directions — as the proverb says, keeping one eye on the future and one on the past. But to Kotomahasolo this was working land, a living forest where his herds pastured among the thorns. "We depend on the forest and the rain," he explained. "People like King A-Thousand-Cannot-Lift-Him or the de Heaulmes may say they own the land, but only God gives the rain."

Kotomahasolo is rich. The tin roofs of his houses shone in the sun. His eldest son, sitting beside him on the mat, wore store-bought denim shorts and a matching sleeveless vest, open to show the amulet lying on his bare chest. On the young man's wrist dangled a modern silver-link identity bracelet hammered from melted-down old ones. (A little too conscious of his own beauty, he kept swiveling around to sit in the foreground of photographs.) These men are simultaneously of Berenty and not of it. They invest their sisal wages in livestock; they run their herds through the plantation to drink at the riverside. Most of their income is not wages but interest on capital in the four-legged form of bawling new calves. Their zebu multiply, building a surplus against the day when Kotomahasolo's funeral will unite his clan in pride, and the son will lead his kinsmen in spearing a whole herd of zebu to accompany the father into the afterlife.

Kotomahasolo is royalty. He descends from King A-Thousand-Cannot-Lift-Him. "That was a great king: just the way ten men could not lift a tractor, so a thousand could not raise that king off the ground." He complained, though, that royalty means less than it used to. "For instance," he said scornfully, "if there were a glass of water between us in the middle of the mat, and someone said, 'This glass of water goes to the person who is the true descendant of kings, somebody — just anybody — might put up their hand and say 'I am!' just to get the glass of water! But *I* am the true descendant!"

Why did he make the prize a glass of water? Because it was so trivial or so important? So important! He went on to apologize. "We do not even have water to offer you." Normally, if visitors come to your village, you should give them drink. But now, in midafternoon, there was no water at all, for the women had not come back from the river. They were still trekking five kilometers uphill, each with a gallon bucket on her head, even the ten-year-old girls — chatting merrily the whole long way. Meanwhile the men waited with their thirst. It seemed to me that old traditions were alive and well a hundred yards outside the limits of Berenty estate.

Who are these Tandroy, whose traditions have survived for so many years alongside the commercial economy? By extraordinary chance, we have a written record of one slice of their history, from a time when white men were only first beginning to influence Madagascar. In the early eighteenth century, a London midshipman named Robert Drury was slave to the Tandroy.

"Would you like to visit Drury's king?" Georges Heurtebize sprang that question on me as we shooed the boldest of the ringtailed robbers away from our breakfast in Berenty's thatched cafeteria. (This impressive ancient female, more than fourteen years old now, haunts the tables with her current infant on her back, a juvenile in tow, and a deft tongue into the jam dish.) I took one look at the quick-smiling, leather-skinned anthropologist seated across from me and leaped at his invitation.

Georges is the only white man since Robert Drury who has spent much of his life as a Tandroy. He was enchanted originally by a night of full moon, when his village hosts sent him out to join the young people wrestling in the ringa. He dropped out of his original profession, geology, and settled among those proud, hospitable people. Now, years later, his diary has become the prime modern account of the tribe. His painstaking genealogical researches have revealed the history of his clan, the oral record of a people supposed to have no history. In 2000 Georges was revisiting Berenty to put the final touches to the Androy Museum, whose collections he assembled and mounted, helped by the American anthropologist Sarah Fee. (I was right, so long ago, in thinking that for the de Heaulmes, having a naturalist in their forest was not unlike having an anthropologist in their museum.) What better guide could there be to modern Androy — and to the three-hundred-year-old mystery of Robert Drury? I certainly needed a guide, because the more I hear about Tandroy customs, the less I feel I understand them.

Tandroy are a paradox: simultaneously some of the most conservative and the most enterprising people in Madagascar. In the old days men raided for cattle and women. Nowadays they migrate throughout the country to earn money — for cattle and women. Young men leave home, but the goal is usually to return to the family with riches enough to buy a wife. If the man already has children by his bride, he has to pay extra cattle to become their official father and incorporate them into his lineage. A second paradox: to outsiders the Tandroy appear egalitarian, equal in poverty except for a tin roof on the house or rare new clothes. In fact, some are descendants of nobles and some are descendants of slaves, rich men with cattle and poor men without. In the villages, everyone knows who is who.

Men and women both expect to marry several times in their lives, though women marry only one man at a time. Divorce is easy, especially if the man is the one who wants it. He just tells the woman to go away, usually negotiating a gift of livestock or money. When she returns to her father's village or goes off to marry another man, she leaves her children behind. A nursing baby or toddler stays with the mother but goes home to the father's clan at least by the age of five, where other women will take over the care.

A third paradox: in spite of their mothers' absence, children have a clear and constant identity. Their father's village is home. His lineage is their family, though they do not lose touch with their biological mother. The most horrible sanction that can be imposed on a criminal is to be ostracized from the paternal clan. In a ceremony full of curses of banishment to outer darkness, a person is punished for an unforgivable sacrilege like incest. Not just casual incest or a single transgression, but repeated incest and an insolent failure to make sacrifices to lift the taboo. Even the curse of ostracism is usually reversed within a couple of years, however, because leaving the clan is so unthinkable a fate.

The final paradox, the one that baffles me most, is that women do not act submissive in spite of their almost total formal disenfranchisement. They don't inherit land or cattle. Divorce means leaving their children behind. However, women laugh loud and stride free. They rush to greet visitors to the village, they walk with a spring in their step, they are always making jokes — and unmarried girls have remarkable freedom to choose lovers. Even married women make their own calculations about how to have both old, cattle-rich husbands and young, lusty lovers, though jealousy occasionally leads to murder. Perhaps be-

ing raised by stepmothers makes girls independent because they have
to be.

Philibert Tsimamandro, the only Tandroy anthropologist, once
tried to explain his people's attitudes to a group of my students. Young
Erica, heir to a mix of English sentimentality and Argentinian passion,
burst out, "But don't Tandroy have a concept of romantic love?"

"Of course," answered Philibert readily. "Lots of people take
lovers."

"No, no!" cried Erica. "I mean *real* love. The kind of love where you
would give up everything, *everything,* to be with the other person!"

Philibert considered. "Hmm — just how much of everything?"

Patriarchal inheritance does allow a certain backhanded liberty.
Men and women can marry whom they please, even outside the tribe.
They are not constrained, as the tight-lipped plateau families are, always calculating who will inherit the family rice paddies. The Tandroy
father's lineage is continuity; women and cattle are life and riches,
though the relative positions of women and cattle are in some doubt.
The only novelist of the Tandroy remarks, "I never knew a man to
commit suicide over the death of his wife and children, only sometimes if a man loses his herd."

Perhaps the simplest summary is that Tandroy admire strength.
"Better," they say, "that a child's umbilical cord is cut by a strong
woman than a weak man." In Androy the strong survive.

*Prickly pears around the king's compound glowed deep green in the
sunset light.* Ambondro village lies some ninety kilometers northwest
of Berenty, along a faint track across plains and spiny forest, which
Georges somehow traced in an indomitable four-by-four. The prickly
pear, one of the many resistant varieties introduced since the catastro-
phe of the cochineal, delimited the family precinct with a six-foot wall
of spiny lobes impenetrable to man or beast.

We skirted it to the opening on the west side. Malagasy have compass directions ingrained from birth. Living people approach a house
from the secular west; dead people and spirits from the sacred east.
(Malagasy are all too aware that foreigners do not know this and must
be instructed to go out of a village to the west to relieve themselves. As

far as villagers are concerned, foreigners are not even toilet-trained.)
Inside the compound stretched a grass, dust, and zebu-patty open
space a hundred yards across, with a dozen houses and stick-fenced
corrals for cattle and calves. The houses were the usual tiny wooden
dwellings, except for a larger one some twelve feet tall and easily fifteen
feet on a side. Its eaves and doors were beaded with the segmented
knob patterns that, world over, mean vertebrae as well as the vertical
chain of descent from the Ancestors.

Women rushed forward to welcome us, led by the king's rumbus-
tious middle-aged daughter, while a very old and infirm man tottered
from the royal dwelling without giving us a glance. He wore nothing
but the remains of a pair of turquoise shorts around his loins, a copper
bracelet, and a leather string at his neck with a pair of iron beard tweezers hanging from it. (If necessary, beard tweezers also serve for pulling
prickly pear spines out of one's tongue.) King Tsihandatse, the Not-
Sarcastic, sat down on a white stone (not hewn, just a squarish stone),
with his back against a small tree. It was not casual: it was his stone,
and he was facing east, the honorable direction. Then he nodded to us.
We came to greet him, crouching so our heads were not higher than
his. After Georges's ceremonial introduction, the king regally invited
us to put up our tents in his compound and sleep there through the
night of the full moon.

The villagers plied us with habobo yogurt and invitations into their
houses. One house was in the oldest Tandroy style. The few posses-
sions hung from the eaves in dirty straw baskets and a battered plastic
airline bag. There was no floor, other than the hearth on the north side
and bare earth where bed mats would be unrolled at night. The building of even such a simple house would have begun on an auspicious
day, with corner posts and roof beams placed according to a strict traditional sequence. Presiding spirits, though, may change over time.
From the rafters hung small, half-finished cups of woven straw with
the ends sticking out, signs of a brand-new spirit cult recently imported from the Sakalava tribe of the west and north.

Another hut, the same externally, was rampantly modern inside.
The teenage wife was the village's champion mat weaver. She had lined
the walls and floor of her little house as if it were a bird's nest, with

sweet-smelling palm-frond mats crisscrossed in green and purple lines. Her fifty-year-old husband had once been a soldier, traveling even up to Antananarivo, the capital. The family owned a bedstead! And a trunk! And on the trunk was a stack of Christian books. Above the trunk hung a shotgun, ready to be fired in the air at funerals. The wife's round face beamed as she asked us to photograph their fine establishment and above all her new, fat little baby, his similarly round face topped by a tiny straw hat of her own weaving.

That night, under the moon, I listened entranced to the lullaby of bleating sheep and lowing zebu in the corrals and the distant midnight drumming of young people playing at the ringa, the wrestling match in which village youths try to throw each other to the ground while young girls sit with feet outstretched and drums on their laps, beating quick rhythms with their palms so the tournament becomes almost a dance. At three A.M. someone nearby began to strum a *marovany*, a rectangular wooden box with strings on two sides, a distant, gentle cousin of harp and guitar, the instrument of choice for the new spirit cult. The marovany's soft chords blended with the pouring silver moonlight and the black moon shadows under the prickly pear palisade.

But I have never, never, never learned to appreciate roosters.

Three hundred years ago, one-eyed King Kirindra gave audience to a crew of shipwrecked sailors near where we lay in the moonlight. In May of 1703 the *Degrave,* a merchant ship bound home to England from India, foundered on the southern coast of Androy. Warriors of King Kirindra (the Stubborn) herded its hundred and fifty crew members inland toward his fortress town. One of the crew was a fifteen-year-old midshipman: Robert Drury, nicknamed Robin.

On the evening of the third day's march the ship's company came to the king's town, Fenno-arevo, "Full of a Thousand." Midshipman Drury gazed up at a stockade some twenty feet tall made of living trees. He later wrote that the trees

> seem to have been planted there when very young. They grow very straight and tall, and so near together that a small dog can't pass be-

tween them. They are also naturally armed with large strong thorns, so that there's no breaking through nor climbing over. There are but two passages, or gates, no wider than for two to go abreast, one to the northward and one to the southward. The whole compass is about a mile.

The trees were fantiolotse, the dominant trees of Madagascar's spiny forest. (As yet there was no prickly pear.) To plant a fortress wall, one cuts lengths of branch some two yards long and sets them into the ground in a row. They take root, thicken, and grow branches like the bunched fingers of a twenty-foot hand pointing at the sky. Against an orange desert sunset the silhouette of a traditional palisade of thorn-studded giant fingers seems a surrealist nightmare, even today.

King Kirindra welcomed the ship's company "sitting on a mat, cross-legged in the open air, just before the door of his house, having a gun leaning on his shoulder, and a brace of pistols lying by him." He would have placed himself at the ceremonial northeast door, so the sunset loomed at his left hand, highlighting that side of his face in an orange glow. The king "having but one eye, and thin jaws, his countenance, when he frowned, seemed the more terrible." Beside the king were ranged "his sons and kinsmen in the same manner sitting on the ground on each hand with guns and lances." Another row of warriors stretched on both sides, "forming together a half-moon. They too were most of them armed with guns and lances. There were mats spread from one end of the people to the other for us to sit on, so that when we had joined them, the whole assembly made almost a circle. We were a little concerned to see them all armed, . . . [but] it was their custom never to go from one house to another without their guns and lances."

The king tossed down a draft of local liquor without toasting or sharing it with anyone. Captain Young of the *Degrave* was then offered drink in a dirty cup. The captain refused it and pointedly asked for the king's cup. The king said that by custom no one shared his cup, which is still true of kings today. Robin offered the captain his own silver mug, the only thing he had saved from the shipwreck. The king "was so wonderfully delighted with it, that he begged it." Robin pertly retorted that "seeing so many people had drank out of it, I did conceive it could not be proper for his use. At this he, and his people too, laughed heartily."

Was Robert Drury's ghostwriter Daniel Defoe? The book *Madagascar, or Robert Drury's Journal During Fifteen Years' Captivity on That Island* became an eighteenth-century bestseller. However, Drury has sometimes been considered as authentic as Piltdown Man. The literati pursue delightful academic arguments as to whether or not Drury's "Transcriber" was Defoe himself, the master of docudrama, the author of *Robinson Crusoe*. Perhaps the transcriber even invented most of the tale. Or perhaps Drury was actually a pirate who made up a story of captivity in Androy, the most inaccessible part of Madagascar, so he could go home to England without being hanged.

There are deeper reasons for readers' discomfort with Drury. In the nineteenth century, some could not admit that a white man would slave for blacks. In this century few of us wish to remember that black men and women also slaved for blacks. Slavery was widespread within Africa at the time, and universal in Madagascar. Slavery was a norm for people of all colors, throughout the world, until a bunch of mad English Quakers declared it inhuman.

Robin's account of the Tandroy gives us the key to their society. This was a nation of warriors, village against village, clan against clan. Their social structure still reflects the legacy of recurrent warfare and capture of animals and people. Anyone who has been in Androy believes that Drury was here — without necessarily believing every word of his book. Of course the transcriber fixed the story up. He (or just possibly she) could not keep his fingers off it, any more than I can.

A prologue. The King's Head in Old Jewry, Cheapside, London, sometimes called the Beefsteak House. The King's Head was an upscale pub, catering to merchants and gentlemen, paying taxes on twenty windows. Its proprietor, John Drury, belonged to the Worshipful Company of Innkeepers, and he served as an alderman of his parish. The birth of John's first son, Robert, was entered in the parish records for July 24, 1687. Robin might have inherited the inn, but at the age of thirteen the boy prevailed on his parents to let him go to sea. He tells us that his mother begged him on bended knees to stay at home. When he persisted, his father entrusted him to old Captain Young, a well-known skipper of the route to East India. Midshipman Drury was number 118 on the surviving crew list of Young's ship, the *Degrave*, "of 700 tonnes burthen, and mounted 52 guns."

Sailing out of the lower reaches of the Thames, the ship rounded the corner of Kent on February 19, 1701. Drury writes that they saw a squadron of men-o'-war preparing for sea under the command of "Admiral Bembo" (Benbow). The boy would have glimpsed the men-o'-war through hovering fog over the gray English Channel: the flagship's logbook also noted the *Degrave* passing by in "fogge weather." Admiral Benbow himself may well have followed the *Degrave* through his spyglass, because his nineteen-year-old son John was fourth mate aboard her. And if Benbow's name sounds familiar, the inn at the start of *Treasure Island* was named for him — a book born of sea tales like Drury's.

King Kirindra's largesse would be unimaginable today except at funerals. The king offered the *Degrave's* crew camping space and beef to eat. Apparently he hoped that the hundred and fifty men of the ship's company would join his warriors as a band of white mercenaries and help him vanquish all his foes. He was rich enough to support them, since he owned some two thousand field slaves. The sailors thought, though, that the king meant to poison them. They had little leadership, for wise old Captain Young had died on the voyage, and his twenty-five-year-old son was now captain, seconded by twenty-one-year-old John Benbow. Young Captain Young's own mistakes were largely responsible for the shipwreck. As the *Degrave* broke up on the wave-pounded reef, Captain Young made it to shore carrying a bottle with his dead father's heart in it, to honor the old man's dying wish that his heart should be buried at Dover.

A few days after the crew's arrival, at their regular morning audience, the officers laid hands on the one-eyed king, his queen, and his nephew, Prince Mananjaka (Who-Has-the-Right-to-Speak). The ship's company fled the town with their captives, heading for the Mandrare River and Port Dauphine (modern Fort Dauphin). In those days, river valleys were disputed no man's lands. If they could make it far enough across the Mandrare they might be safe.

"There is no torment like the torment of thirst," writes Drury. The spiny forest has evolved to offer no relief from the sun. The best one can do is crouch against a baobab trunk. Some *za* baobabs, the species of this corner of Madagascar, are thicker through than the length of a long-wheel-base Land Rover, but that is still not enough shade for a hundred and fifty men. The hostages suffered silently, their hands bound day and night. Each night a retainer from the following hordes of warriors came to offer the king one cow horn of water on bended knee. The king and prince did not reveal to their captors that baobabs hold water a thirsty man can tap. In their eastward march the company struggled to within two hundred yards of a murky pond, but King Kirindra and Prince Mananjaka claimed there was no water for miles.

The first night the sailors let the queen go. In fact, they had not wanted her as a prisoner, but she had insisted on staying with her husband. The king told her to go home and take care of his children.

The second night they let the king go. They bartered him for six good guns and the warriors' promise to leave them in peace, which the naive captain desperately wanted to believe. From a distance across the plain, the sailors could see the king being greeted by people who crouched down and licked his dusty feet in gratitude.

The third day "we were almost parched to death, and to so great an extremity were we reduced that we crawled on the ground to lick the dew, and this was all the means we had to moisten our lips." The officers forced the men to continue their trek by night. They came in view of the Mandrare River, "the sun just rising," with the eastern mountains silhouetted beyond and the dawn light glinting off the water. "It was a great way off, yet the hopes we had of getting water to quench our parched bodies gave us no small pleasure, and our spirits began to revive even at the sight of it."

The sailors stumbled forward. The Tandroy followed

> like so many greyhounds . . . They began to slaughter our men . . . I was one of those who could not travel well, but there were twenty

behind me; the woman who was saved in our ship was next to me. I, seeing them kill our people as they overtook them tore off my coat, and afterwards my waistcoat, throwing them away that they should not hinder me in running. For the foremost of our people being got over the river, and I not far off, took courage, but as I looked back at the pop of a gun I saw the woman fall, and the Negroes sticking their lances into her sides. It was my turn next, for the same Negroes came after me, and I was just got to the river side as they fired a gun at me; but I jumped into it . . . Even so, I would not go over the river without stopping to drink two or three times out of my hat, till I was swelled with water.

The survivors waded through the river neck deep, then ran a mile or two beyond it through scrubby woods until they came to a "sand hill," with at the top a "sandy open place we could see no end to" — most likely the dunes near the river's mouth. From the top the sailors would have seen the seacoast a mile or two to the south, the water indigo blue in the sun, waves breaking white, as though the water was far more substantial than the gray-green forest. The dunes themselves are living dunes like those of the Sahara. The sea wind sifts their crests into parallel ridges like the flutes of a scallop shell, each riffle crest outlined with shimmering mica grains and floored with black titanium ore.

The *Degrave's* crew turned on their pursuers although

we were a poor handful to withstand an army of two or three thousand. When they found we made a stand to oppose them they did so too, being also beneath us down-hill we could see only their heads. Their shot flew very fast over us, and we kept them in play from noon till six in the afternoon, by which time all our shot was gone. Our people who had money made slugs of it; and when that was done they took the middle screws out of their guns and charged their pieces with them . . . [then] they knew not what to do.

They had no more hostages, nothing left to bargain with. The Tandroy again promised amnesty — in the morning, if they delivered up all their arms that night. Captain Young agreed, but John Benbow recognized final disaster. He slipped away in the night with a few of the company and headed toward Port Dauphine.

In the morning the warriors surrounded the weaponless crew. "One of the princes took hold of me and delivered me to one of his men . . . [with] three or four youths much about my age . . . [they] bound our hands with ropes . . . I was just tied when I saw the same prince stick his lance into Captain Young's throat." The Tandroy "soon murdered every man; they then fell to stripping them of their clothes, and even butchering them, for they ripped open several of their bellies." Only Robin and three other boys remained, "the eldest not above sixteen years of age." A Tandroy warrior lifted his lance to strike Robin, but another said the boy was reserved for one Lord Miavaro.

The boys were dragged away behind their new owners. "All the way we went I had the ghastly prospect of our men's mangled corpses in passing through the woods to the river." Malagasy orators use a Homeric phrase for a great sacrifice of cattle: "the crows and the birds of prey came from miles around to the feast." The hooded crows and black kites and brown Madagascar buzzards and proud, crested Madagascar harrier hawks must have gorged themselves. Even the big black housekeeper ants, scavengers of the forest, would have carried morsels of meat above their heads like Roman legionnaires under a formation of shields, down into holes as wide around as a man's arm. Finger bones joined abandoned feathers and the skeletons of mouse lemurs around the gaping ant holes. There is no further mention of that bottle with old Captain Young's heart. I picture it slowly rolling in the Mandrare's current, past indifferent crocodiles, to be buried at last in sand at the other end of the world from the white cliffs of Dover.

The new slave had not eaten in three days of marching. On the way from the battlefield, Miavaro's men stopped and cooked beef "cut into long pieces, like ropes, with the hide, and dressed and eat it half-roasted according to their custom, and gave it me in the same manner. This I thought the sweetest morsel I ever eat in my life, though a beggar in England would not have touched it." (Meat is sometimes cooked the same way today.)

They walked for another day

homeward, for now I must call it so . . . and arrived at a pretty large town, with three great tamarind trees before it. One of the Negroes carried a large shell, which, as soon as he blowed, sounded like a post-boy's horn. [Conch-shells are still used as village trumpets.] This brought the women to a great house in the middle of the town about twelve feet high, which I soon found to be my master's. He had scarce seated himself at his door, when his wife came out crawling on her hands and knees till she came to him, and then licked his feet, and when she had done, his mother did the same; and all the women in the town saluted their husbands in the same manner.

Milela-padia, the custom of licking feet in extreme submission, lasted at least in token form well into the nineteenth century.

"My Mistress beckoned me to go in and sit down. I perceived a great deal of serious discourse pass between my master and her, and by her looking so earnestly at me, while he was talking, I conjectured he was telling our tragical story, and I observed the tears to stand in her eyes." His new mistress was a king's daughter who had been taken in war herself. "For this reason she took compassion on me, being herself a slave, and in a strange country, and only preferred to be wife to my master by courtesy." She was probably nearer Robin's age than her husband's, for women are married in Androy in their early teens. She fed Robin "carravances": garbanzos, or chickpeas, which looked to him like "grey peas boiled in dirty water." She then added milk; he accepted her gesture and ate. "She talked a great deal to me, but I understood not a word she said. My master was all this while sitting with his brother without the door, regaling themselves and drinking toak [distilled honey-liquor]."

Robin was told to sleep "across close at his Master and Mistress' feet [for] the whole house was not above twelve by fourteen feet." A Tandroy house aligns to the noble and the ignoble directions of the compass, so Miavaro slept on a woven mat with his head to the east, on the southern side of the young wife who had waited for his return. Robin, at their feet, lay cramped over toward the western, ignoble door used by servants and menstruating women. Robin's master called softly to the new slave three or four times in the night. The wakeful boy answered every time. "I fancy he would have been better pleased if I had slept sound." Robin was packed off to stay at an aunt's even smaller abode. Where whole families live in one-room houses, people normally don't expect privacy. Sex is treated with either tact or ribald gusto. However, Miavaro swung between generosity and violent hatred of the mere existence of his white slave, and that night's impotence could have been the start of it.

Lord Miavaro had some two hundred working slaves. He did not need more field hands. At first Robin was a household pet, an echo of the black pageboys of eighteenth-century Europe. His mistress fed him and chattered. He herded cattle with other boys his age. He learned to start a fire by twirling the male firestick on the female one and to dig up fat, prickly tenrecs from their winter hibernation. He rightly notes that tenrecs may have more than twenty young ones in a litter — indeed, they set the mammalian record, at thirty-six. Robin's interest was to roast them so "their skin is as brown and crisp as a pig's."

One night Miavaro put on his generous mien. He took Robin off into the woods to join in serious sport. "I saw preparations for killing and dressing a bullock, or some such thing; but seeing none to kill and it being now dark, I observed them to walk about with caution, and to talk softly, and all the symptoms of some secret design. I presently fell a-crying, and thought they were going to kill and eat me." But they were merely stealing cattle. Two men dragged in a bullock, and Lord Miavaro cut its throat with a lance. They butchered it, each man taking his share away secretly and separately. Robin got a big chunk to give the aunt he lived with.

Cattle stealing led on to stealing women.

It is common practice for parties to go out and surprise their enemies by night, when least expected. On these expeditions every man generally carries a piece of meat in his hand, and getting into town in the dead of night, they throw the meat to the dogs to prevent their barking. When they are entered, one fires a musket, and making no other noise, the inhabitants suddenly rising, and hastily getting out of the doors of their low huts in a stooping posture, are stabbed with lances; the young ones and women they take captive,

Sifaka *(Propithecus verreauxi)* in the crotches of a tamarind tree, Berenty Reserve. *Frans Lanting*

Moonrise over the Mandrare Valley. Berenty Reserve is the band of large trees by the river in the center, a well-watered forest in a dry land. The mountains beyond were thrust up by the volcano whose explosion rifted Madagascar from India. *Colin Radford*

The beach near Fort Dauphin is a graveyard for ships. Onshore winds clothe the mountains in lush rainforest *Colin Radford*

West of the mountains lies the lunar landscape of Madagascar's dry spiny forest. Ninety-five percent of its plant species are unique to Madagascar. Tandroy carry water to distant villages by ox cart. *Alison Jolly*

Shadow's troop of ringtailed lemurs confronts Fan's troop in 1997. The two small saplings ringed with spur marks act as territorial goalposts. Shadow's troop is facing away from us. Two of Fan's troop face us and defend their own goal. Few lemurs take an active part in hostilities. *Alison Jolly*

Shadow's troop huddling in 1992, when it was not clear they would survive. This lineup was all females and young; no males had yet committed to joining them. *Alison Jolly*

Lemurs of Berenty.

Above: A white sifaka. *Cyril Ruoso*

Right: A gray and red mouse lemur, a newly discovered species. *Russell Mittermeier*

Below left: A lepilemur at its nest hole. *Nick Garbutt*

Below right: The brown lemur Cream Puff, an excellent mother and probably a serial killer. *Alison Jolly*

Rekanoky, the chief reserve guardian, cradles a two-gallon egg of the extinct elephant bird. Behind him are "octopus trees" of the spiny forest.
Frans Lanting

Sisal fields during the drought of 1985. Recurrent droughts shape life in
the south of Madagascar. *Frans Lanting*

The dance of the cattle: Valiotaky stampedes zebu through his village during the funeral at the Lucky Baobab. *Alison Jolly*

Valiotaky and Sir Richard Jolly dance to each other during the funeral. *Alison Jolly*

and drive away with them all the cattle they can find, burn the town, and return home by unpracticed ways.

On returning from one of his larger sorties to war, Miavaro "made his entry into town in a triumphant manner, the trumpet-shells blowing and some people before him dancing all the way with guns in their hands. At the entrance the foremost men fired their guns toward the ground, which is the signal of a return with victory. Lord Miavaro and his brother, Lord Sambo, came after them with attendants; next followed the cattle and slaves he had taken from the enemy." Sambo is still a Malagasy name. It means the Ship, a sign of the zodiac. You can be sure, though, that anybody named Sambo was not born under that sign. No one gives strangers power over their child by advertising his real horoscope.

The women licked Miavaro's feet. He then called Robin to do the same, but Robin's knees refused to bend. Miavaro asked if Robin thought himself better than his own mistress, who was a king's daughter. He "fell into a passion . . . he rose from his seat and with his lance made a strike at me with all his force, but his brother giving it a push on one side, he missed me . . . Miavaro . . . took me by the hand to lead me out of the town and kill me." Lord Sambo declared "he would that moment leave him, and see his face no more, if he offered to act such a piece of cruelty . . . When Lord Miavaro saw his brother going in good earnest, he called him back, and told him he would spare my life, but I would have a very tiresome one with him, for he would be revenged on me one way or another for my contempt of him." Sambo winked at Robin to lick Miavaro's feet, which he did, asking pardon, "then of my own accord kneeled down to Lord Sambo, and licked his feet very sincerely and heartily, thanking him for having thus . . . saved my life."

Robin came of age as a Tandroy. Banished from his favored position in the house to become a cattle herder, he thrilled with a pastoralist's pride. He declared that zebu are fine beasts:

> They are very nimble and unruly — they would jump over high fences. They have a hump between their shoulders, almost like a

camel's, all fat and flesh, which might weigh about three or four-score pounds; they are also beautifully colored, some streaked like a tiger, others black with white spots, and some white with black spots; or half black and half white. They do not give so much milk as our cattle in England, nor will they suffer themselves to be milked at any time, till the calf has first sucked.

In time he was allowed a patch of ground to farm for himself. He set himself up to raise bees for honey.

Andevo, the word for Robin's status, might better be translated as "serf" rather than "slave," or something between the two. Andevo were not worked to death, like slaves shipped to white-owned plantations in the West Indies. They were in some intermediate state, serving a lord but with fields allotted for their own use, a not too distant parallel to the work system on colonial plantations like Berenty, where wage earn-ers have areas allocated as their own gardens. Most of the andevo were forcibly captured in war, but some were poor men who sold themselves and their family into slavery to survive — again with all too clear paral-lels to men forced into labor by the head tax. However, andevo had no right to leave if they wished, and their masters had powers of life and death over them. Robin reports that the herd boys with him were cas-trated by their masters for killing one of the cows to eat themselves. Robin himself escaped castration only by pleading with Miavaro to shoot him instead, from any distance his master chose. He suspects that Miavaro was generous that time and missed on purpose.

Robin gives us an endless list of battles, with over a hundred names of the warring clans' leaders. When a town was attacked, the women would flee into secret places in the woods, brushing over their tracks with branches. Robin often went with them as a guard. It finally dawned on him that Miavaro trusted him with the women only be-cause it would be obvious if his young mistress's next child was half white.

One-eyed King Kirindra and his sons and nephews fell into civil war. "The epidemical evil of this island is their frequent quarrels with one another, and the very cause so many of them are sold to Europeans for slaves." Kirindra attacked Miavaro in force.

The lances now began to fly at one another; one of which went through my lamba, and scratched me; I was a little scared at first, but soon recovering my spirits, I returned them the lance over the fortification, in the same manner that it came to me. The cattle were very troublesome to us, several being wounded, they ran up and down and disordered the rest, like so many wild bulls. We fought thus for four hours, with great fury on both sides, till King Kirindra . . . called off his forces and retreated to his camp . . . We buried the dead under the fortification.

In the course of the war Miavaro's town was burned. The people rebuilt it in a new place, with its back to a patch of dense forest and the front reinforced with a triple stockade. The war dragged on. Crops were burned, most of the cattle were killed, and famine ruled in the land. Mothers snapped if their children wanted food two days in a row. Nonetheless, no chief would lose face by proposing peace.

At last an ambassador arrived from the people on the west coast around the port of St. Augustine, near modern Tulear (Toliary). He proposed ending the civil war and forming an alliance against a third tribe. Then the ambassador spotted Robin and called out in English, "You, white man, come hither!" Robin, ashamed, could not remember English words to reply. The ambassador turned to Robin's master and said: "Here's a white bird among crows; in our country they are common, ships coming there frequently: but they wear clothes, eat and drink with the lords. This poor young man looks piteously . . . Don't use him cruelly."

Lord Miavaro growled, "I have not used him cruelly enough; you don't know how his friends served King Kirindra!"

The ambassador declared, "If [my own king] had this white man he would give him some clothes which his countrymen have left behind, and take care of him as his own son till a ship comes to carry him away."

Robin now knew where to seek sanctuary if he could ever escape from Androy.

If weird foreigners turned up on Main Street in a tank or a flying saucer, would you be terrified they would cut out people's hearts, or would you believe they really want old broken dishes? It is to the great credit of King Tsihandatse, the Not-Sarcastic, that he played host to archaeologists searching for Robert Drury's village. A couple of years before my own visit to Ambondro, archaeologists Mike Parker Pearson, Karen Godden, Ramilisonina of Antananarivo's Museum of Art and Archaeology, the Tandroy archaeologist Retsihisatse, and Georges Heurtebize himself all tumbled out of one Land-Rover at the entrance to the Ambondro village stockade. Retsihisatse and Georges explained to the highly dubious villagers that the team had come to honor and respect their ancestors, not to do sacrilege.

In other places that team has sometimes been held at spearpoint. Mike worries that someday a visiting scientist will be killed in one of the remoter parts of Androy. The traditional story of *mpakafo,* pale white spirits who wander at night and steal hearts, is all too likely to be attached to any pale foreigners. The old superstition now circulates with the new twist that foreigners may have AIDS and want to take out people's brains to search for a cure. In spite of all that, King Not-Sarcastic trusted the archaeologists' explanations. He welcomed them in.

Near the present village grows a sacred wood on the site of an early royal town whose king is still revered in local legend. His name was Roandrianjoma, King Friday, for Friday is an auspicious day.

Like all Tandroy royalty, Drury's king, one-eyed Kirindra, was given a different name at his death. Georges Heurtebize's oral genealogy suggests that Kirindra lived at just the right period to become the famous King Friday. A marvelous irony, if the transcriber was indeed Defoe. In *Robinson Crusoe* Friday was the all-purpose black servant, while the Tandroy king Friday was the black ruler perhaps served by a white slave. Unfortunately, the dates mean that the similarity of names is sheer coincidence. *Crusoe* was written years earlier, and Drury did not record Kirindra's death name.

In King Friday's sacred grove you must not gather a stick of firewood; in fact, you must not even enter. You must not defecate or urinate nearby. Georges and I went to see the grove from the outside: a lovely tuft of spiny forest, too small a fragment for large animals, but densely grown with all the forest plants, their spires rearing up against the sky. What were the archaeologists to do? All the evidence of history and geography led them to this patch of woods, and now they could not go in. Mike Parker Pearson has a swashbuckling Indiana Jones exterior. Most of his face is a piratical grin between beard and bush hat. Indiana Jones or no, he does not violate local taboos, especially taboos about ancestors. Nobody who wants to keep working in Madagascar can be disrespectful to the Ancestors.

King Not-Sarcastic solved the problem. He asked permission from King Friday himself for Mike to survey the sacred forest. The present king went into trance, made sacrifices, and communed with his great royal ancestor, who was well disposed to let the archaeologists enter his village — once. The team found in the woods a five-hectare spread of fragments of early eighteenth-century red-slip pottery. It was the remains of a town of exactly the right age, perhaps half a mile in diameter (Robin had said the circumference was a mile). However, the tantalized archaeologists knew they could never betray King Friday's permission by turning one trowelful of dirt.

In later seasons they found and excavated Miavaro's town, the one built during the civil war, with the post holes of its triple stockade. They located the place where the *Degrave* apparently foundered, where the sailors heaved their cannon overboard to lighten the ship and reach the shore. One British-made cannon of the right age lies buried in sand; another is on the reef, beneath the roiling waves, encrusted with red and yellow sponges.

From the bits of broken potsherds, from the discolored dirt of ancient post holes, and from the stories of the local people who know where cannon are buried, the weird foreigners were able to confirm the details of Drury's life in Androy. His account is studded with names and descriptions of demons and famine foods and places still current today.

To me the most exciting result is a negative one. No sites in the region of Kirindra's and Miavaro's villages date to before Drury's time. That means that the tribe had just expanded into that part of Androy. Robin tells of pasturing the cattle in open plains. Miavaro's stockaded new town was built with its back to a woods, but its front faced a long view that would let Miavaro's people see approaching enemies. The woods is still there, though its edge has retreated some hundreds of meters. The long view is there, too. This means that the openings in the forest predate settlement and that the mosaic of landscape in Drury's time was not so very different from what we see today. In other words, the romantic Western view that in the past endless forest blanketed other people's countries and that forest destruction has all been caused by wicked, careless villagers is just not true. Modern studies of West Africa and pollen analyses in Madagascar's plateau also show that those places held open land long before human settlement. People do not always destroy forest; sometimes they even foster it. A strange way to learn about landscape history — from the book of an eighteenth-century midshipman!

It is all too tempting to read Drury's story as continuous present. His account is only a snapshot of one period in time. The archaeologists found evidence of much older peoples living in the south before the Tandroy. The earliest may have been settlers from the Swahili coast of East Africa. By the twelfth and thirteenth centuries people were living beside the rivers, building in stone, and treasuring a few celadon dishes from far-distant China. Those people disappeared for unknown reasons. Later, proto-Tandroy migrated south from the interior. Not until the sixteenth and seventeenth centuries did the "typical" Tandroy lifestyle develop, as warring clans drove one another away from the rivers to live deep in the spiny forest.

The clan of kings was apparently from foreign parts! In legend a lighter-skinned family sailed into Fort Dauphin and somehow imposed itself as royalty on three adjacent southern tribes. The kings' power waxed, then waned. Other great families rose up to hold their own funeral celebrations and build huge stone tombs. Eventually, of course, the French marched in. French soldiers dictated peace among the clans, confiscated guns, proclaimed slaves free. The society of proud warriors themselves now faced servitude, to a whole new class of colonial rulers.

King Tsihandatse the Not-Sarcastic nowadays is respected as the senior member of his line. He is poorer in cattle, though, than many other men. In the morning, before leaving, we took his picture with both of his elderly wives and the thirty-odd members of each of their nuclear families. He dressed for the photos in his regalia: a whitish felt hat with strips of bright emerald cloth sewn from crown to brim and hanging down a couple of inches all around over the basset-hound wrinkles of his face. Some fussing ensued, as a bit of trim dangled in front of his eyes, but that was finally tucked up inside by his ebullient oldest daughter. He wrapped himself in a green plaid cotton lamba like a bedspread and posed on the step of the royal dwelling's ceremonial northeast door. Like most of the hereditary royalty of Europe, he has a head full of traditions but a home-sewn crown.

Love tempted Robin to stay forever; sorcery made him flee. Without the sorcery, we would never have heard his story.

When the civil war ceased, his irascible master, Miavaro, still carried on raiding. Robin now acted as a warrior, proud that he had a slave of his own to carry his bedroll and musket. In one attack, Robin captured two women: an old one and a sixteen-year-old girl, whom he loved on sight.

> I comforted the mother as well as I could, and told her "not to lament too much for her daughter, she should live very well. I would take more care of her than of myself, and though I was not a black man, I had as tender a heart as any black man whatever, and designed to make her my wife, if she liked it." . . . I was very careful of my pretty prisoner, tying a rope about her middle, with the ends about myself, and laid her close to me, holding her fast also in my arms. She only laughed and jested with me for it, but I was so fearful of her getting away that I could not sleep . . . [I] was formal enough to mimic matrimony as far as I could, by taking her hand, and saying I was willing to make her a tender, and faithful husband, and asked her, if she was willing to be a faithful, and loving wife; to which she cheerfully agreed. And so we lay down, and were as happy as our circumstances would admit of, notwithstanding we had no bride-men and maids, nor throwing of stockings.

When they returned to the town all the women licked their husbands' feet. Robin thought, "I had now a wife, and as fine a one too as the best of them, and the next time we returned from such an expedition, I should have homage done me! My Mistress sent and desired to see my Lady . . . She would have her set down on the same mat as herself, and could not forbear shedding tears, it having been her own case [to be captured into marriage] and charged me to use her tenderly."

Robin was now a unique and valuable slave. Miavaro again turned suspicious. He decided to called in an *ombiasy*, a sorcerer, to ensure that Robin could never escape. The curse sounds like those still in use.

> At length enters the wrinkled old wizard with solemn pace and a leering sneer on his haggard countenance, shaking his projecting noddle . . . Away goes the fumbling old fellow to work, scraping a root and mixing of things which I knew had neither good nor harm in them (for I was afraid of nothing but his nose dropping into it), muttering all the while betwixt his few broken teeth words that neither himself nor any one else knew any meaning to. When the dose was prepared he called it the Fermonner and put it into carravances boiled on purpose, and it was given to me in a calabash. But before I ate it he hung several roots about me, one over my eyes, one at my back, one on my breast, and one on each leg, giving every one a name. Then scraping a little from each of them, and putting it into the mess of carravances, I was ordered to eat it, which I did without any concern. In the meanwhile he pronounced his prayers and curses over me.

Robin now knew that he had to escape. He didn't believe in the curse — even his transcriber describes him as a Christian bigot. (Remember, his father was a church alderman.) He saw all too clearly that if he fell sick with any disease at all, it would be seen as proof that he had planned to get away. Miavaro would at last have a convincing excuse to kill him. Ironically, the sorcerer's curse ensured that while his health still held, Robin must flee.

He offered to take his wife home to her father, but she was terrified of the charm.

She begged and cried, but there was no staying any longer for me here, my life was every day in danger. Had I been in any other part of the country, where I could have lived free, easy, and safe, I don't know what effects the love I had for her might have produced. At length she was a little appeased from her first passion, and I broke from her arms by break of day — with what pain those of my readers who are tender lovers can better imagine than I describe.

Thus Robin fled Androy. He traveled to west-coast ports, where once every three or four years a ship might come from Europe.

He had many more adventures, still as a slave or quasi-slave to other tribes. At last, in 1716, Captain William Mackett of the good ship *Drake* took him on board, giving Robin's current owner "a handsome and very good buccaneer gun, also some powder and flints, and a case of spirits." In return, Drury says, "I presented the captain with my own slave, Anthony."

The sailors cut Robin's matted hair and beard. They gave him trousers instead of his loincloth. Captain Mackett then handed him this letter:

To Robert Drury on the Island of Madagascar.
LOUGHBOROUGH, *Feb.* 27, 1715
SON ROBERT DRURY,

I am informed by one Mr. Thornbury, that he left you in health on the island of Madagascar; which I was glad to hear. My very good friend Mr. Terry hath a friend, commander of a ship, the bearer hereof, that hath promised to do all he can to get you at liberty. I therefore desire you to do the captain all the service that you can in your country. And in so doing you will oblige our good friend Mr. Terry, and your ever loving father until death,

JOHN DRURY

The letter is probably real. John Drury did know his son was alive on Madagascar; two months after the letter's date he drew up a will leaving his property to any surviving grandchildren "provided their mother was white."

Captain Mackett was a slaver. Robin made himself obliging, as his father asked. He helped the captain buy Malagasy for sale to Jamaican plantations and the grim rock of St. Helena. In spite of his lamentations over his own plight, it did not occur to him to question the institution of slavery. For almost all of human history, in eighteenth-century England and in Madagascar up to the French conquest of 1897, an ordinary man like Robin never asked if slavery itself was wrong.

Robert Drury was buried in Lincoln's Inn Fields, London, on March 15, 1733. His birth and his burial are sure. The crew list of the *Degrave* included his name in 1701; the *Drake* returned to London in 1717. In Robin's Madagascar, three centuries on, the fantiolotse still lift their giants' fingers, studded with thorns, against the desert sky. Men still follow their zebu, each one armed with a razor-sharp spear. Women still are exchanged between households for a bride price of zebu. And whole villages of people in Androy, who look just like their neighbors, are forbidden by custom to marry the children of freemen, because they are still, to this day, known as the descendants of slaves.

5

I Begged My Grandmother to Tell the Governor-General

Famine, War, and Revolution: 1940–1948

ᏉᏘᏆᎶ

They called it Maro Taolo, "the Time of Bones." Anyone who lived through the Androy famine of 1942–43 remembers. Tsiaketraky, He-Who-Cannot-Be-Thrown-to Earth, was lucky to be seven years old. Children under five in his village died. Then old women died, then old men. His family dug up spongy wild tubers from the woods. They pounded tamarind pulp to swallow, slaking its acidity with chalk and wood ash. Tsiaketraky's parents had an uncle they hoped could help them, in Tulear on the west coast. They set off and walked across the island for many days, two hundred and fifty kilometers, following the route of Robin Drury's flight from Androy two and a half centuries before. Tsiaketraky was old enough to walk with his parents, so he survived.

The father of Philibert Tsimamandro, the Unexpected, the only Tandroy anthropologist, walked the seventy kilometers from near Berenty into Fort Dauphin to buy two baskets of manioc. He was so weak that he ate one basketful to gain the strength for the walk home, so he arrived with only one for his hungry family. He was a strong man. Others simply fell down dead as they walked. Their bodies lay in the ditch by the road. Also by the road lay little mewling bundles wrapped in leaves: babies put out in hope that a passerby would take them from the starving mothers. There are people in Fort Dauphin today named "Exchanged-for-Corn."

I asked Jaona Tsiminono, the Never-Suckled, if he knew people who died in that famine. He said, "My father." I blurted out, "But how could you give your father a funeral in the Time of Bones?" He looked at me and answered, "He was a Christian. I buried him as a Christian." I did not dare ask further. Perhaps he meant that a small funeral sufficed. When there is absolutely nothing left, Tandroy die as Christians.

I knew the sequence from the famine of 1991–92. You sell the remains of your herd, then you sell the cooking pots. It is shameful to sell cooking pots: when secondhand pots appear in the markets, famine has come. The men send their daughters and then their wives to Tulear or Fort Dauphin to become prostitutes. The final humiliation of all is to turn Christian. An adult must die with at least one zebu, whose breath carries the person's breath onward to join the ancestors. Sometimes in a forest there stands a rock — a big pebble — beside a kind of mast with a single cow skull on it. That is a pauper's grave. If there are no zebu at all, you do not even die in Tandroy tradition; your spirit roams the nighttime forest as a homeless ghost. Only Christians can be properly buried and mourned without the sacrifice that dignifies death.

One day when Jean de Heaulme was fifteen, he went hunting in Berenty forest. It was supposed to be a reserve, but the de Heaulmes claimed the right to hunt guinea fowl, especially in the Time of Bones. The crown prince of the de Heaulme estate fired his shotgun, then started back in terror. A dead limb of a tamarind tree fell right at his feet, broken by the blast — and on it was the desiccated corpse of a woman. She had climbed up into the tree to die, knowing no one would bury her, to save her body from the starving dogs that ran in packs and fed on corpses.

People of means did what they could. Madame Rasamimanana, the mother of Hanta, my lemur-watching colleague, lived in this region as a twelve-year-old girl. She was called Norosoa (the Beautiful-Sweet). Her father was a civil service doctor, the government medical officer in Ambovombé, the market town beyond Berenty. Norosoa and her family traveled by automobile to Fort Dauphin in February of the wet season of 1942 before the famine struck. When they reached the Mandrare River, they loaded the car onto a ferry-raft. Some thirty men held ropes to pull the raft. The river was so deep that they lost their footing and actually swam, hauling the ferry through the current. Norosoa remembers the heads of the men swimming, she says, because of her mother's and grandmother's dismay. Her mother kept exclaiming, "It is horrible, horrible, to cross a river like this!"

Then came the drought. People dug deep pits in the sand of the dried-out riverbed to reach water. Norosoa's father tried to care for the starving. Their family, elite people from the plateau who had always eaten rice, now boiled up meager rations of dried sweet potatoes, manioc, corn, and beans and thought themselves lucky to get anything at all. One day a skeletal old man wandered into the yard, his ribs like a ladder down his chest. Her grandmother, who lived with them, was so appalled at his condition that she gave him all the food she had cooked. He wolfed it down, then walked some meters away, curled up under a tree, and died.

"But I fed him!" protested Norosoa's grandmother when the doctor came home. The doctor was furious. He shouted that his mother-in-law had killed the man. To aid someone who is truly starving, you must start with water, then add gruel and, gradually, solid food. Eventually he calmed down enough to apologize to the old lady. "Never mind," he said to reassure her. "A man in that state would have died anyway."

Soeur Gabrielle, the nun who began life as Marthe de Heaulme, led her convent into action. Her outpost of the Daughters of Charity lay in Amboasary, the dusty little town established beside the new river crossing ten miles below Berenty. The nuns in their winged white headdresses boiled up gruel in cleaned-out oil drums. (In the famine of 1992 I watched a family stagger in from the country to the same kind of oil-drum soup kitchen run by Soeur Gabrielle's successors. The adults and their teenage son were totally naked, having bartered even their clothes.) The de Heaulmes and other newly settled French colonists of the Mandrare Valley fed their workers and the workers' families — another reason old Rehomaha said he would let his head be cut off for the de Heaulmes. Monsieur Confolent, the richest of the plantation owners, took in two hundred abandoned children and fed them throughout the famine. He certainly saved their lives. Most were not orphans. Their parents had tied little amulets around their necks to identify their sons and daughters if they also managed to live.

Famines are never just about food. There is always food somewhere, if not in the region, then in the next region or the next country. The Nobel laureate Amartya Sen points out that what fails is people's entitlement to food. If society accords them relief because of their own saved money and cattle herds, or because of their political power, or because of the moral claims of shared humanity, there is no famine. Sen argues that a real democracy has never had a famine. During the famine of the 1930s after the elimination of the prickly pear, Androy's Governor Decary demanded that the colonial government send grain to feed the people in his charge. His decisiveness saved at least some Tandroy who flocked to feeding stations. In 1942–43, Androy had no entitlement at all that was recognized by the outside world.

The outside world was fighting World War II. One tiny, insignificant spinoff of that war, but the only one that mattered to the starving Tandroy, was that the pretty port of Fort Dauphin had almost completely closed. The British fleet clamped down on Madagascar.

In the late 1930s the ebullient Governor-General Léon Cayla, having made an economic success of the colony, began to prepare Madagascar for war. His cortege of plumed, scarlet-coated horsemen were not much help when Hitler's menace loomed. In 1938 the French decided to mollify public opinion by returning the ashes of the exiled Queen Ranavalona III to Madagascar. Cayla arranged ceremonies for her reinterment at the Queen's Palace, amid general rejoicing. During the wave of Malagasy goodwill toward France, Cayla mobilized drafts of colonial soldiers for the coming conflict.

Hitler's blitzkrieg thundered across the Low Countries in May of 1940. The Germans swept the British off the Continent at Dunkirk and marched triumphant into Paris on June 14. By then, 34,000 Malagasy troops were already in France, with 72,000 more soldiers and 20,000 workers on the verge of sailing. On June 22, Marshal Henri Pétain signed his Vichy government's armistice with Hitler. The armistice threw Madagascar's colonials into confusion. When General Charles de Gaulle broadcast a call to arms from London, ordering Frenchmen of spirit to follow him, one group of patriots in Madagascar telegraphed their support. Governor-General de Coppet, who replaced Cayla, made a speech on Radio Tananarive urging all Frenchmen to join de Gaulle's Free French, and follow him in the path of honor. The Vichy government immediately redispatched Cayla to regain control. On July 3, 1940, the British bombed and sank the French fleet at Mers-el-Kebir in Algeria, for fear the ships would sail under Vichy orders and thus deny Britain supremacy of the seas. In far-off Madagascar, French opinion swung fiercely against Britain — aided, Cayla remarked, by the overenthusiasm of the British missionaries, who made it seem that de Gaulle was somehow fighting for Britain, not France. Tananarive subsided into obedience to Vichy. Henry and Alain de Heaulme, like almost all the other Frenchmen, were back in uniform as a Vichy militia, though in the end, never on active duty.

"After all," explained Jean de Heaulme, "we had always followed France. If France was Vichy, French in Madagascar automatically became Vichy. When Britain invaded Madagascar, of course we fought the British. If Germany had invaded, we would have fought the Germans instead."

Fort Dauphin looks as though wars could never touch it, only wind and waves. If you stand above the sea on the town's little peninsula, a scalloped headland indented with bays, and look eastward, a crescent of white sand curves off to your left, backed by the rainforest ranges. The silhouetted mountains sport at least one gray cloud with its trail of slanting rain or, in season, the drifting smoke of two or three brush fires. The sunlit bay is a fifteen-mile half-moon, satisfyingly punctu-

ated at the farthest end of the curve by the distant granite hump of
Evatra Peninsula. The waves roll straight toward you, blown by southeast trade winds that riffle the sapphire water with whitecaps. Below
them a long-reach swell is ready to simply pluck a boat from its anchors and toss it onto the sand.

Three hulks of freighters seem to be parked in parallel at the near
end of the beach. They were wrecked in recent years as onshore gales
drove their bows up the shore in nearly identical poses. Subsequent
storms are dismantling them. Their carcasses will soon join the other
underwater humps you can make out when the water is still: a buried
museum of defunct shipping. The port did not wreck just the love-
ship of the pink girls. When the first French governor, General Gallieni, visited Fort Dauphin in 1903, his warship, *La Perouse,* blew
ashore after he landed. He was greeted by French settlers and their
wives in Victorian dresses and flowered hats; a hand-sewn banner over
the road read "Welcome to Fort Dauphin." One other wreck is currently visible in the exact center of the harbor. Its bridge and bow still
rise above water, while amidships it forms a particularly nasty shoal.
It supposedly carried vanadium metal ore; perhaps it just carried insurance.

If you are in luck, one active ship may be in port. (I have even seen
two at once.) The most frequent visitor has a brilliant orange hull, as
though for maximum contrast with the cobalt bay. The boats unload
gasoline and diesel oil into a pipeline. They drop cases of condensed
milk and French butter into the attending lighters and load up bales of
sisal. The sisal goes only as far as Tamatave, farther along the coast,
where it is transferred to containers within larger-draft ships. Small
cruise ships with Zodiacs stop at Fort Dauphin, but the huge, high-
sided ones will not take the risk of winching their cosseted clientele
down into lighters to reach the shore.

Walk over the ridge from the port, another hundred yards on. Look
south. The rollers break on cliffs and "stacks" — isolated pinnacles of
rock with white foam at the base. This is the kind of granite seacoast
that awes holiday visitors to Brittany, Cornwall, and northern California, but this coast is tropical. Purple nudibranchs — sea slugs — bigger

than a man's hand crawl in the tidepools. The lobsters have blue shells with orange bosses. A grove of huge old *filao,* casuarina trees, hides wood-framed houses built at the turn of the century by American Lutheran missionaries. They called the place Libanona, for the Cedars of Lebanon. They came to relax from their labors inland in the desert regions, to sleep while the sea wind soughed through the filao needles. Round to the leeward, the little scallop of Libanona Bay is protected by a reef, so you can swim in warm waves safe from sharks. Climb up again and look west to another long, long arc of sandy beach. It's not very good for swimming: I have seen a fisherman carrying a hammerhead shark as big as himself draped over one shoulder. It is a good spot, though, to sit with a drink in your hand, watching the sun set suddenly behind the mountains in a vermilion sky.

This idyllic picture supposes that you have enough to eat. Preferably Three Horses beer at sundown with the prospect of tiny greenish oysters in baroquely carved shells, or grilled garlic shrimp en brochette, or fresh-caught tuna steak, or pungent lobster curry with rice. In contrast, the fisherfolk who confront the sea so picturesquely in their pirogues may be on such a tight margin that if the catch is bad that day, their family will not eat at all. If there is famine inland in Androy, best not to think about it.

In World War II, though, you would have peered out to sea in desperate hope that a ship, any ship, would run the British blockade to bring food, any food. You might even have seen the black silhouette of a submarine slip into that blue bay, like a shark in a paddling pool.

"With a deep muffled eruption the for'ard magazine tore her bows apart . . .

> Swept by infernos of blazing flames, she began to settle forward. Our quarter-deck by this time was covered with disheveled prisoners. We looked enthralled as the Italian's fo'c'sle dipped below the mirrored surface. Water climbing slowly up her bridgeworks, propellers already many feet above the surface, she still belched dense smoke which drifted several hundred feet towards the horizon . . .

Flame and debris flying . . . her complete stern floated lazily upward, somersaulting forty feet above the Indian Ocean. Prisoners
and crew alike flashed face down on the decks as the shock passed
overhead.

Jack Harker, radio operator of the British cruiser *Leander,* was
"raider hunting" in the Indian Ocean in the early years of the war.
Leander's crew was proud to sink cargo vessels heading for Vichy terri-
tories. The two most strategic French ports were Diego Suarez and
Djibouti. Diego Suarez is a deep-water harbor on the extreme northern
tip of Madagascar, a thousand miles north of Fort Dauphin. Djibouti,
on the Horn of Africa, is still a French military base today. British and
Free French ships concentrated their blockade there. By June of 1941,
Djibouti was famished. Captain Paul Maerten, the commander at
Diego, tried a ruse to revictual the besieged defenders. Instead of warships, he sent native craft — *botry* and *goelettes,* Arab-designed boats
that still ply the waters between Madagascar's ports with perpetually la-
boring engines and masts to carry sails. Their smokestacks belch black,
greasy diesel fumes; on the afterdeck an answering plume of white
woodsmoke rises from the cooking fire. Ensign Paul Cazalis de Fou-
douce commanded the first of the little fleet. The three Frenchmen
aboard donned turbans and stained their faces with walnut. They
sailed brazenly into Djibouti's harbor and unloaded seventy metric
tons of food. Djibouti was not fully relieved, though, until the day before Christmas, when a Vichy sloop carrying 138-mm guns thumbed
her nose at the British patrol boats and delivered three hundred tons of
food from Madagascar.

The pretty but treacherous port of Fort Dauphin was simply not
worth that much trouble. No French military garrison was starving
there, merely unknown tribespeople. Early in the war, submarines
from Diego Suarez did put in because they could dive under the
patrolling Britishers. Eventually a privateer reached Fort Dauphin with
a full cargo of flour. "A real privateer, a corsair," recalled Jean de
Heaulme. "She would leave a port with one smokestack and come in
somewhere else with two — one of them made of canvas. She simply

sneaked past the British. The flour was full of weevils and cockroaches, but that just made more protein. It helped against the famine." At last, at the end of 1943, the rains returned, and the Tandroy went back to building up their herds.

Diego Suarez would fall to the Japanese like a ripe mango. Madagascar's northern port is a superb harbor commanding all the vital routes to the Red Sea. By the spring of 1942, Germany controlled most of France, eastern Europe, and the Balkans and was marching inexorably deeper into Russia. The Japanese advanced even faster than Hitler's blitzkrieg. They bombed Pearl Harbor on December 7, 1941, and within four months they held almost all of Southeast Asia. Vichy France simply handed over its own Indochinese bases. The Japanese fleet sailed in strength into the Indian Ocean, sinking British warships off Ceylon and India. Little doubt about their next prize: Diego.

To save the Red Sea route to India, the British had to secure Diego Suarez. A battleship, two carriers, two cruisers, eleven destroyers, six corvettes, six minesweepers, five infantry assault ships, three personnel ships, and six mechanical transports sailed from Durban, South Africa. They reached Madagascar in absolute secrecy on May 4, 1942. (Imagine that, in the present age of ubiquitous spy satellites!) The northern tip of Madagascar is a sculptured peninsula, like Fort Dauphin in the south but magnified in scale. The British fleet crept up on the western, leeward side by night, across the narrow isthmus from the harbor. The flotilla threaded its way among reefs and floating mines, with the destroyers serving as lightships, and minesweepers clearing the way. At five A.M. the landing party attacked in force, up a steep ridge with rock outcrops on top, one of which has ever since been known as Windsor Castle. British airplanes from the carriers dropped leaflets on the town of Diego, demanding unconditional surrender. They bombed French planes sitting on the airfield. In the harbor they sank a cruiser, three submarines, and a sloop. Vichy France was still, in theory, a neutral power. Britain did not stop to declare war before attacking.

Captain Maerten and Colonel Édouard Claerebout, the two French commanders, radioed to the British: "Diego Suarez will be defended to the end according to the traditions of the French Army, Navy, and Air Force." Eight hundred French and thirty-two hundred Malagasy fought off the invaders on the rocky ridge with mortars and machine guns. Some two hundred men were killed, but they did not yield their positions.

The British decided on a diversion to distract the defenders — a suicide mission. They would land fifty marines at night in the town itself from the destroyer *Anthony*. The British admiral admitted afterward, "The *Anthony's* chances of success I estimated at about 50 per cent, my advisors thought 15 per cent, and of the Royal Marines I did not expect a score to survive the night. The next few hours were not happy ones."

The destroyer slipped through the narrows under fire from Diego's guns. Lieutenant-Commander Hodges, who brought the ship's stern to a jetty against a strong offshore wind, was later officially praised for "superb seamanship." Marines ran into the dockyard. Defenders fired back with machine guns, but the marines seized strongpoints. Soon they "were embarrassed by the large numbers of men from the naval headquarters and the artillery depot who came in to surrender." Britain won an almost surgical victory through seamanship, determination, and daring. Or, from the Vichy point of view, by a dastardly attack on a neutral and unsuspecting base, including sneak invasion of a sleeping town. It promptly became known as "the Rape of Madagascar."

De Gaulle, predictably, was furious. He had wanted Madagascar taken by Free French troops, not British. He was almost equally angry that the British stopped after taking Diego, instead of marching on Tananarive to confront what he called the Vichy Fascists.

Madagascar was a minor pawn in the leaders' game. Churchill wanted to safeguard India, jewel of the British Empire. De Gaulle wanted to squash Vichy. Roosevelt was in favor of the invasion as long as America could pretend ignorance. Marshal Jan Smuts wanted to show that South Africa was in the war. (Some French feared that Smuts simply planned to annex Madagascar.) The Boer leader Daniel Malan was appalled at the prospect of black South African troops killing whites — that might give them bad habits. Among them, the Allies mounted a second invasion force in September to march from Majunga and take Tananarive. Armand Annet, the new Vichy governor-general, tried to negotiate an honorable defeat. The Vichy leader Pierre Laval cabled from Paris that Annet must instead defend Madagascar "as long as possible, by all possible means, and with no other considerations."

Governor Annet knew he was outnumbered. It also occurred to him that a humiliating defeat, let alone a war fought to the last man and lost, might just be noticed by the *indigènes*. Annet compromised with delaying tactics. His troops retreated, felling trees across the road to slow the British advance. Finally Annet signed the articles of surrender. But he held off until one minute past midnight on November 6, 1942, which would grant his officers the medals and extra pay appropriate to a full six-month campaign. He still believed that men who fought on the Vichy side would wish to be remembered!

The Malagasy did take note. Philibert Rakotosamimananana, later a distinguished medical doctor, told me of watching the British enter Tananarive when he was a boy of ten. He perched on the long flight of steps leading down to the marketplace while the tanks rolled into town.

"There were so many tanks! And so fast! As fast as cars! Not like the antiquated Vichy tanks doing about six kilometers an hour. After the tanks came jeeps and trucks. Some of the jeeps had quarters of whole pigs on board. We all thought 'Well!' And then there were the Zulus [actually East Africans — South Africa did not send black troops]. Some Zulus were military police. British discipline was impeccable. White soldiers obeyed their policemen, whether black or white. No one stepped out of line. We were used to seeing whites beat up on blacks, but not the other way around. Again we thought, 'Well, well!' But then, people like my parents watched to see what flag the British would fly over their camp on the ridge. To our dismay, they raised the French flag. They were going to give our island back again to France, to de Gaulle."

You might think that Fort Dauphin could stay comfortably aloof from politics. The nearest the British ever came was a base in the southwestern town of Tulear, which had Catalina seaplanes to patrol the Mozambique Channel. However, when Gaullists took over the government changed, and a few French settlers tried to prove they never had supported the Vichy side. Monsieur Seyrig, an Alsatian who ran the fuel depot in Fort Dauphin, owned a radio so he could check on the weather as boats came into port. He was denounced for possibly trying to communicate by radio with German submarines. He was tortured and died in prison in Tananarive. The Jenny family, second-generation residents of Fort Dauphin, were also thrown in jail. Their father had been one of the first Europeans to settle in the south. As early as 1905 he sent barges from Fort Dauphin up the Mandrare River to collect the latex of the endemic *Euphorbia intisy.* The Jennys shipped intisy rubber out to Europe, where it was made into thin, delicate goods like surgeons' gloves — and the very first Michelin auto tires. Fort Dauphin Europeans had known the Jenny family all their lives, and yet, because they were Swiss-German, they were denounced as enemies.

Today Bertrand de Guitaut, a second-generation settler himself, looks back and remarks, "We think the Malagasy are paranoid today about invasion by phantom submarines. They are no different from us. If anything, they learned that particular paranoia from us French in World War II."

Plantation owners prospered in the war. Mica was a strategic material, used as insulation for all the electrical parts demanded by the world's war machine. The few ships that came into port wanted to buy the de Heaulmes' mica for both sides of the conflict. Exports continued to reach America under cover of Vichy "neutrality."

Sanctions have a double edge; they can operate like protective tariffs to boost local initiative. The de Guitaut family discovered how to grow tobacco for a closed local market. They bricolaged every input out of local materials. With one hundred workers, they dug irrigation canals, which they lined with waterproof clay. Tobacco seedlings need shade, so they improvised little parasols of *fia* tree bark, stuck on lengths of river reed. Women picked caterpillars off the leaves. (The de Guitauts did try to have ducks clear the insects, but the ducks shredded the leaves while grabbing for caterpillars.) They constructed shady hangars thatched with reeds, brought in in ox carts, and suspended the leaves from poles of local bamboo to cure. Then the leaves were piled up to ferment — a delicate process, since if the pile grew too hot it could burst into flame. At last the tobacco was baled, and the bales wrapped in local palm-leaf mats.

The de Guitauts' tobacco was not for smoking but for chewing, a women's habit. A corps of tough old-lady tobacco tasters checked that the final product was the best mix of leaf and wood ash. Only one local tree made the right kind of ash. The de Guitaut brothers discovered that by adding lime, any old wood ash would do, and the process became a jealously guarded trade secret. To market the chaws, they made wrapping paper for their little sachets out of a slurry of bark from the local elephant's-foot plants. All that for a bad habit!

One further problem: the island was almost out of fuel. De Guitaut and de Heaulme trucks ran on gasohol: 95 percent ethanol distilled from sugar cane. It worked fine in the trucks, although the drivers kept drinking it.

In good years there was plenty of local food even during the war. In the eastern rainforest, people wove their own clothes from raffia; in the west, from native cotton. Chantal de Heaulme, Jean's younger sister, remembers her father crafting sandals for the children from discarded rubber tires — standard third-world footwear. Their mother sewed little slippers out of scraps of old silk to wear on Sundays to church. The de Heaulme children had two pairs of homemade shoes; the vast majority of people, as always, went barefoot.

In those years Chantal loved traveling to Berenty. Her sister, Huguette, three years older, was a town girl like their mother. Huguette blossomed in the social life and relative civilization of Fort Dauphin. Their older brother, Jean, was off at the prestigious Lycée Saint-Michel in Tananarive, where he seemed devoted to Boy Scouting, undeterred by Uncle Alain's experience with the Scout troop that died of plague. Chantal was free to be the tomboy. She would climb up and sit at her father's side in the high cab of Baghdad, the Chevrolet truck, heading west to the plantation. She especially liked watching the cows and goats being milked and the spinning cream separator. Her family took the cream, while the skimmed milk went to plantation children. Each child had the right to a "kapoky" of milk a day — that is, the empty Nestlé milk tin that is the standard measuring cup all over Madagascar. They drank it on the spot, their dark eyes peering above the drinking bowls.

Chantal may not have been old enough to speak at the dinner table before dessert, but in Berenty she pestered her imposing father with questions. However stern he seemed to others, he was always happy to explain his knowledge of Androy to his daughter. Whatever she asked, about a flower or an insect or a traditional folk tale, he knew the answer. His delight in his adopted landscape burned brightly even in the years of war.

One day when she was about ten, Chantal visited the de Guitaut family for a whole week at their plantation house, which was a morning's run downriver from Berenty. She traveled alone, in the care of Jaona the Never-Suckled, the aeropousse runner. Chantal arranged herself on the wooden seat of the aeropousse, her small suitcase tucked behind her and her dolls in her lap. They passed through about five villages along the way. As they reached each one, Jaona and his teammate lifted the aeropousse shoulder high into the air, iron wheel, little girl, and all, and displayed her to the villagers. Women rushed up to greet her and to offer her bowls of habobo, zebu yogurt. Come to think of it, some of them might have been greeting Jaona.

"My God," exclaims Chantal, "but Jaona was a handsome man!"

"I have to tell you," I agree. "He is over eighty now, and he still is."

A month before his eighteenth birthday Jean de Heaulme joined the French army. He passed part one of the baccalaureate at the Lycée Saint-Michel, but he saw no point in wasting another year studying for part two. He planned to do his military service early instead of waiting till the regulation age of twenty. If he enlisted from Madagascar, though, he would be sent to Burma, a country that held no attraction for him. He wanted to serve in France as his father had before him.

He flew off all alone at the end of 1946 in a Dakota DC3, the workhorse of World War II, to the "mother country" he had never seen. He went to stay with a cousin in Toulon, where he put in his name for early military service.

He still had to wait six months. Monsieur de Heaulme, not one for letting a son sit idle, informed Jean, "I do not want you to stay there without doing anything. You can go to a factory to learn to work." Jean apprenticed as a mechanic at the Pont du Sud factory in Toulon. He learned to weld and to do machine-lathing well enough to work without supervision. After all, Monsieur de Heaulme could put together Chevrolet trucks and railway steam engines; the son should be able to do likewise. Jean remarks that an interval of manual labor is now common or even fashionable for middle-class students, but in his day it was almost unheard of. Henry de Heaulme invented the idea from first principles, just as he had invented the idea of a private nature reserve in Androy.

On Sundays Jean, with nothing much to do, fulfilled another dream of his father's. He learned to fly. His instructor at the nearby military airport of Cuers was a dashing man named Bernard Astraud. An electrical engineer at the Pont du Sud plant, only a few years older than Jean, Astraud was passionate about aviation. Jean quickly caught his instructor's delight in piloting. Jean says, "I loved Madagascar, and everyone knew I came from Madagascar. They kept asking me questions: 'What is it like out there?' Bernard Astraud said to me. 'Bon, beh, it seems like a fantastic country!' Well, he saw my enthusiasm!" In the end, Jean changed his instructor's life when he found a way to bring Astraud to Madagascar.

Jean joined the Nineteenth Artillery Regiment on April 14, 1947. He was a "blue," a rookie, along with sixty others. The Nineteenth Artillery was full of seasoned army men who told tales of the battle of Bir-Hakim, of the bloody landing on Antheor Beach. They adored their leader, General Jacques Leclerc, and, still higher in the stratosphere, General (later Marshal) de Lattre de Tassigny. The older men regarded the blues as fluffy new-hatched chicks, but for the first time in his life Jean was surrounded by comrades and equals, all under the same discipline.

His unit moved up the Vallée de la Vésubie. They retook and occupied Tende and La Brigue, border enclaves claimed by Italy during the war. Jean's first experience of adult comradeship was in an army on a wave of recent victory, during spring in the Alpes Maritimes. His unit then served with the 454th Anti-Aircraft Regiment of the Second Armored Division stationed in the French Zone of Occupation, the pretty, relatively unscathed region around Lake Constance and the Black Forest in occupied Germany. Jean met hardly any Germans, though. The overseas French may have distrusted the British invaders, ancestral maritime enemies of France, but they hated Germans. If Jean had befriended a German at that time, his Réunionais grandfather might have disowned him.

After six months, when a new draft of recruits came in, Jean and his friends were no longer raw blues. They could now apply to be non-commissioned officers. He keeps a photo of himself as a very young man, cap smartly over one eye, the cleft in his chin outlined in soft side-lighting. (The photographer clearly specialized in photos to send to girlfriends.) A very beautiful young man, gazing at you over the shoulder turned toward the camera. His regiment's insignia — a dagger crushing a swastika — shines from the epaulet, and on his sleeve is the first chevron of rising rank.

In the summer of 1947 he was given special leave to head up the Madagascar delegation to the Boy Scout International Jamboree. It was the first jamboree to be held after the war. Lord Baden-Powell himself officiated. Acres of tents, ceremonies and sing-songs, pow-wows with real Sioux Indians in eagle-feather headdresses! The Madagascar Scouts erected a ceremonial gate made of sticks in front of their tent, in the outline of the Queen's Palace in Tananarive.

At the jamboree Jean met up with a family of his own cousins: Jean, Alain, and Richard de Heaulme de Boutsocq. Their father had left Réunion to seek his fortune in French Indochina, as Jean's father, Henry, had gone to Madagascar. The two Jeans confided in each other that each dreamed of a career in the regular army. The army offered everything in their family credo: discipline, hard work, upright morality, the responsibility of command — and patriotism to a country that for them reached far beyond the borders of metropolitan France. There were new chances for excitement and glory; an actual war seemed to be brewing up in Indochina, in a place not yet called Vietnam.

Jean demobilized from the army as a master sergeant. He felt no surge of freedom but, rather, unease. It seemed very strange to give up his rifle and face Europe with no weapon in his hand. He hoped to join up again soon. Perhaps his father would encourage him to enter Saint-Cyr, the French military officers' academy founded by Napoleon.

His cousin Jean de Heaulme of Indochina remains an image of the path not taken, the Might-Have-Been. That other Jean did enter Saint-Cyr. He captained a squadron of parachutists in the desperate battles of the French Indochinese war. There he met, and eventually married, Geneviève de Galard, a heroic army nurse known to all of France as the Angel of Dien Bien Phu. At the end of his army career he retired with honors: General Jean de Heaulme de Boutsocq.

For Jean de Heaulme of Madagascar, out of the question. Monsieur Henry de Heaulme was adamant. Did the boy long for life in a structured hierarchy, where he could accept orders from other men? A regiment of comrades-in-arms? Namby-pamby officers' quarters? Abdication of the kingdom of Berenty, which Henry and Alain had spent their lives to build? Monsieur de Heaulme telegraphed his son just four words: RETURN IMMEDIATELY TO MADAGASCAR!

Jean says, "Well, I was a dutiful child."

On March 20, 1949, he boarded a British troop carrier, the *Al Soudan*. It was full of Germans! Of the 2,500 French soldiers and ex-soldiers on board, 1,500 were Foreign Legionnaires, mostly German, dispatched to quell Madagascar's own War of Independence. Jean was too young to see action in World War II, and he did not go to fight in Indochina. Now he sailed home — into war. It was a war kept totally secret from the outside world.

March 1947: a Tandroy nobleman tried to warn Monsieur de Heaulme. Tolo, heir to King A-Thousand-Cannot-Lift-Him, made a special trip across the Mandrare River to Berenty. He sat down on the porch of the de Heaulmes' house as though he'd dropped in for a leisurely afternoon of conversation. He remarked that if Monsieur de Heaulme ever needed help, he should send word: Tolo, his friend, his honorary blood brother, would stand by him. Henry de Heaulme answered, "Of course, of course, I'm always sure of your help and friendship," thinking Tolo's words mere courtesy. Later he understood. Tolo meant to stand by him if it came to life and death.

On the night of March 29, at separate points all over the east and north of Madagascar, Malagasy attacked French prisons, guard posts, and homes. France called it a rebellion. For the Malagasy, it was their War of Independence.

As early as 1943, during the worst of World War II, de Gaulle had assembled colonial delegates in Brazzaville, French Congo, to discuss limited delegation of power. In 1945 the new United Nations charter proclaimed that all colonies would eventually be free. In 1946 three prominent Malagasy — Ravoahangy, Raseta, and Jacques Rabemananjara — were elected to the French Chamber of Deputies, the parliament. Then France tried to turn the clock back to total colonial domination.

Robert Dama, a simple Malagasy soldier, listened inspired as Deputies Raseta and Ravoahangy made an oration to Malagasy troops still serving in Germany: "You will soon go back to Madagascar! It will be up to you to protect all Malgaches!" Dama had been a German prisoner of war; he had also guarded German prisoners alongside GIs from America. The Malagasy veterans expected to gain political rights and financial rewards for their overseas service. Instead they were dispatched back to their villages amid rice rationing and the reinstitution of forced labor for the government. Madagascar was soon full of very angry men with military training — and firsthand knowledge of how to kill Europeans. Dama became a general in the 1947 revolt.

France imposed a total news blackout. The rest of the world did not know and did not care that there was a war of independence in Madagascar. Most of the fighting was in remote rainforests, the only place guerrillas could hide for long, with the freedom fighters increasingly isolated from each other and from any general knowledge of the course of events. It was easy to blockade news to the outside world.

Testimonies give us snapshots of 1947–1949, sudden illuminations like strobe flashes in a very dark room. In Manakara (where the de Heaulmes had bought their steam engine from the railway) some forty Frenchmen were killed in the first attacks of March 29, 1947, a Saturday night and Sunday. Attackers hesitated before men with Malagasy wives, surrounded by their families of half-Malagasy children, then struck the Frenchmen down anyway with spears and stones and machetes.

The railroad stayed open for some days. An adjutant in the French army named Maître commandeered an engine and ventured up the line from Manakara to see if any other Frenchmen were still alive. Wild rumors circulated among the rebels that freedom-loving America would send troops and airplanes to help them. By chance, Maître was wearing an American-made uniform, like many soldiers who had fought in Europe, and he had a ruddy countenance that seemed stereotypically Anglo-Saxon. His troops ran into a group of insurgents who greeted him with joy. The Americans had really come! Maître seized his chance. Affecting fractured French, he claimed he was indeed American. There seemed to be just one Frenchman left alive in the region, a redoubtable Breton coffee planter named Carlet, who had been holding off attackers for several days with the help of his locally born wife and a half-dozen workers who considered themselves his family. Maître went with the rebels to "capture" Carlet. He had to keep up his pretend American accent while trying to find a way to tell the suspicious Carlet that he was really French and had come to save him. In the end, both Frenchmen survived.

The three Malagasy members of France's Chamber of Deputies were arrested as ringleaders. Rabemananjara, the youngest, told afterward how he was dragged before the police chief, Monsieur Baron. Baron ordered him to confess. When he refused, Rabemananjara was left with a Senegalese soldier who made him kneel, then sat astride his back, grabbed the nape of his neck, and plunged his head up to the neck in a bucket of water that stank of piss and petrol. Over and over, each time bringing Rabemananjara to the point of asphyxiation. He finally yielded, not to the torture but to the horror of being accused by colleagues. Baron showed him a declaration written by Ravoahangy, the older deputy, whom Rabemananjara had always followed and admired. (Ravoahangy was also tortured.) "He could not care less about having you shot," said Monsieur Baron, laughing. "Not him nor the others, either. You are so young, almost a child: the truth is those other people have cheated you." In the end, Rabemananjara wrote out a declaration accusing Ravoahangy in his turn. Armed with the forced confessions, the courts condemned Ravoahangy and Raseta to death and Rabemananjara to a life sentence of hard labor. A year later all three sentences were commuted, although the three deputies were not allowed to return to Madagascar until after the nation became independent.

"Pacification" of rainforest villages by French and Senegalese soldiers continued over the next twenty months. Estimates of the dead range from 11,000 to 90,000 killed — the higher number is more likely. Patrice Ndrova of Fasina, near Mananara, left a notebook of memoirs for his family. He wrote:

> It was completely impossible to stay in the village; we had to take the women and children to live in deserted places so as not to be discovered by the whites and the Senegalese, for it was catastrophe if they got their hands on you . . . We had to abandon the ripened rice in the fields, the manioc and bananas, the sweet potatoes and taros, so we endured famine. Besides, we lived in the midst of the forest, in miserable huts, with rain day and night, without ceasing, in the cold, without either blankets or clothes to put on our skin other than filthy rags. There was no salt. No sugar for the coffee. Mosquitoes and leeches to make you shudder: little children carried along in the flight had their mouths, their eyes, their ears and their whole bodies covered with leeches. At night, men went out hunting food. In short, we lived like wild beasts. Terror of the Senegalese stopped us coming out into open spaces, and terror of "Bandits," the revolutionaries, from staying in the village, so the only course was to remain, dead or alive, hidden in the forest.

(It would be interesting to hear a Senegalese version. I once traveled with Ibrahima Fall when he had just arrived in Madagascar as the UNICEF representative. Ibrahima was one of the handsomest men I have ever met: tall, with bitter-chocolate skin that was almost blue-black in the shadows. Long, curly eyelashes. Visibly Senegalese. I watched people watching him, and finally asked, "Do you know why they look at you like that?" He answered, "Of course I know why. My grandfather served here in 'forty-seven. He told me stories of what the French made him do.")

France blamed the MDRM for orchestrating the revolt. This was the Mouvement Democratique de la Renovation Malgache, the political party of the three delegates elected to the Chamber of Deputies. MDRM members were mostly elite townspeople who had been through the French educational system. They knew of the fall of the Bastille, they had school copies of *Les Misérables;* they were contemporaries of Jean-Paul Sartre. They demanded that France should live up to ideals of Liberté, Égalité, Fraternité.

France took revenge. The official list of tortures is all the more horrifying for its dry, bureaucratic detail. It includes the "wooden horse": forcing a man to kneel with a squared stick at the back of his knees and his hands tied to a kind of bridle around his neck. If he lowered his arms, he slowly strangled himself. One group of 166 elite Malagasy were taken in railway cattle cars to Moramanga. Some were shot in the railway cars; the rest were taken into the forest at night to be machine-gunned by French and Senegalese, as they stood before their own mass grave. Just one wounded man crawled out from under the pile of corpses several hours later and eventually told the tale.

Jean de Heaulme was promptly remobilized when he returned from France in 1949. The army gave him an officer's commission — an officer who spoke Malagasy and had a talent for organization. He took charge of a unit of the Foreign Legion, most of them German. One German became Jean's close friend. This man had been an officer in the Luftwaffe, but he served in the Legion as a private. He explained that he had joined to take away the shame of defeat. Back in Germany he would have been unemployed, unwanted, beaten. The Foreign Legion gave him discipline, esprit de corps, and, above all, a chance to start again. (Men join the Legion under false names and officially have no past.) Jean was surprised that German soldiers and French officers could work together, but they all submitted to the same discipline, with the enemy now Malagasy.

"What did you actually do, then?" I asked.

"Mostly chase rebels who were running away as fast as they could. I was set to organize transport along the coast from Mananjary to Manakary. Every convoy had military units before and behind, with rifles. There was not much trouble."

In Berenty and Fort Dauphin the French had no need to panic, but they did so all the same. The mass of the people never rose. Monsieur de Heaulme's blood brother, the chief named Tolo, never had to choose between his loyalties. Still, white civilians of Fort Dauphin lived in fear. Men went to their offices and carried on business during the day but kept a rifle at their side. At night most of them assembled their families to sleep in the fort or at the Jennys' house — ironically, since the Swiss-born family had been jailed by their neighbors only a few years before as suspected German spies. The Jennys had built their small mansion on a little ridge, unlike the secluded de Heaulme house. The Jenny house was surrounded by porches set with two stories of lovely white pillars. The porches, pillars, and steeply sloping gardens gave it sightlines for defensive rifle fire on all four sides. The women and children slept while the men mounted guard.

It was the Malagasy elite who suffered. The Fort Dauphin police threw 231 suspected rebels into the prison, which is still in use today. It is just a square sand yard measuring thirty by fifty meters, surrounded by a ten-foot-high wall topped with broken bottles. A couple of buildings inside hold rooms for sleeping. The prison is next to Fort Flacourt, still a military post, on the end of the tiny peninsula. If the inmates could see over the wall, they would have a vista of blue sea and granite coast. Today you can casually climb the ruins of an eighteenth-century bastion and wave down at the prisoners, who wave back.

In 1947–49, people died there of starvation and abuse. Some still live to tell of being dumped head first into oil drums of water that red peppers had been boiled in. One Malagasy warder in particular would shit in prisoners' cells and piss into their mouths. A summary police tribunal condemned 117 of the men and three women to be shot. The names remain: some were doctors, some governors or canton chiefs, and one is identified as a writer and interpreter. The army stationed in Fort Flacourt under a Captain Martin then refused to carry out the death sentences. Henry de Heaulme and other prominent settlers also protested. Eventually a "Crisis Cell" composed of military officers, judges, and two settlers, Felly and de Heaulme, commuted the sentences to a mere five years' hard labor.

Prince Pierre Ramahatra lay on royal blue sheets, covered by a sunshine-yellow duvet, with a crimson woolly hat perched on his bald head as though defying fate. He gestured to me to sit down with a twitch of his left hand — the only limb he could move a little, after the stroke that had felled him two weeks before, in September 2000. His face lay on the pillow, a talking head, an isolated mind, a fistful of memories on its Technicolor background.

His son Roland urged me, "Ask him! He is ready to tell you the whole story of 1947. It is better than any antidepressant, after such a blow, to know that there are people who still want to hear what he has to say." Roland was his father's attending physician: a medical doctor, a philosopher, and former governor of Tananarive Province.

The Ramahatras are quite a family. Most famous of all was the turn-of-the-century Great Prince, the great-uncle of the prince on the Technicolor bed. Roland's brother Olivier gave me his own slant on their distinguished ancestor. (Olivier is a professor of economics, a profession with wide latitude for eccentricity.) He pointed out a photograph of the Great Prince in top hat and frock coat, seated in a filanzana, his team of bearers in uniforms consisting of striped rugby jerseys and bare feet. Then Olivier seized the framed family genealogy from the living-room wall. The chart, with its multiple links to the Malagasy royal family, made my head swim, but I got the gist of Olivier's exposition.

"Prince Ramahatra was, of course a *traitor!* He always came out on top. First he was a privy councilor to the queen, one of the grand powers in the ancien régime, but then the whole Malagasy government surrendered as soon as the first two French shells landed in the garden of the Queen's Palace. Did he get caught up in the revolution against the French? No, not him. He waited to see which way the cat would jump. When General Gallieni arrived — even before he arrived — Gallieni decided that the way to subdue Madagascar was to shoot a prominent aristocrat and a prominent bourgeois so the rest would crumble. Of course Great-Grandfather was picked as the most prominent aristocrat. But did he wait around to be executed? No, not him. He managed to shuffle off that honor onto Prince Ratsimamanga, who became the heroic martyr. Great-Grandfather turned himself into the most trusted adviser of the French instead. You cannot blame him. He was born to rule. Our family have always ruled. You could not expect him not to rule, whatever the government, even if it happened to be French. You can't expect my brother Victor not to become prime minister or my brother Roland not to be chief of province for Antananarivo. What can you do if you are born into a family like this! We are all princes, whatever we do. So I mostly live in Paris now. Do you know the Champs-Élysées, the River of Light, the most beautiful avenue in the world? Where else do you expect a prince to live?"

When I escaped from Olivier to the bedchamber, Pierre Ramahatra also began his tale with his great-uncle the Great Prince. He spoke in a low voice, with hardly a repetition, the speech of a man who had been orating in public — and in French — all his life, even when he had to dictate his speech from a royal blue pillow.

"I tell you, the Great Prince Ramahatra, when I was born on the fifteenth of March, 1917, he came to the house . . . As soon as he arrived, as soon as he crossed the threshold of the house, he cried out, 'If the child is a boy, I will be the godfather!' In my time the would-be godfather called out like that. As he climbed up to the first floor, he kept on shouting. Just then a person in the childbirth chamber opened the door a crack and said, 'The child is a boy!'"

The Great Prince did become godfather to little Pierre. Later, in 1933, the dying Great Prince formally declared Pierre Ramahatra inheritor of his title, though by then, of course, the old titles had no official value. In Madagascar titles pass not to the first-born but to the member of the next generation deemed most worthy.

Still later, in 1946, twenty-nine-year-old Pierre took a job — as a police inspector for the French. He was posted to Fort Dauphin. Rabefialy, the traditional king of Fort Dauphin, received the prince royally. The king sent geese, turkeys, and ducks as presents every

Sunday until the young man really did not know what to do with them. Some he managed to give to a new friend, Andreas, a police inspector like himself, who hailed from a little village in the rainforest above Fort Dauphin that had the charming name of Eminiminy — the Rainy-Rainy.

"But I have been to Rainy-Rainy!" I exclaimed. "A six-hour walk over the mountains. Beautiful!"

"And do you remember the leeches up in Rainy-Rainy?" the head on the pillow asked me. We burst out laughing together.

He turned suddenly serious. "So you want to know what actually happened in 'forty-seven?

"On the twenty-ninth of March, 1947, at ten A.M., the police received a letter from the governor-general saying that the doors of the prison in Moramanga had been forced open by the prisoners . . . They killed a Frenchman. Fearing that the revolt would spread, the governor-general organized a command for a level-two alert of the police. That is, shifts day and night for police at the gendarmerie. Then, to seize the documents of the MDRM [the Mouvement Démocratique de la Rénovation Malgache], who were, according to the declaration, the instigators of that event. The MDRM Fort Dauphin secretary was called Jacques Raharijaona. He held the documents. They seized all the dossiers, searched through the papers to requisition them, but they found nothing.

"Then the torture started, to make Raharijaona say that the Malagasy colleagues of the MDRM intended to kill all foreigners. Raharijaona denied that he had received such an order. And he fainted three times. In spite of that he was beaten up again — three times. Then they let him breathe for a little, and then they plunged his head in a bucket of dirty water.

"Well, excuse me, it was urine.

"Raharijaona denied everything. And for three days it went on like that. Since in the end they had learned nothing, they let Raharijaona go, at seven in the morning. No, it was ten in the morning, because he attended Mass. Then he washed himself and started out for his house. There he fell unconscious. And then he died.

"Learning about it, all the Malagasy of the town nearly revolted.

They were calmed by my colleague Andreas, by myself, and by prominent Malagasy and Frenchmen [including the commander of the fort; Monseigneur Silva, the bishop; and de Heaulme] . . . Yes, de Heaulme as well. All those people met at the police station . . .

"The crowd wanted to take revenge. Then the people with us said to the crowd, 'We are your side, let us work together, but do not let us attack the police.' Then they went to the police commissioner, led by Monseigneur Silva, the bishop. They said, 'Stop the tortures, otherwise we will tell the crowd to take action . . .'

"The police commissioner, the man who ordered all that torture, was called Henri Gervais. He was a Creole from Réunion. Abetted by a Malagasy inspector . . . called Jules. Jules André."

Roland broke in to clarify. "That means that the bishop, de Heaulme, the commander and all the rest of you, you were against the police commissioner who wanted to torture people?"

"Yes, indeed."

"Right," said Roland. "The others were isolated, then? Commissioner Gervais and Jules André were all on their own?"

"No, there were other Frenchmen with them. Frenchmen, but above all Creoles. Creoles from Réunion were with them. Those fellows, they did not like the Malagasy. Malagasy did not like them."

The people he called Creoles looked like Malagasy. Their ancestors had been shipped to Réunion, mostly from Fort Dauphin. The racist term for them was "sold for guns," meaning they were descended from slaves, though many actually left Fort Dauphin as indentured laborers after slavery had ended. Because Creoles were Réunionais, they held full French nationality. That put them in the classic position of the oppressed turning into oppressors.

"Madame Henry de Heaulme was president of the Red Cross at Fort Dauphin. Henry de Heaulme threatened that they would alert the International Red Cross if the torture continued . . . But that did not stop them putting in prison all the members of the MDRM, thirteen of them, nearly all the Merina and Betsileo [plateau people] of Fort Dauphin. That meant the elite, the cadres. At that time there was no school in Fort Dauphin for boys above the age of twelve. That means that nearly all the Malagasy professional people of Fort Dauphin were Merina and Betsileo.

"They wanted to put me in prison, too, even though I was in the police. But de Heaulme, he was very tough with them. Several times he forced his way into the police station. Our office was beside the de Heaulme house. Madame de Heaulme and her family could hear the cries of people being tortured. As for me, the de Heaulmes said, 'If ever they try to touch you, we telegraph Tananarive. We will raise all the French of Tananarive to help you, people like the de Lastres and the Villentroys.'

"But that did not stop the torture of other people. On the contrary. The political prisoners, if I can so call them, were all in jail. I was nominally in charge of the prison, though I had no power to stop the abuses. Every morning the political prisoners were waked up. They stripped to naked torsos, and they crawled on all fours, and people hit them. Yes, hit them. As they crawled three times around the prison yard. Three times around. They were hardly fed, either. In the prison there are two rations: half-cooked dried maize, the official ration, and then what the families bring to the prison gate. But for those prisoners, the guards threw away the families' food. And they had been arrested without doing anything, without any proof!"

Roland cut in on his father's story. "Even according to the official orders, one needed some reason to imprison people. But there were no reasons! There were no archives, no proofs. Nobody in Fort Dauphin had any intention of killing French — there was no reason at all!"

"Commissioner Gervais called the Merina and Betsileo civil servants into his office one by one. Then he called their wives one by one. One of them managed to escape by jumping out of the window. The commissioner's office was beside our office. We saw a woman jump out of the window nearly naked. I ran to throw her all I had in the office, a black photographer's veil. In those days, photographers covered their heads with a big black veil.

"I threw her that cloth, and I said, 'Cover yourself with that, Madame!'

"She said, 'He propositioned me! He wanted to rape me!'"

"As she was crying out very loud, all the people of the area came out of their houses. And Gervais, the commissioner, opened the door of Andréas's office and said, 'You have nothing to do with this. It does not concern you.'

"We told Madame Bakoly to return to her house, which was only fifty meters from the office. The people were furious as anything, eh? And the commissioner hauled us back to tell us, 'You have nothing to do with this story. And you do not know anything.'

"So we said nothing.

"There was never a riot. It never happened. Never. There wasn't even a demonstration in the streets against the French. Never — except for the wives of the men who had been arrested. There were thirteen of them, and some of them were raped by the French. In the Frenchmen's offices! That was what nearly destroyed Franco-Malagasy relations.

"A month later I was sent to Tananarive. By airplane! Monseigneur Silva paid half my fare, Monsieur de Heaulme a quarter, and the Jennys the final quarter of the fare. I was sent to ask if the Catholic brothers could send teachers to open a school for boys of twelve to fourteen years old in Fort Dauphin. That mission failed. They said there were not enough teachers to spare. But the first thing I did, as soon as I arrived at our house, was to ask my mother to send for my grandmother, the widow of the Great Prince Ramahatra. I told her *everything*. I begged my grandmother to intervene."

Roland asked, "You didn't go yourself?"

"Oh, no, no, no. I would have been diverted by Commissaire Baron, the chief of police. Baron was — he was *cruel*. If Gervais tortured in Fort Dauphin, Baron was doing it at the national level. People like Ravoahangy."

I suddenly understood what the father and son were telling me. Almost anyone else in Madagascar who tried to complain about the police in that dark time would wind up with Baron, the chief of police who had tortured the deputies. Neither French nor Malagasy could check the power of the police and the army. There was just one way to circumvent the French hierarchy, and that was to reach the pinnacle of the Malagasy hierarchy. The Frenchmen of Fort Dauphin who bought an airplane ticket for a young police inspector who was born to be a prince were taking the one clear path to the governor-general himself.

"So I begged my grandmother to tell everything straight to the governor-general, de Coppet. My mother and my grandmother went right away. They were there from eight in the morning until afternoon. I think they were received by the governor-general about ten A.M.

"The governor-general was absolutely furious, eh? He called me in for an hour in front of him. First he said — I was standing up in front of him — first he scowled at me and demanded in a solemn and menacing tone: 'What is this story you are going to tell me now!'

"And me: 'Monsieur Governor-General, I am going to tell you things — that are true.'

"'What's that, then?'

"I laid out everything for him, notably the case of Madame Bakoly.

"'That's true, is it?'

"'You can send an emissary, in the eyes of everyone, to check up on what I have told you. Here is a list of the names of the women, one, two, three, four . . . And a list of the men, one, two, three . . .

"'Right. If I arrive at Fort Dauphin and find it is not true,' said Monsieur de Coppet, 'you are going to be sent to prison in Antanimora.'

"I said, 'Yes, but what I have told you is true, and you will have the proof when your emissary returns.'

"Then he said, 'How are you going back to Fort Dauphin?'

"I said, 'I am going back by road.' I had come by airplane, but I expected to go back by truck, five days on the road. It was expensive, too, because at every stop it meant paying for a night in a hotel.

"He said, 'No, no, no, no, no. You are going back by airplane.'

"And then he said to his secretary, Razanamasy, . . . 'Give Monsieur Ramahatra an airplane ticket to return to Fort Dauphin.' So I went back by airplane! I came and I went by airplane!

"When I got back, it was a Thursday. Commissioner Gervais ordered me to the office. He asked me furiously, 'What's wrong with you? You have been telling lies to the governor-general!'

"'I did not tell him anything. What is it you want me not to tell him?'

"'Oh, great!' shouted Gervais. 'Go away!' . . .

"Monday, the secretary of the district telephoned me. 'I don't know if you know the news. A Frenchman came here Saturday. He went on foot, with no hat. He was not carried [in a filanzana] and nobody was with him. He went straight to the prison. He called all the prisoners, and he spoke to each one. He came in the morning by special airplane, and he went back in the evening by special airplane.'

"So I understood. Good.

"Tuesday, to everyone's astonishment, SEVERAL Frenchmen got off the airplane. A chief administrator, a doctor, a magistrate, a surveyor, and a new chief of police called Texier, as well as three or four gendarmes. They replaced all the French civil servants of Fort Dauphin, except the postmaster. Four of them came straight to the police office. The new magistrate asked: 'Where is Ramahatra?' I heard, and said, 'Yes, sir, what is it?' He said, 'Let us work well for France!' I added, 'Yes, and for Madagascar, too!' He burst out laughing. The new police commissioner, Texier, became known as the man of good will, a man who liked Malagasy, who played with us on the football team.

"But the old officials had to leave by the same plane that brought in the new ones. Word went around the whole town instantly. The crowd gathered, and screamed insults at them all the way to the airport . . ."

"Screamed insults! I can understand that!" echoed Roland.

As the wise man on the blue pillow ended his account, Dr. Roland Ramahatra concluded his father's story. "Trying to separate people by color during the events of 'forty-seven is Manichean: good against bad — simplistic, invented, with no relation to reality. There were people of good will, whether Malagasy ready to save the honor of the lady Bakoly, or French like Monseigneur Silva, and the de Heaulmes, and all the other people my father named. Then, on the other side, there were Malagasy of ill will, like Jules André, and French of ill will, of whom the chief culprit was Commissioner Gervais. Manichean divisions are simply *wrong*."

6

Me? I'm a Lathe Operator

The Golden Fibers, 1948–1960

࿇

Madame Marcou was a short, busy woman with blond curls. Royal blue earrings. Blue pedal pushers and matching high heels. A sleeveless top of royal and turquoise and begonia pink, with a long gold chain holding a gold medallion of filigree palm trees, made by the Indian jeweler in Fort Dauphin. Monsieur Marcou in his turquoise sport shirt almost outshone his wife. The hot June sun made their lawn glow emerald beneath the willow trees, the grass sloping down to a tiny streamlet that flowed into the Dordogne. Above the lawn rose a white terrace, inset with a pond of fifty or sixty goldfish schooling in synchrony under a wire heron screen. The pond was bordered by rectangular boxes filled with orangey pink begonias to match Madame's blouse, all blooming at once with military precision, like the schooling orange fish.

Monsieur and Madame greeted me warmly, delighted at my delight, and led me to a patio with an awning, where we could sit at ease. I couldn't sit down straightaway, though, because just beyond stood three small plastic greenhouses, where I could see tree-sized fantiolotse.

Madame is an enthusiast of succulent plants. She grows cactus, euphorbia, and Madagascar's peculiar plants in the family Didiereaceae. Her plants mostly bristle and prickle, though a whole series of her favorites sheath themselves in long white hairs. Right in front, its pot on a pedestal of honor, was a *Pachypodium vigueiri* — a variety of elephant's-foot, its bulbous base like a smooth stone, its top a maze of woody stems with baby-pink flowers. I had never seen a pink elephant's-foot before. Madame confirmed it as a Madagascar "rarissima." Most of the plants she had grown herself from seed or tiny cuttings.

Their house was no château, just a normal modern house with add-ons. Monsieur built the add-ons: the three greenhouses, the terraces, the fish basin, every one of the stone steps leading up to the terraces, and the shed for his big power lawn mower and his power tools.

"After all," he said, "a terrace is pretty small stuff after what I have built in my life."

"There's a revolt in Madagascar — we can do our military service early!" Guy Marcou's friend came running to tell him. They were in the class of '48, meaning they would normally begin their two years of French national army service in 1948, when they turned twenty. But in 1947 notices appeared all over France, including the Champagne district, where Guy Marcou grew up, inviting boys with special skills to volunteer at age nineteen. In the town of Nancy alone, three thousand nineteen-year-olds applied to go put down Madagascar's revolution. Marcou counted himself lucky to be one of five hundred chosen. He had already served his apprenticeship as a lathe operator, a machinist who could turn and cut metal, a skill the army needed. His photo album holds a tiny black-and-white snapshot of a gang of very young men in uniform, grinning and clowning as they board their troop transport in the port of Marseilles.

Three weeks later they had just reached Djibouti on the Horn of Africa. The new soldiers were wild for shore leave, but their commander ordered them to stay on the boat. A bunch of the recruits threatened to dump a general overboard in Djibouti Harbor. They actually got their leave, at least for long enough to watch a parade of black colonial troops in white shorts and kepis stand at attention while a white trumpeter sounded the call — another snapshot in the album. Marcou recalled Djibouti as so hot that if you opened a faucet, the water would evaporate before hitting the ground. The upstart volunteers were promised punishment for their insubordination, but it was deferred until they reached Madagascar.

Their punishment came. Marcou and his friends spent three solid weeks on guard duty at Fort Duchesne, the French military base in Tananarive. The new recruits stood at the doors and the gates and under Fort Duchesne's brick arcades, confronting a hostile populace who came daily to jeer and taunt them.

The mob never did mount an attack on the armed soldiers, even on soldiers as green as Marcou, but the government had good reason to fear it. Just before Marcou's group arrived, five leaders of the '47 revolt were executed at Fort Duchesne. One of them, Rakotondraibé, the "generalissimo," was a supposed leader of the rebellion. The Malagasy did not riot to stop the executions, but in Madagascar, killing is not so grave a sin as denying decent burial. The crowd wanted their martyrs' corpses back. The bewildered young soldiers stood on guard, wondering what they were in for in this bizarre country.

After that Marcou worked as a lathe operator in the army until an accident sent a bolt into his foot. He was demobilized with only nine months' service. He decided to stay on in Madagascar. He heard there might be jobs in the sisal plantations, which were just starting to function after the war, as markets opened and the plants matured.

He traveled down to Fort Dauphin in a four-engine Junker airplane with benches along each side, which brought on a fear of flying. When he applied for a job at Berenty the head of the Fort Dauphin Electricity Board interviewed him, since Monsieur de Heaulme was traveling. He reported, "He'll do." Marcou rode out to Berenty in the second Chevrolet truck. Old Baghdad was now retired to service in the mica mines. Baghdad still ran, but the radiator had fallen off, so the engine was cooled by a jerry can of water and hoses. There was clearly work for a mechanic and machinist.

Jean de Heaulme, meanwhile, was banished to a mica mine. Betanimena, "the Place of Red Earth," lay in the mountains northeast of Berenty, at the end of seven hours of driving in a four-by-four. Seven hours if Jean was lucky and did not bog down or break down on the way. So the boy was tempted by a career in the military hierarchy? If he was a man and not a boy, let him command a workforce of several hundred miners instead, as the only European in the valley of red earth. Henry could do it. Uncle Alain had done it. The test of Jean's mettle was whether he could do it too.

Jean stuck it out for three full years before he passed the test in his father's eyes.

Mica is a silicon oxide that splits into fine horizontal layers, the best of all natural insulators for heat and electricity. The thinnest layer of it that still has mica's properties is just two molecules thick. The modern world runs on silicon chips: microcircuits channeled within a kind of artificial mica. Two generations ago, high-tech electronics depended on real mica, on men like Jean de Heaulme blasting away at Gondwanaland's mountains in places like godforsaken Betanimena. Or, in the glorious part of his job, tramping with his geologist's hammer over farther, wilder mountains, following leads suggested by wandering Tandroy cow herds, to prospect for high-grade mica seams.

Wherever mica has been mined, the hillsides gleam in the sun with mirrored flakes, as though the ground itself were sanctified by a shower of glittering communion wafers. Men dynamited the hillside, then dug out rock slabs from deep horizontal mine tunnels. They literally dug; there were no electric drills. No electric headlights: the men's hard hats carried miners' traditional carbide lamps. The tunnels were braced with hand-sawn timbers, the ore dragged out in hand-pulled wagons on hand-laid rails. After that the slabs went to the splitting women. They sat under shade trees, wearing a wrapped lamba or shreds of a dress, with a dusty straw basket of raw mica on one side and another basket for the finished work on the other side. They would seize a mica chip in one hand and the clawlike toes of one foot. They hacked at it with large knives like kitchen knives, splitting and trimming until each flake was a thin translucent oblong a few inches square and free of any flaws. From their baskets the flakes began their journey toward the industries of France and America. The glittering communion wafers are the debris discarded by the splitting women.

Once a month Jean loaded the big mine truck with three metric tons of mica flakes and slabs. He and Rekidja, his chauffeur, cook, and lifelong friend, drove the truck into Fort Dauphin. Then they delivered the cargo, bought the next month's supplies of food and fuel and dynamite, and drove back to Betanimena. There Jean hung up his water bottle on a tree to evaporate and cool in the wind. He slept in a shack made of mud with a grass-thatched roof. His house was literally smaller than his Willys Jeep.

America's Marshall Plan boosted Madagascar's sisal. France was a country in need of postwar reconstruction, and Madagascar was French. Jean's Jeep, and all the other new materials for mines and plantations, came from America.

When Guy Marcou arrived at Berenty, in 1949, the plantation produced just twenty metric tons of sisal fiber a year; by the time he left in 1964, production was six hundred tons. The golden fibers went out of Fort Dauphin's harbor in bales, to end up as rope, carpets, packing, and insulation all over the world. In the 1950s sisal was in huge demand. Later it seemed that nylon would replace sisal completely. Now it is clear that for certain uses the elasticity of natural fibers is a crucial asset. For instance, when a boat tries to make fast in a high swell, a nylon rope can tear the bollards out of boat or dock. Sisal rope eases into the strain. In its agricultural uses, sisal does not cut into growing plants or baled fibers. Ecology-minded purchasers like the idea of natural vegetable fiber instead of spun petroleum, though it takes a lot of idealism to love a sisal plant.

Marcou's first workshop was the central room of the building that later became Jean de Heaulme's house with the airplane shed, which is now the Museum of Androy. Marcou's forge and soldering area is now the site of the false Tandroy tomb in front of the museum, right by the dropoff to the forest where sifaka come for siesta. Sisal leaves were squashed into fibers in the present restaurant; the noble 1928 steam engine powered all the machinery from the site of the present bar. The leaves rolled into the maws of the two Robbet defibering machines on paired chains. The chains were always fouling or breaking, which meant that Marcou was perpetually welding them. Marcou mildly described the machines as *casse-pieds* — very annoying. I suspect his language was stronger at the time.

In 1950 Henry de Heaulme got his grant from the Marshall Plan. American tractors rolled into Androy — John Deeres and Massey Fergusons and, the king of them all, the Caterpillar treedozer.

Each of the treedozer's tires stood as tall as a man, so the driver sat above other men's heads. Two four-meter-long steel arms projected forward, linked by a metal bar that would strike a tree trunk perhaps ten feet off the ground and tip it away from the approaching Caterpillar. As the root ball lifted, the tractor's bladed prow, built (as Marcou pointed out) exactly like a snowplow, scooped the roots from the ground and nudged the tree out of the monster's way. The spiny forest fell like traditional ninepins.

I saw the treedozer in action after I arrived in 1963. The de Heaulmes were still clearing land then, for the 1950s and '60s were the golden age of sisal, when the fiber's price peaked on the world market. When Monsieur de Heaulme took me out to watch the orange monster demolish trees, he pointed out with pride that he left ten meter-wide strips of original forest between his giant fields. He didn't do this purely for conservation. The canny landowner knew that trees help the soil retain water and tame the south wind. In Androy's summer months a wind sometimes blows that can dry out your eyeballs if you look toward the south, and it layers the whole world with fine red sand. Nothing stands against that wind better than a strip of indigenous spiny forest.

All I could see, though, was the forest falling. After the trees crashed down and the Caterpillar moved on, a family of sifaka hopped out of the remaining stand of trees and sat on the tumbled logs. A male throat-marked, rather tentatively, on a fallen trunk. White sifaka are intensely territorial animals. With the family's home destroyed, they would have to challenge other owners for living space, if, indeed, they had any hope of survival. I took a photo, but all it shows is an animal sitting on a log — not what it meant to him that an hour earlier that log had been one of the proud scent-posts of his home.

The forest fell. The tree trunks were cleared away. Gangs of men planted out little sisal seedlings from the nursery beds in long straight rows three meters apart. Baby sisals are like small green hedgehogs, except that hedgehogs are cute; sisals are just spiky. After four years the leaves are so long that you can only just walk between the rows, carefully.

"Leaves" does not convey what sisal looks like. Think of a green bayonet blade, not so sharp at the sides, but filed to a hardened needle point. Now think of it a meter and a half long. Now think of a hundred such blades arranged in spirals around a squat, bulbous trunk, so you can just see over the tallest leaves. Think of rows of such plants going on and on, over 5,000 hectares, 12,500 acres. That, plus the 1,000 hectares still in forest is the de Heaulme estate: multiply it by five to include the other sisal concessions, and you have the Mandrare Valley. Stand where the sunrise throws crisscross shadows of bayonet leaf upon bayonet leaf, in dizzying geometry to the horizon — and then imagine how you would turn that stuff into a harvest.

Work assignments start at six A.M. — five A.M. in the summer — with the *Appel,* the Call. Half an hour earlier the Berenty gong — three long iron bars planted in the earth — is struck by a man with a ringing hammer to signal time for rising, then ten minutes before the hour for warning, and again on the hour for the Call itself. (Even today only the richest workers own watches, and you wouldn't wear a watch sisal-cutting in any case.) At the Call, the courtyard fills with several hundred men and women, who squat, immobile, in the gray dawn in ordered rows. Each is wrapped in a cotton lamba, which blocks their outlines into the solidity of Egyptian sculptures, each head topped with a tiny, conical Tandroy straw hat. Each chef d'équipe receives his assignment for the day. He and his crew of fifty men and twenty-five women climb into flat, slatted carts pulled in series behind a tractor. They reach their field to cut at first clear light.

The men bend to work. They do not swing machetes the way cane cutters do. Their tool is a homemade knife with a wooden handle eight or ten inches long and an almost hemispherical blade about the same length. A man slices a lower leaf loose with surgical precision, leaving a white half-moon scar a little smaller than his knife blade. The sheared sisal bole begins to look like a giant green pineapple. The cutter deftly reverses the leaf, nicks off its spearpoint tip, and flings it parallel to the others on the ground. He cuts three rows of leaves from a four-year-old sisal, two more rows the next year, and three in the final year. After that the plant is fit only to grub up and burn. If left in the ground it will bolt a seed stalk as tall as a green telephone pole, with flowers at the top. In the daytime, ringtailed lemurs come out of the forest and climb the stalk to drink the sisal nectar; at night, Madagascar flying foxes flap down to lap from the alien plant.

When I borrowed a knife to try, I found it surprisingly easy to cut the leaf base as long as I kept the knife's razor edge perpendicular to the fibers. I felt rather clever to start out so well with my first three leaves, severing each with a juicy crunch and managing not to impale myself on the tips. I forgot, though, that the edges are rows of minute serrations. As I grabbed the leaves casually to throw on the pile they left deep cuts in my palm. I had to keep my hand curled up to get through the rest of the morning without bleeding on people.

As soon as a man cuts ten sisal leaves, a woman bends to bundle them up. She turns those sharp edges to the inside, leaving the round, safe backs outside. She ties the bundle with strings of green sisal fiber she has separated and twisted out of a leaf the night before at home. She tosses the ten-leaf bundle onto her head — or hugs three or four bundles — and walks them to the end of a row. There she lays ten bundles alongside each other, then a ten-bundle layer on top at right angles to the first, until she has made a cube of one hundred bundles, a thousand leaves.

Each man's daily task is three thousand leaves, each woman's six thousand. A few ambitious young couples work together; the man cuts six thousand in a morning, working fast, while his wife waits for him instead of gathering leaves for two men. Nobody wants to work much more than four hours a day, though. It isn't just that the work is physically hard, and that the sun by nine A.M. in summer is already too hot for anyone to think of cutting sisal. The point is that paid work has to allow space for real life. Women must fetch water, pound corn, mind children. Men must look after their cattle. Few Tandroy choose a life that separates them from their cattle, even today.

As each thousand-leaf stack is built, the chef d'équipe comes to check that the leaves are not short or broken or blemished. Then he takes a foot-long hunk of discarded leaf base and a leaf-tip thorn and scratches the cutter's name on the green surface, down to the white fibrous layer below. That chunk of leaf is the tally for the day's task. Of course, the fastest ones trot off toward home before the less efficient.

At the end of the morning the tractor comes back with another work crew to toss the leaves onto slatted flat-bed trailers and cart them to the factory.

In 1950, when the de Heaulmes aimed to expand their sisal operation, the cutting process simply needed more people. They solved that problem by having three separate Calls — one run by Monsieur Alain de Heaulme himself, one by Monsieur Fruteaux, the first French employee, and one by Alexandre, a Tandroy, the son of a Protestant pastor. Alexandre was literate and knew how to command, and he became an overall leader like the others.

Another key employee was recruited in 1951: Tsiaketraky, He-Who-Cannot-Be-Thrown-to-Earth. Just eighteen, he already had a black mark against his name. He had tried to better himself by joining the army. But, born to a noble Tandroy clan, he found he couldn't stand taking orders. After eight months he deserted, running away in the plateau town of Fianarantsoa. The army caught him, hauled him back, and threw him in jail. That in itself was not shameful for Tandroy — a great many did time in jail just because the French did not agree with the grand old game of cattle theft. However, Tsiaketraky's cell was a punishment hell-hole so small that he could not even stretch out when he lay down. It was only for fifteen days, though. Then the army spat out the offender and told him to go home. Instead he went to Berenty and asked for a job. Henry de Heaulme knew the whole story. He hired Tsiaketraky as a simple laborer, while watching the man who could not take orders step easily into roles of command. Tsiaketraky soon became a chef d'équipe and then a sisal commander over hundreds of men. Along the way he picked up whatever skills he needed, starting by teaching himself to read and write.

Processing sisal, however, needed machines as well as people. In the early 1950s Monsieur de Heaulme went to Rhodesia to visit similar plantations there. He came back with a head full of ideas. He bought three new Stock sisal-stripping machines from Holland to replace the hated Robbets. To strip sisal, you start by throwing a bundle of ten leaves onto the belt of a machine. Three men heave the bundles from the heap in front of the factory. A fourth man, using a *coupe-coupe* (machete), whacks off the fiber ties that the women put on in the fields. Three more men spread the leaves to lie separate and parallel. The belt then goes around a large roller that simply squashes the leaves, which are then liberally washed with river water to remove the green pulp. The belts circle a second roller for a second squashing, and from the far end emerges a hank of clean, pale green fibers, one or two meters long. At the end of the belt two men collect as many fibers as they can lift on a five-foot-long shoulder pole, then transfer the pole to a primitive homemade trolley on tracks, which has notches for five of the two-man poles. When the trolley is filled, another worker shoves the cart off along its metal tracks toward the drying fields.

When the Stock machines came, the ancient steam engine was retired. The Stocks ran off Marshall Plan tractors. These Case tractors sported an attachment so they could power machinery — in this case the belt that drove the crushers. Guy Marcou installed the Stocks where they stand today, near Monsieur Henry's and Monsieur Alain's houses and the ever-growing workers' village of Berenty. He built a large concrete shed to house the crushers, open along two sides for loading leaves and taking away the fiber hanks. Then he laid out a drying field, with termite-proof wooden crosses linked by wires, like a long-haired cemetery, where the wet green fibers bleach to golden white in the sun.

So far, though, they were losing a valuable byproduct. The longest fibers, which originally converge on the leaf's spearpoint, come out neatly parallel on the crusher belt, ready for drying. Short fibers, though, washed down into the concrete gutter under the machine, where they bubbled along in a thick soup the color of a spinach milkshake. In Rhodesia Monsieur de Heaulme saw how to reclaim the short fibers from the runoff channel. He sketched out three brand-new machines for Guy Marcou to build.

They are essentially simple scaffoldings about six meters tall with metal conveyor belts running up to them from the central drainage channels of the three crushers. The fibers are whirled in a primitive centrifuge, a huge metal drum pierced with holes like a colander. At the top they transfer to another belt that takes them off to yet another drying field, where fluffy balls of short-fiber sisal pile up, ready to be used as a packing material. Marcou is intensely proud that his machines can still run after forty-five years, having worked twenty-four hours a day for much of sisal's golden age. They haven't even had an oil change! He soldered the motors into oil-filled aluminum boxes to protect them from sisal fibers and the acidic water. The boxes have never been opened again. The water reservoir he built for the Stocks, a kind of giant swimming pool with a 510-cubic-meter capacity, has never changed or cracked either. To ensure adequate power, the de Heaulmes bought a Poyaud diesel-powered generator, and then a whole row of Duvant generators. And Marcou erected another building for the electricity supply.

He obviously did not do it all alone. Monsieur de Tourris, a cousin of the de Heaulmes from Réunion, soon joined as Marcou's assistant, but they needed masons, carpenters, metal workers, and electricians. Marcou made a formal announcement on the informal "bush telephone." Any laborer with the ambition to specialize should come for an interview on a given Thursday morning. About fifty arrived, and most were chosen. One man Marcou somehow liked on sight turned up straight from his village in loincloth and tiny Tandroy hat, carrying a hatchet instead of the usual spear.

"Jeremia," asked Marcou, "would you like to become an electrician?"

Jeremia had never heard of a resistor or a circuit breaker, let alone held one in his hand. "Yes, of course," he said readily. He ended up as the plantation's chief electrician, masterminding 2,500 horsepower of generating capacity, power not only for the sisal but for a tourist hotel as well.

For a while the later stages of processing stayed in the building that is now the restaurant. One day as Monsieur de Heaulme was talking to Marcou, he looked around, found a clean old plank and a bit of charcoal, and began to sketch plans. Marcou took the plank home under his arm and stayed up till two A.M. transferring ideas to graph paper. The next day he presented the concept of a building sixty meters long by twenty-seven meters wide (including how to hold the roof up). That structure is still the processing barn.

Dried sisal fiber, again tied in hanks, is dumped on the floor at one end of the barn. A shift of women attacks the pile, each one lifting her share onto a huge platform scale to measure the 250 kilos of her daily task. Then she carries the load in armfuls to her own cement table. She checks each group of strands for black discolorations, which would make the fibers break in the final spinning for rope or rugs. She also checks for color: premium grade is almost white; lower grades are spotted and yellowish. It takes a new woman at least a month, maybe longer, to train her eye and hand to sort efficiently. As she seizes each hank, she beats it on the table to straighten it. The air is soon full of tiny flying snowflakes of sisal. Health studies in Tanzanian factories indicated no lung damage from breathing sisal, but the de Heaulmes did make an attempt to impose cloth masks as a health precaution in the processing shed. These were roundly refused by the workers. They preferred to have their faces free to talk to each other as they worked, and the employers did not insist.

Honnette, at fifty, is the oldest of the sorters today. Younger women work right through pregnancy up to the day they go into labor. After giving birth, they get two months' unpaid maternity leave. This is skilled work, much sought after and lighter by far than bundling sisal in the fields. Here too the women work a four-hour shift — or less if they finish their task ahead of time.

The sorted sisal is carried to the brushing machines, where young men seize one end of a hank the size and width of a horse's tail in one hand and flick the other end into the narrow maw of an almost closed cylinder. With roaring and clanking and an even wilder blizzard of sisal snow, the machine currycombs the fibers so they are long and parallel. The brush man eases the sisal out, grabs the combed end in his other hand, flicks the first end in, then casts it off, fully combed, onto a table while reaching with his first hand for another horsetail. It becomes an over-and-over rhythm, like paddling a single scull. The brush men's shoulder muscles ripple and gleam under their dusting of sisal flecks. To tell the truth, they know it — the twelve or twenty young men strut and preen and grin and speed up their already impressive rhythm if ever they see visitors.

Brushed sisal is baled by men or women, who lay armfuls in a slatted wood frame five feet tall. Then three of them climb in on top and jump up and down. The final compression, though, is done with a mechanical press that squeezes the original six-foot pile down to the dimensions of a bale of hay. Sisal ropes hold it together. A forklift moves the solid mass to the storage shed, where it awaits its journey by Mercedes truck to a freighter in Fort Dauphin's blue harbor. From there it goes off across the world to be turned into rope or carpet or agricultural ties and sacks.

Monsieur Marcou recalls, with a twinkling grin, the time when a whole delegation of high-powered engineers came out to see how sisal is processed. One of them, a woman, turned to him at the end and said, "Very impressive! And who built this factory complex so far out in the bush?"

"I did, with Monsieur de Heaulme."

"You did! Tell me, did you first train as an engineer or as an architect?"

"Me? I'm a lathe operator."

"Try to come back with a wife!" joked Monsieur de Heaulme. After five years, Guy Marcou asked for home leave to see his family — and, if possible, to marry. It wasn't really a joke. Young bachelors could be hired cheaply, but after a while they were bad news in a tiny plantation community.

Back in Champagne, Guy met the beautiful Éliane. He set himself to a whirlwind courtship. He told her early on that she would have to share his life in Madagascar or else they should stop seeing each other right away. Éliane was intrigued, but she was an only child. Her parents had laid her future out on rails: marry locally, take over the family grocery business, and care for them in their old age. No Guy Marcou. Definitely *no* Madagascar.

Éliane began to take rather a long time making grocery deliveries.

When Guy's leave ended, she finally promised to follow him. Somehow she prevailed on Guy's father to help her make a mold of her own house key. She could face running away from home, but she couldn't leave a French bourgeois front door unlocked behind her.

At two o'clock of a Sunday afternoon, when her parents were out in their garden, she laid a letter on the table and tiptoed to the door carrying a tiny suitcase. The dog in the garden began howling furiously. She shut the door and locked it and ran.

She stayed with her future parents-in-law from August to October, then boarded an airplane for Tananarive. She had packed a wedding dress in her suitcase. "What courage!" exclaims her husband, even now. "And basically I could have been telling her anything. I might have been a deadbeat with no job, or taken her and dumped her, or never even come to Tananarive to find her at all."

The groom, however, was so eager that he hitched a plane ride to Tananarive with Bernard Astraud. The de Heaulmes had combined with two neighbors, the de Guitaut and Confolant families, to build a sisal-spinning factory in Fort Dauphin. Such a factory needed an electrical engineer. Young Jean de Heaulme persuaded the families to hire his closest friend, his flying instructor from Toulon. Astraud arrived in Fort Dauphin with all his magnetic charm and proceeded to teach everyone in sight to fly — everyone but Guy Marcou, who had a phobia about airplanes. Still, it was worth flying with Astraud to reach Éliane.

Éliane never doubted that Guy would meet her, but she had never really imagined Madagascar. Tananarive is built like an Italian hill town, with tiers of red-brick, peaked-roofed houses. She marveled at the marketplace with its white umbrellas and the long flight of white steps leading up to an open square fringed by lavender-flowered jacaranda trees, which hung above the market like a balcony. In back of the square stood French-style government offices and the ever so French Provincial residence of the governor-general. Only — the hill town was inhabited by dark people. Éliane somehow had not pictured that.

The couple flew back to Berenty almost at once. Chantal and Uncle Alain took in the runaway fiancée so she could live properly chaperoned until her marriage. Chantal showed her how to light and trim kerosene lamps, how to wash without running water. Outhouses would replace the plumbing Éliane had always known. Meanwhile Chantal and her sister, Huguette, and Madame de Tourris, the wife of Guy's assistant, had long pretty dresses made so that Éliane could have bridesmaids. A month later Guy and Éliane were married at the church in Amboasary, the dusty roadside town that had grown up ten miles away by the new river crossing.

As we talked on their terrace, Monsieur Marcou rose and told me, "Come indoors. I have something for you to see." In their upholstered living room, with its Madagascar coffee table and sideboard with rickshaws and zebu heads carved in elaborate high relief, he switched on their magnum-sized television. The screen lit up in the bleached tints of the 1950s: a tape of their wedding film. There is petite Éliane, wearing bouffant white, on the church steps in a shower of rice, her cap and curls just reaching the shoulder of slim young Guy. There are Chantal and Huguette, in New Look dresses with wasp waists and gored skirts of large-check red and black plaid, and Madame de Tourris in cream. The bridesmaids fuss with the bride's veil, then climb into plantation cars to drive back to Berenty for the wedding lunch. The newlyweds take the lead in a pick-up truck while Chantal waves exuberantly from her Jeep. At Berenty, Bernard Astraud announces his wedding present. He will take the bride up in his Chipmunk airplane and do a loop-the-loop. She climbs in, but Guy pleads his phobia and escapes. "I assure you," Madame Marcou recalls as we watch the film, "my stomach did a loop-the-loop on its own quite independently from the airplane." Afterward Astraud takes off to leave. The snippet of wedding film ends as everyone ducks and Éliane grabs her veil, while skirts and veil and all are enveloped in a swirl of airplane exhaust and dust, like the Sahara in a sandstorm.

"What courage she had!" Chantal today echoes Guy Marcou's remark. "A well-brought-up girl from a comfortable home in the north of France, taking on our life at Berenty! She threw herself into decorating their house with bright red window frames and fancy sewn pillows and curtains with red trim. She planted out little euphorbia in old car battery cases: their descendants soon grew all around the factory. It finally came right after a couple of years, when she had a baby and enough to do, but at the beginning it really took courage."

A row that Guy and Éliane look back on as the lowest point of all came only six weeks after their wedding, when they set out on New Year's Eve for midnight Mass in Amboasary church. Éliane put on stockings and high heels. At last she could go out properly to a familiar ceremony, just as if she were back in France.

Ten miles down the road at the river crossing, the Mandrare was in flood. In the 1950s the bridge was a *radier,* a low causeway that allowed high waters to pass over it. You do not drive over a flooded radier. The driver's eye inevitably is tricked by the current, so the car veers off into the deep pool below. However, you can feel your way walking if the water is not too deep. Guy told Éliane to take off her high heels and her stockings, tuck up her skirts, and wade across a hundred and fifty meters of slimy water flowing over a concrete ramp at nearly midnight in the far south of Madagascar. It is true that almost all the crocodiles had already been shot by a Swiss named Monsieur Boetchi, to the great relief of the local population.

Éliane cried and screamed and said she wouldn't. Guy pointed out that she would not reach midnight Mass. In the end she waded. And waded back again to return home. That was perhaps the moment when she accepted her new life. From there, she could even face the next day's great annual feast. On New Year's Day at noon, Monsieur de Heaulme killed ten steers and distributed the meat in bleeding gobbets to the hundreds of families on the plantation — Éliane and Guy among the rest.

Bernard Astraud, grinning beside his airplane in every photograph, changed the meaning of distance. Airplanes relieved the need for roads — for the elite. They flew their own planes or used Mad-Air as a taxi service. Mad-Air linked almost every town (as opposed to village) on the thousand-mile-long island continent. An hour in a plane today still saves you a week on the road, because streams flood, bridges wash out, and inevitably the car breaks down under intolerable strain. The first Mad-Air flight I ever took was a DC3 that landed on a grass airstrip marked out with white lines, like a long-haired tennis court. The red-faced pilot helped unload by kicking cargo crates out of the space behind the baggage net into the arms of nearly naked black men. I think someone was kind enough to hand down the live goat from the baggage space more gently. I was a little sad when Mad-Air grew self-conscious and renamed itself Air Madagascar.

Meanwhile, much of the populace walked, and still walks, or submits to the tortures of superhumanly overpacked bush taxis, which leave no place for goats except on the roof, or for the chickens except on your lap. On top of the children already in your lap. Then, when the *taxi-brousse* breaks or bogs down, ox carts plod inexorably past you. Madagascar's roads shock even visitors from Africa. In the colonial era, all the political pressure was to build airstrips instead. Bernard Astraud established a training school that met for a few weeks every year at the perpetually sunny town of Behara. It attracted pilots from all over Madagascar and adhered to French-recognized standards.

Jean de Heaulme was released from bondage in the mica mine in 1953. He then joined his father running the businesses at Berenty and Fort Dauphin. Some of his innovations shocked his father and uncle. Calculating machines! Why, grumbled Uncle Alain, should you buy a machine with wheels clacking around when clerks can add up figures perfectly well? One of Jean's time-saving moves, though, won wholehearted family approval. Jean could fly.

Berenty from Fort Dauphin became a short hop over the mountains. Even the Betanimena mine was twenty minutes from Berenty instead of the excruciating seven hours in a Jeep. Jean loved the controls in his hands, the exhilaration of flight. His father, as visionary as ever, championed the new machines.

No pilot himself, Monsieur de Heaulme was shortly elected president of the Aeroclubs of Madagascar. He set about equipping clubs of new pilots on a quasi-industrial scale. In 1953, Bernard Astraud learned that the Royal Rhodesian Air Force had twenty-four Chipmunks to sell. These were two-seat training planes, ideal for teaching pilots. When the air force upgraded, it offered the planes to the Madagascar Aeroclubs for less each than the price of a car.

Huguette de Heaulme fell in love with a pilot. Jacques Lalut was a *commandeur de bord,* or captain, for Air Madagascar. He had trained in America on wartime fighters. Monsieur de Heaulme swept his pilot son and his daughter's pilot fiancé into helping fetch their Chipmunks from Rhodesia. Lalut now lives in the south of France and writes. His novel *Have by Now Become Two Beautiful Trees* is a wonderfully mixed creation. He tells a lyrical wish-fulfillment love story anchored in details of airplane engines, takeoff times, radio reports, and weather conditions, all punctuated by a very French list of menus and bottles of wine consumed at each landing stage. In the novel Lalut describes the Flight of the Chipmunks just as it happened.

It took a combination of military-style organization and amateur gusto, with international paperwork masterminded by Monsieur de Heaulme. Nine amateur pilots for the first convoy traveled to Bulawayo, Rhodesia, in a plane lent by the French navy base in Diego Suarez. It was an ancient Junker 52, a trimotor with a cabin that Lalut claims was made of corrugated iron. Inside the iron cabin, morning turbulence caused "paper bags to appear in the hands of two or three of those knights of the sky, with empty gaze and greenish tint." Even the Junker needed three stops to reach Bulawayo.

The Chipmunks were single-engine planes designed for aerobatics, with low-set wings and a cockpit in which the passenger sat behind the pilot. (You may have seen a Chipmunk in flight in the film *The English Patient.*) Their Gypsy 135 motors were renowned for robustness, the "heavy cavalry" of airplane engines. Lalut admits that they "sometimes presented little disquieting vibrations, but they had the advantage of not stopping completely." That was just as well, since the homeward route lay across the Mozambique Channel.

The Rhodesians received them royally. A yellowed clipping from the *Bulawayo Herald* shows the only picture I have seen of Henry de Heaulme smiling, indeed grinning, as Jean grins back from an open cockpit, while Astraud laughs out loud. To start with, the pilots learned to fly in formation. Lalut was used to that from his fighter training, but the amateurs were understandably queasy. They soon found that flying in closer formation (within reason) made it easier to follow the leader's moves. A couple of days later the nine little planes left Bulawayo, waved off by the French vice-consul, press, photos, and cinema.

The Chips had a range of only 350 kilometers, which meant nine refueling stops on the flight to Fort Dauphin. The welcoming circus continued at each stage: Que Que, Salisbury, and Umtali, Rhodesia; Vila Pery, Beira, Quelimane, Antonio Enes, and Lumbo, Mozambique; the medieval streets of Mozambique Island. Receptions! Cocktails! Consuls and mayors! English fried fish fillets and chilled Portuguese white wine. A hilarious race in which the pilots pulled several rickshaw drivers, installed in their own vehicles, around a hotel yard. (The drivers were pale with fear — after all, the rickshaws were their only capital.) Jean sparked off that race and won it. The "Marseillaise" was sung in all its verses by their Portuguese hosts, while the French hummed in embarrassment through the Portuguese national anthem. The group made an excursion to the great game park of Gorongosa while the airplanes spent three days in Beira for mechanical checkups. Hippopotamus! An elephant barring the road! Jacques Lalut and Jean de Heaulme, sharing a cabin, dashed across to the lodge at night for a drink of water, imagining that every moon shadow hid a lion or leopard. (Madagascar has just one occasionally lethal land animal — a biting spider.) One evening in the game park, Lalut was hypnotized to see a file of naked women dancing in the distance to the sound of a drum, dancing for themselves, with no men present.

The most dangerous leg of the trip came next. After taking off from Lumbo, the convoy of little planes had to refuel at Juan de Nova, a tiny island in the middle of Mozambique Channel. Pilots and their passengers bundled up in inflated Mae West life vests, complete with powder to dye the water around a downed airman and to "make the sharks throw up," as Bernard Astraud put it cheerfully. (The channel is a favorite haunt of great whites.) Astraud drilled the amateurs in how to ditch the plane at sea if anything went wrong — not easy, given the Chips' fixed landing gear. If all went well, they would land on a hard sand beach.

I asked Jean, "Weren't you even a little bit afraid of that landing?"

He chuckled and said, "Oh, we were young! We were — no, we were not afraid of landing on Juan de Nova, because the Chipmunks were easy to handle and very solid airplanes. But we were afraid of not *finding* Juan de Nova! We had only a quarter of an hour of gas to spare. So if we didn't find it right away, we had not much time to look for it. I remember taking off in the morning from Lumbo. If there was a contrary wind of more than ten knots, we would not arrive at Juan de Nova. We had to fly very early in the morning, when there was no wind. And at four in the morning, I remember we had warmed up the motors and rerefilled the reservoirs, and we left as soon as the sun — no, not even sunrise, but first light — to profit from the calm and actually reach Juan de Nova." One after another the little airplanes put down on the beach, each waiting for the one ahead to be pulled away. Lalut touched down last after two hours and twenty-five minutes in the air — with only five minutes left in his Chip's fuel supply.

Juan de Nova was home to a fertilizer mine, thanks to the guano of the millions of seabirds that nested on its northern beach. (The Chips landed on the southern beach, whose sand was too coarse for the birds' taste in nesting.) Sixty-three men lived on the island, mostly Seychellois of all colors. They exported bird excrement to South Africa for the Potassium Company of Alsace. But of all the menus Lalut lists in his book from that journey, I most envy him the lobster, oysters, and raw fish marinated in lemon juice and coconut milk served up by their hosts at Juan de Nova — though definitely not the succeeding dish, sea turtle ragout.

A second convoy of nine Chipmunks followed some weeks after the first, and then a third. But on the third flight, fog came down, a radio failed. Bernard de Guitaut and his wife, Aleth, were killed flying into a mountainside in Rhodesia.

Still, the colonials soared high as if their world would never end. In 1953 Jean de Heaulme and a couple of friends drove their Land Rovers all the way from Cape Town to Cairo and then on to the Rover factory in Manchester, England. They were only the third group ever to do so. (The team that came in ahead of them was led by Peter Townsend, later the lover of Princess Margaret.) Jean still has the newspaper clippings of their arrival, with the Rover officials holding high a welcoming magnum of champagne.

Then came the maiden flight of Monsieur de Heaulme's twin-engine Beech Baron D55, call letters 5R-MBX, Cinq Romeo Mike Bravo X-ray. To take delivery, Henry and Jean de Heaulme and Jacques Lalut went all the way to Wichita, Kansas. They were astounded by the Beechcraft factory, as clean as a hospital, with workers in white coats and gloves. They bought cowboy hats and bet each other that they would wear them all the way home. Jean can still recite the stages of their flight by heart. Wichita, Chicago, New York, Toronto, Gander. Then the long hop: eight hours over water from Gander to the Azores, navigating without modern radio guidance, and depending on a tricky extra tank of fuel in the spare back seat beside Monsieur de Heaulme. From the Azores to Bordeaux, Ajaccio, Malta, Benghazi, Cairo, Khartoum, Juba, over the wide-spreading swamp of the Sudd, where the Nile loses half its water far away from the sea, and over the already vicious skirmishes going on between north and south Sudanese. Kampala, Nairobi, Dar-es-Salaam, Majunga, Tananarive, and finally Fort Dauphin. The three heroes disembarked amid the familiar coconut palms and casuarina trees of Fort Dauphin, still wearing their exotic cowboy hats from Kansas.

Bernard Astraud built central electrical plants for Fort Dauphin, Farafangana, Ambalavao. He set up the sisal-weaving plant, SIFOR, that he had been hired to run and helped found a new company called DIFMAD to sell machines and construct other factories. (He still pulled the occasional stunt like flying under the newly built bridge at Amboasary, fifty feet high, that replaced Éliane Marcou's slimy underwater ramp.) He left Madagascar in about 1972 to found Air Djibouti, taking with him airplanes from the Fort Dauphin Aeroclub. Some years later, Astraud returned to France and opened one of the first firms to lease helicopters to industry.

In France one day he was demonstrating how helicopters could be used to take emergency mechanics and spare parts to a combine harvester broken down at the peak of harvest. It was all being filmed: the golden wheat, the orange harvester, a helicopter swooping to the rescue from a blue sky. Perhaps because he was concentrating on the filming, Astraud did not see a power line. He crashed. There was a pause while no one dared approach, though he was still moving, still alive. The camera went on turning. The helicopter burst into flame, and Bernard Astraud died in its charred remains.

Jean finally found a reason to settle down. Colonel Arthur Loumange arrived to take charge of the military garrison at Fort Dauphin. He had faced the Vietcong revolt in French Indochina a little before the time when the Vietcong artillery demolished the cream of the French army at Dien Bien Phu. Fort Dauphin was a peaceful reward for Loumange after Indochina, a post to which he could bring his wife and only child, the sparkling, elegant, eighteen-year-old Aline. Inevitably Jean and Aline fell in love. However, Aline's family were not nobles. They were deeply Catholic, conservative, upright. Their morality and ideas echoed the de Heaulmes' own credo, but they did not share the same antique caste. Monsieur and Madame de Heaulme, with the weight of three centuries of Réunion aristocracy behind them, absolutely forbade Jean and Aline to marry.

They waited five years for his parents' permission. At last Soeur Gabrielle, the supposedly unworldly family saint, broke the impasse. She confronted her imperious brother with the irrefutable fact that Jean and Aline were in love. Five years of waiting had not driven them apart. Would Jean become like Uncle Alain a generation before, who never married after losing his own heart's desire?

Not even Henry de Heaulme could withstand Soeur Gabrielle.

The engagement was announced. Soeur Gabrielle in her starched nun's coif delightedly advised Aline on the wedding dress. The couple were married at Berenty. The new bridge over the Mandrare River at Amboasary, the longest bridge span in Madagascar, opened just in time to bring the whole French community of the region out to the wedding reception. One lot of guests celebrated a bit too well and ran into a bridge truss going home, but that did not dampen the merriment.

Jean took over many of the family responsibilities, but he never stopped flying. One day he and Bernard Astraud left Tulear, on the other side of the island, to fly back to Fort Dauphin in the four-seater Beech Baron. Behind rode Aline, heavily pregnant with her second child (Henry), beside the toddler, Bénédicte. After the plane — fortunately — had gained full height above the sea, Jean started to circle back toward Fort Dauphin. Suddenly both engines stopped dead at once. The two pilots looked at each other and laughed out loud, because the situation was so bad no other response was possible. Meanwhile Jean's hands and eyes automatically ran down the sequence of checks that Astraud had first taught him. The last check of all was a stopcock on the fuel line, down between the front seats. No one going on mere logic would have checked it, because the airplane simply could not have taken off if that stopcock was closed. Now it was closed. Jean turned it, the engines kicked into life, and the two friends laughed again. Pregnant Aline had gone to sleep as soon as the plane started to move, and the two-year-old had played with an intriguing handle . . . The story of Berenty might have ended there.

Independence beckoned: Monsieur de Heaulme stood for election. Madagascar's 1947 War of Independence had been crushed, but by the late 1950s, French lives and fortunes were hemorrhaging in Algeria and Vietnam. General de Gaulle was returned to power in 1958 with a mandate to dissolve an overseas empire that had turned into a nightmare.

Plantation owners, the people who owned sisal, vanilla, and coffee estates, now faced a choice. Should they welcome the inevitable change or sell their property and get out? Madagascar had never been more prosperous, certainly for the rich, but also to some extent for the poor. New enterprises like SIFOR and DIFMAD bloomed. In Fort Dauphin export companies — the Marseillaise and the Lyonnaise and the Boetchi family and the Jenny family — sent out not only sisal and mica but ten to thirty thousand head of cattle per year from the herders of Androy. Cattle and secondary products such as wild castor oil beans allowed the Tandroy to profit from their own holdings. The de Heaulmes employed some two thousand Tandroy workers, as did the other plantations of the Mandrare Valley.

Henry de Heaulme believed the country would do even better economically when it took charge of its own affairs. His family was not so sure. In 1959 he purchased ten thousand hectares of forest from the Electricity Board, which was selling off its assets before it was nationalized. The land lay far away, on the west coast of the island near the town of Morondava. His wife, Madame Marcelle, pointed out that for the same money they could purchase three hundred hectares of beautiful vineyards near Bordeaux and move to a civilized life in France. Or, if they learned English, they could emigrate to supposedly stable Rhodesia (later Zimbabwe). Monsieur de Heaulme prevailed, as usual. He bought his new, vast forest as an act of faith in independent Madagascar.

He wrote magazine articles urging independence. He was elected a provincial representative and soon became president of the Provincial Assembly. His imposing manner, personal wealth and influence, impeccable French credentials, and proverb-studded Malagasy oratory made him an obvious leader. He became vice president of the National Assembly, the body charged with drawing up Madagascar's new constitution. Jean lovingly shows off the official book of black-and-white photos of the "Historic Days" in October 1958, at the signing of the constitution. There is Henry de Heaulme with the future President Tsirinana from the north; jovial, rotund Botokeky from the west coast; the fiery Tandroy Monja Jaona. Monsieur de Heaulme is granite-faced as usual, his mouth a squared line in a square visage, but that is how photographs always showed him, except for that one smile next to the Chipmunk airplane in Bulawayo. He was intensely proud to be one of the founding fathers of Madagascar's independence and to count its future leaders as his friends.

Malagasy politics comprised three broad groupings, fragmented into a bewildering number of rival parties. There were the French. There were the Malagasy of the plateau, including the Merina of Tananarive. The third major group were the Malagasy of the coast, so-called Côtiers. The Tanosy of Fort Dauphin and the Tandroy of the far south are just two of the sixteen or so Côtier tribes that ring Madagascar, though the tribes subdivide into many more local clans.

Madagascar's independence was originally championed by the Merina. Of the three deputies who were interned in France after the War of Independence of 1947, Ravoahangy was a member of the highest Merina nobility, and Raseta came from a leading Hova (upper bourgeois) Merina family. Jacques Rabemananjara, politician and poet, came from mixed plateau and Côtier parentage, but the movement was made up largely of French-trained intellectuals from the plateau. Rabemananjara pleaded eloquently with the French to honor the ideals of their own revolution. The patriots' unifying pledge, the Oath of the Mountain, referred to no symbol-laden peak of Madagascar, but to Mont St. Geneviève in the Latin Quarter of Paris, where most of them met as students.

These radicals of the plateau demanded independence from French political control, the French franc zone, and French private ownership. A few outspoken Frenchmen worked with the plateau movement. Committed Communists, they proclaimed the perpetually revolutionary creed that all men are created equal, with equal rights to life, liberty, and even the pursuit of happiness.

Except — many Côtiers suspected that equality did not include them. Independence under a plateau government might simply return them to domination by the Merina. Their grandfathers remembered Merina extortion and forced labor and the days when "Blacks," that is, Côtiers, were sold as slaves to the "Whites," the Merina. To many Côtiers, the French seemed better masters, possibly even less racist. They looked for a solution that would grant political freedom but with a soft transition that retained French guarantees and economic stability. This was a cause that suited farsighted colonists like Henry de Heaulme.

Enter Philibert Tsiranana. "Beneath a bluff peasant demeanor he concealed a shrewd politician's brain," says historian Mervyn Brown. The son of illiterate Côtier farmers from the far north, Tsiranana seized his chance to be educated as a schoolteacher and then drove ever upward through his party's ranks. I saw him just once, wearing his trademark peasant's straw hat with its ten-gallon brim. Beneath it, his broad face shone out with a beaming smile like a Malagasy Santa Claus. That day he was presiding over a traditional bullfight on a little greensward in the center of Tananarive. It seems totally appropriate that in a Malagasy bullfight, nobody is supposed to get hurt. A loinclothed man simply runs up alongside the hump of a zebu bull, leaps forward to grab the horns, and wrestles the animal to the ground. If he cannot, he jumps or rolls away, and someone else has a go. Eventually the bull gets tired enough to let some human win, whereupon they all go home. Unless, of course, it is the zebu's turn to be steaks.

The genial politician in the big straw hat produced a moderate platform that swept almost everyone to his support, backed up by exceedingly adept maneuvering of votes within and beyond his country. Tsiranana apparently originated the concept of the French Community: a confederation of ex-colonies still tightly linked to France.

In August of 1958, de Gaulle himself traveled to stand upon the spot where in 1885 young Queen Ranavalona III had sworn undying opposition to the French. De Gaulle drew an even larger crowd than the queen had, because the ceremonial ground of Mahamasina had been transformed into a great big soccer stadium. Above it loomed, as of old, the granite cliff and the Queen's Palace. De Gaulle pointed theatrically upward and proclaimed, "Tomorrow you will once more be a state, as you were when that palace was inhabited."

On September 28, 1958, Madagascar held a nationwide referendum on membership in the French Community. Yes meant France would still direct foreign policy, foreign trade, the customs, the military, and higher education. France would balance the government budget and maintain the value of the Malagasy franc in relation to the French franc in Europe. A no vote instead meant disinheritance — excommunication, as happened in Guinea in West Africa, which the French left taking every modern thing they had brought, famously ripping out even the telephones.

In Madagascar only hard-line radicals voted no. The overwhelming vote was yes for a soft transition — a transition that left a Frenchman behind the inner door of almost every government office.

Thus, the three-way tug of war among colonists, Côtiers, and plateau brought a kind of independence. On June 26, 1960, in the soccer stadium of Mahamasina, at the sacred stone of the old royal kingdom, a beaming President Tsiranana at last proclaimed Madagascar free. Free, with equal rights for Côtiers like Berenty's Tandroy — whose dance troop traveled up to Tananarive to dance for independence. Free, with rights maintained for French settlers, whom the new president welcomed as "Madagascar's nineteenth tribe."

And Berenty would be free for another decade to continue business as usual.

7

A Very Cheap Wife

Chantal and Fenistina and Me, 1963–1975

Gmmo

Chantal de Heaulme married in a church that her brother built for her wedding. I married in a pavilion built for a king's mistress. Jeanne Fenistina never married at all. Fenistina is the only Malagasy woman I ever met who just said no.

Sometime in early 1962, my father took me out for a drive in our blue Willys Jeep station wagon, on purpose to have a talk with me. The hills of Ithaca, New York, were streaked with the chocolate and white of January thaw. Pop was clearly ill at ease. I suppose Mom had put him up to it.

"I think you should not be too standoffish about Richard," he finally said. "Here you are, almost twenty-five. Not that twenty-five is old, but most of your friends are married by now. You'll finish your Ph.D. in June. You know, a lot of boys might find you a little bit frightening. It is getting to be a rather narrow field, and the longer you wait, the narrower it will be . . . Your Richard strikes me as a very superior young man. Of course, I don't know if he has asked you to marry him, but I think you should think very hard before you finally say no."

"But he hasn't asked me!" I wailed. "I want to marry him, and he doesn't want to marry me!" My father winced, and looked shocked. We drove home in silence. I went upstairs to the attic study and furiously typed away at my grant application to go study lemurs in Madagascar. Madagascar seemed just about far enough away from Richard Jolly.

A year later, after my first visit to Berenty, I drove the Land Rover back to Fort Dauphin, all set to take possession of the mission house in Amboasary town and settle down for solid lemur-following in Berenty forest.

"But you cannot go out to Berenty yet!" exclaimed Madame Jenny in Fort Dauphin. "Tomorrow night is the Lion's Club Ball! You must stay in our house and then join our table at the ball tomorrow."

Courtly Monsieur Kurt Jenny and his ebullient wife swept me off to their house with the two-story white pillars (the lovely mansion on the ridge where the French community took refuge in 1947 because of its sightlines for firing). My bedroom on the second floor looked out across sloping gardens and sanded paths to tall hibiscus hedges. The mountains beyond raised a black silhouette against a sky of blazing stars. The room seemed wholly furnished by its floor of wide planks of rainforest hardwood. A scented, warm night wind caressed the folds of the high mosquito net. I lay in bed remembering Kipling's lines:

> To the naked feet on the cool dark floors,
> and the high-ceiled rooms that the Trade blows through:
> To the trumpet-flowers and the moon beyond,
> And the tree toads' chorus drowning all —
> And the lisp of the split banana-frond
> That talked us to sleep when we were small.

Pop made sure I imprinted on Kipling early. Now, at long last, I had reached the place inside the books and dreams of my childhood. Who cared about Richard Jolly!

"I have never had so much fun at a dance as the Lion's Club Ball of Fort Dauphin." My letter home to Mom and Pop went on:

> It was odd, since there was no one person there I most wanted to be with, nor did I miraculously turn into a good dancer. But I knew I was going to have a wonderful time, from the moment Madame Jenny voiced approval of [my cousin] Margaretta's yellow satin eve-

ning coat . . . We started to the ball, Madame in nearly strapless silk rose print, with dance shoes in her hand, shoes on to walk over their raked sand paths to the car, and still more shoes to put on afterwards when her feet were tired.

The ballroom was a huge empty sisal warehouse of the de Heaulmes' — huge reinforced cement cross-beams supporting a wood-beamed roof. Very modern in the feeling for the possibilities of cement, somewhat baronial in the contrast of light wall and dark timbered ceiling. Turns out Monsieur de Heaulme designed and built the place 25 years ago.

Monsieur de Heaulme was there, standing at the door with his son and daughter-in-law, looking more than ever like a square-ended battleship. The son is all round and rosy by comparison. The daughter-in-law, Aline, is a dark, slight, beautiful Provençal, and looks as though she might even stand up to her father-in-law — but also as though she understands him well enough not to have to.

Tables were arranged all round the walls, and a 7 course "buffet" served at one's place throughout the evening. Fine system: Everyone sits in one place with 5–10 friends all evening, is amused at intervals by boys bringing food and wine, but is free to dance with anyone. Just the opposite of our system, where you are generally stuck with one escort all night and must therefore perambulate frantically in search of amusement.

I cringe now to think that I actually wrote "boys," not "waiters." That was what my hosts called them. At first I could not make out the funny French word, "bo-ï." Then I thought, "Well, in France waiters are 'garçons,' so I suppose there is no difference." When Richard arrived from East Africa, he shouted, "They are NOT BOYS. They are MEN!"

Our table was the Jennys, a young man and his wife from the Compagnie Marseillaise, the nervous young doctor who is the only one in Fort Dauphin, and the Davids, [the manager] of the thorianite mine at Ambatomika. At another table were the de Heaulmes, the de Guitauts, the de Longueils. Oh — and there was a young Malgache at our table, too, the lieutenant of the army, in command here at Ft. Dauphin. The Malgache officers replaced the French ones at Ft. Dauphin last week, in a ceremony attended by President Tsiranana. This is the first year Malgaches have been invited to the Lions' Club Ball. At the last minute they asked if they could sit at one table all together. Everyone agreed this was very tactful of them, but would disrupt the seating arrangements, so they were spaced. The young lieutenant was very nice and a good dancer and everyone talked to him, but he would have had a better time with the other Malgaches.

Anyway, we all laughed and talked and danced and ate caviar and lobster and cochon laqué [Chinese glazed pig] (which they promenaded whole round the tables) and drank whiskey and wine and champagne and danced and raffled a radio and danced and the winner auctioned off the radio and danced and drank champagne and eventually had confetti and papier-maché things to throw like the French Line [I had crossed the Atlantic with my parents on a French Line ship] and paper hats [I got a red paper military képi], all brought down by stern Monsieur de Heaulme from Tananarive. I was dancing in a sort of Sargasso sea of tangled confetti when I finally asked someone the time, since I was sleepy. He said 4 A.M. This surprised me, because I had been waking up at 4 A.M. and fall-ing asleep where I stood at 9 P.M. The Jennys, fortunately, had just (only just) had enough, so we went home, leaving the survivors say-ing to Mme. Jenny, why are you dragging her home so soon!!

The next morning I was determined to start for Amboasary at 6 A.M. . . . I wound up, of course, having breakfast with Mme. Jenny from 8 to 10, luxuriating in her Sèvres porcelain, the bowl of tea-roses and hibiscus, and the real live pop-up toaster which won't pop up soon enough. Mme. Jenny uses sugar-tongs to extract toast, and was amused to hear about Pop with his miniature trident of a fruit-fork. . . .

Mme. J. told me a long episode which took place in Madagascar at the moment when it became clear the Allies would win the war. The worst of the Vichy sympathizers, to prove their Gaullist devo-tion, framed a number of Swiss and Alsatians as German spies . . . It seems so peculiar to me that people in this remote spot will murder each other, just to prove they are also part of Europe.

I finally left, bumped the Land Rover over the dirt road to Amboasary [to take possession of the mission house] . . . And I was miserable. Amboasary is a dusty valley, and the house was deep in blown dirt. There had been mice in one cupboard, one still was in a drawer, about a week dead. The worst thing was that it is in the center of the Malgache village, between the school-teacher's house and the school. Chickens, children, and a big black pig all wander about the weed-grown yard; you step over them en route to the outhouse. I was not sure I would ever master the pressure lantern, or learn to wash without running water, in spite of the fact that man reached the 20th century without household plumbing or electricity. It all seemed fun when camping, horrible in a house . . . And then I burst into tears just looking at the Wilkins Castle Wilkins cleaners bags. [That was the dry cleaners in Ithaca; I'd used their plastic for wrapping] . . .

Fenistina came. In two days, the house has been scrubbed, swept, and arranged, so I'm proud to live in it. Fenistina is a round-faced, light-colored Malgache, perhaps 35, extremely competent to run a house, extremely gentle with me. She is someone I will love . . . Above all, she is someone who can be left to work, and to figure out how to work, while I go off to the woods . . .

So — to the woods away. The first two days when I couldn't face cleaning I went and worked — I can spend 2–4 hours with these troops! The first day when I saw *L. catta* disputing right of way on a branch with *Propithecus,* I knew I was home!

I called Fenistina my maid, but she was chaperone, bodyguard, and friend. When the missionaries were debating whether to rent me their empty house, I asked them if they could find me a good upright Christian maid. I was not quite sure whether I was concerned more about looking respectable to the missionaries or to the get-drunk-on-your-fortnight's-sisal-wages town of Amboasary. I just had a dim feeling I needed someone exactly like Fenistina.

If she had been Catholic, she might have been a nun. She'd have fit very well among Soeur Gabrielle's Daughters of Charity in Amboasary. Of course Fenistina could never have worn the white-winged *cornette* headdress. Malagasy sisters wore khaki dresses with white aprons and wimples rather like Islamic head scarves. But Fenistina was never ambitious, just good.

She was Protestant, of a Merina family converted long ago in Tananarive. She was a quietly beautiful woman, with smooth black hair drawn back into a bun and normally downcast eyes. Then a sudden sweet smile would light up her whole face. (She is eighty now and her smile is just the same.) When she went to church on Sunday, she wore the distinctive Merina lamba, a long white shawl to cover the upper arms, crossed over the left shoulder. Also a lavender parasol to keep off the sun.

For many years she worked in the home of the Torviks, third-generation American Lutherans who directed the mission cohort in Fort Dauphin. She had been through a great deal with that family. During the cyclone that toppled the stone bell tower from the Protestant church in Fort Dauphin, the whole Torvik family and Fenistina cowered together in the pastor's study, the safest room in their prefab pine frame house. The house had been shipped out in sections from Norway by the Lutherans at the end of the last century. Suddenly Fenistina remembered that she had left her precious sewing machine in her room up under the roof. She bolted for the stairs. The pastor flung himself in front of her and forbade her, in the voice that saved sinners from hellfire, to go upstairs. At that moment the roof blew off, taking her room and the sewing machine with it. (I do confess that I was even more impressed with the next to smallest of the six Torvik offspring recounting that storm: "And we all hid in Daddy's study, and we had to go pee-pee *behind Daddy's desk!*")

Fenistina and I reached a routine quite soon: she did everything. She shopped, cooked, cleaned. One Saturday night a drunken lout came along brandishing a boa constrictor, saying he knew she lived with a sorceress. Fenistina drove him away. The horrifying evening that the fleas invaded and crawled up the inside walls of her room in a solid black sheet of insects like migrating army worms, she slept in the guest room. Then she painted her walls with kerosene until the fleas, too, were vanquished. All this for a "mistress" inept at all things Malagasy.

In another letter home I wrote:

I *still* can't describe Amboasary. I have a *nice* house, a *wonderful* maid, and hay fever . . . I alternately think I'll never learn to keep clean, or when Fenistina does the laundry, that I never had it so easy. When I first tried to figure out how to cook zebu I needed all my Comparative Anatomy training not to give up; but when Fenistina took sweet potato leaves and something green called anamalaho and made them into spicy spinach I decided one can live off Malagasy markets. When I slept on the mattress for a week because you can't buy sheets and my cozy sleeping bag was too hot, I grew disgruntled. Now I have sewn muslin sheets and enough for guests — when I asked about pillows, what you do is go out and collect *vony fotsy*, the "white weed," and stuff it into a pillow. Also if you leave a bucket of water in the sun you have hot bath water.

Meanwhile, I scooted off to work every day, leaving before dawn and returning after dark. I drove to Berenty plantation and straight into the forest, where I parked at the first trail crossing by a huge kily tree that overhung the river.

I told my parents,

A little smiling man pops out in a peaked cap and shirt and shorts, or if I come too early, wrapped up in what looks like a tablecloth. He runs ahead of me to the forest gate, which is three huge logs set loosely on two ladder-shaped stands. He hauls the logs off, hard work, since he has only one arm. We then wave at each other. I will see him later in the forest, guarding it proudly with a spear in his one hand.

I drive through the gate, by the white sign saying RESERVE FORESTIERE #2. CHASSE INTERDITE. Immediately I am in a warm green gloom full of bird calls. Tufty grass springs up between the two wheel marks of the car. Something causes a great stir in the grass — three guinea-fowl with red and blue heads, accompanied by 14 scuttling brown chicks . . .

And the lemurs. Lemurs are everywhere. They leap about at 60 feet in the kily tops, with a great swishing of foliage, and they swag-

ger about on the ground with their tails in the air . . . The *Lemur* go
in gangs of 20, black masks and noses into everything, tufted white
ears forward with interest or back with suspicion, black and white
ringed tails semaphoring their emotions. When upset slightly they
growl, when lonesome they meow, when mobbing me they come
and yap all together very loud like *very* obstreperous terriers. All
these noises are catching. Sometimes at dusk one will throw back its
head and howl, but I don't know why . . .

And then there are *Propithecus,* the sifaka. I am afraid I think of
them as huge white teddy bears, just like Avalanche [the stuffed po-
lar bear I loved dearly from the age of 3]. They live in families of 4 to
8, and they hop. When active they hop 20 feet, when not so active
they hop 1 foot. When they feel like it, they come down and hop on
the ground. They have black faces and a brown or blond skull cap.
The white crescent of fur, between, goes down in the middle and up
to their tufty ears, which always gives them a worried expression.
How can one help loving anything with a perfectly round head and
a heart-shaped face? . . . I am seeing new things every day — things
thousands of Malgache hunters may have seen, but no one ever has
looked at.

And it is a thrill just to be in these woods, wandering happily
about out-doors all day, writing down earnest descriptions of birds I
can't identify and plants I can't identify and something at first
couldn't even classify to phylum but finally decided was a six inch
long flatworm (Oh for Borradaile and Potts on the Invertebrates)
and getting rained on and eating bread and oranges and sitting on
lianas which are not as comfortable as they look in the movies and
watching lemurs. . . .

One morning I was sitting watching *L. catta,* way into the
woods, when I heard a liquid whistling far in the distance. The *catta*
sat where they were, too, ears forward, tails hanging down. I sat still,
too, which makes one practically invisible to people. The whistling
changed to singing — a repeated minor cadence, not particularly
African, maybe like a herdsman in the near east. The man had a
beautiful high baritone voice. He sang loud, without forcing, so that
his singing seemed to fill all the spaces between the trees. He would
start on the same high note and hold it, swelling, while he decided

how to descend with grace notes and quavers and bits of fast talking rhythm — perhaps he was telling some long story — to the low note he always ended on. I could just catch just a glimpse of his herd through the leaves: white humped zebu, looking suddenly huge after the lemurs. Then they passed, the singing gradually faded in the distance but went on for a long, long time with an obbligato of bird calls.

The lemurs shook themselves and stretched in heraldic poses and began to talk again.

I did not even think of becoming Chantal's friend. I loved being almost alone, with just Fenistina and the lemurs as companions. I was happy enough to spend weekends with the Jennys and the Torviks, but I had no energy to reach out across cultures. I was just beginning to recover from graduate school. I thought vaguely of writing up the previous four years as a novel about a novice in a very peculiar convent, awash in faith, in hero worship of her elders, with sexual undercurrents and intrigues all around that somehow became sublimated into studying for rites of passage called General Examination and Final Public Oral. Initiation into the Science Tribe leaves scars as obvious as African slashed cheeks or Maori tattoos, as personal as circumcision or clitoridectomy. I didn't write the novel, but I realized that a year alone with animals that don't talk back might be the best therapy.

I was actually pleased that I did not have to relate to the de Heaulmes. Their formal manners, and the privacy that grows up around people who might otherwise be living in much too close quarters, meant that they and I were quite content to ignore each other. Not until this year, indeed this book, did I ask Chantal to tell me her own story. There we were, two young women on one plantation, both in love and both passionately fond of our work. And we never became real friends! Of course I admired Chantal, but I was far too squeamish for the profession she chose.

Monsieur Henry de Heaulme had four children. Jean, born May 18, 1928, was the baby who first traveled to Fort Dauphin in the Harley-Davidson sidecar. Huguette was born on May 23, 1929; Chantal came next, on May 30, 1932; and finally Jacques, on May 27, 1935. The two oldest found their roles in life without much questioning. Jean, for all his high spirits, his airplanes, his driving the length of Africa, was destined someday to head his father's business. Huguette — beautiful, sensitive, artistic, poised — would obviously live in a town as her mother did and marry someone who would care for her. Jacques, always called Jacqui, escaped from his father's shadow as far as the other side of the Mandrare River, where he set up a farm to grow and sell vegetables, meat, and milk.

But Chantal? She loved her sister, and they were best friends, but they were also opposites. Until Chantal was sixteen they wore the same clothes, always dresses, though in summer the dresses were very simple cotton ones. One day Chantal came down to lunch in a pair of shorts. Short shorts. Her father and Uncle Alain were both considerably shocked, but Chantal had her way and dressed as she liked thereafter. Chantal was not content with Huguette's partying in Fort Dauphin. She was not interested in school, either. Let Chantal tell it:

"My professor said to me, 'You will never amount to anything. You are too lazy.'

"'Well, fine, then. No point in going on studying!'

"'If you carry on like this, no point at all!'

"I went back to our house. Papa asked me, 'What have you decided to do?'

"I was seventeen, and I said, 'My professor told me that it's useless to go on working the way I work because I'm too lazy and don't give a damn, so I am just wasting your money.'

"So Papa asked me, 'What do you actually want?'

"I said, 'I want to take care of people at Berenty, to cure them. Me, I'd like that.'

"So he said, 'Right. You will go to Tananarive and learn.'"

There was no nursing school open to French women in Madagascar. Malagasy could study to be nurses' aides and medical assistants, but a proper French girl with an interest in medical care was expected to train in France. Monsieur de Heaulme turned to the chief medical officer of the military hospital in Tananarive.

"Papa contacted the *médecin général* and said, 'My daughter wants to learn nursing, but what can you do with a girl like that? She wants to treat Malagasy!'

"The médecin général said, 'Leave it to me.' He got me in to train in a Malagasy hospital. For no pay, just as a volunteer apprentice. So I started out at Befelatanana Hospital in Tananarive.

"It was in such bad shape after World War II and then the 'forty-seven revolt, that the army [in 1949] asked for nursing sisters from St. Joseph de Cluny to come out from France to put it in order. They took it over, and me with it. We started by cleaning the hospital. We had rats the size of cats that would run between your legs. It was unbelievable filth. Everything was scratched, because the hospital wasn't made of tile, but of wood. Thick planks that must have been waxed at the beginning, but by the time we took over, they were waxed with black grease. So we washed it all down with eau de Javel and black soap and scrubbing brushes. I started my training by scrubbing the filth off walls and floors.

"Finally we installed ourselves as a hospital. The sisters told me, 'Now it is time for you to learn nursing.' I started from zero. I did not know anything. They had to say, you wash a person like this . . . and then little by little I learned."

Meanwhile the first postwar Malagasy doctors started training in the hospital. One of them remembers Chantal working with the sisters, because he thought it was so extraordinary to meet a girl with green eyes! Chantal stayed for eighteen months. Then the nuns said, "We cannot keep you any longer — after all, this arrangement is all a bit special."

"So then I went home. I opened the clinic at Berenty."

The five sisal growers of the valley got together and paid for a Polish doctor to come, bringing quantities of medicines. He also gave out suspiciously large doses of the medicines, and at the end of a year he left. Other doctors served the clinic, but for long periods between doctors, Chantal was on her own.

"The hospital was not yet built. I had a tiny room, no bigger than that, and a table. But we had what was needed. My only help at that time was a nurse who had learned during the war. An old man named Julien. It turned out he claimed he could only treat syphilis.

"I let him get on with that. All day long he would give injections to the personnel who turned up with those lovely maladies. But then I saw what he was doing and got furious, and I said to him, 'All the same, Julien, you are sterilizing your syringes and needles, you are boiling them?'

"He said to me, 'What use is that, Madame? I have alcohol to burn my knife, I pass it through the flame.' So then I forced him to have boxes of clean syringes laid out, and clean needles in another box. In fact, he was a very good nurse, but he just didn't care about cleanliness. Sick people in those days had to be good and tough, so in fact they *were* tough."

Things gradually improved. Perhaps ten years later Berenty built a much bigger infirmary. When Chantal was twenty-eight or thirty, she was joined by a midwife called Madame Marie-Rose. She had trained in the same general period and the same tradition as Madame Martine, who had delivered Chantal in Fort Dauphin. Madame Marie-Rose was a very large lady with very small hands and an extraordinary sureness of touch in turning a baby that was presenting the wrong way. A magnificent person. The Berenty clinic delivered three hundred and fifty babies a year — about one a day! Traditionally, though, Tandroy women went into the forest to give birth, attended by just one other woman friend. Chantal persuaded these women, too, to bring in their newborns to have the umbilicus cut and dressed with a sterile bandage, safe from the risk of tetanus. And, very importantly, the nurses inscribed the births in a notebook. The baby's father took the notebook across the river to the civil offices at Behara. (The mayor's office of the canton, then still at Behara, was later moved to Amboasary.) At Behara the clerks copied down in the official register what was written in the notebook and signed that they had received it. Then they gave the father the crucial *acte de naissance,* the birth certificate, which would allow the child access to school.

There was a school at Berenty. Those babies Chantal and Marie-Rose delivered were assured an education if their parents wanted it.

The school director, Mahatamba, later joined Monsieur de Heaulme before independence as a deputy to the National Assembly from the south. A second teacher, Madame Regine, taught the entry-level classes for the smallest children.

Chantal treated the children as well as the mothers. "Look here," she said to me. "Here is a photo of me giving out Nivaquine." The young Chantal sits with spoon in hand, a bucket of milk beside her. Two little boys, perhaps six-year-olds, press up to her knees, very bare and black against her white nurse's coat, as she spoons the medicine into their mouths. "The government sent us a measured packet of Nivaquine to dilute in a liter of water. I used to put it in milk — better for the children, and it cut the bitter taste a little. And of course I gave them a bonbon right after, so they could have something sweet. Even so, there were kids who could not take the taste of quinine and spat it all right back in my face!"

In childbirth in Madagascar, you do not scream. While Chantal delivered the sisal workers' babies, townspeople went to the *maternité,* the maternity clinic at Amboasary. Only a couple of hundred yards from my little mission house, the clinic was a silent building I never wanted to visit. One day Fenistina told me that her younger sister was coming to stay with the sister's mother-in-law to be near the clinic. Fenistina's sister was expecting her third child at the age of twenty. For your first baby you go home to your own mother; for the second and third you stay with your mother-in-law, if you have a husband.

Fenistina's sister was a very beautiful woman with soft, smooth skin and a placidly hopeful expression. We did not talk much, since she spoke little French. I stood by with the Land Rover every night in case she needed to go in to the mission hospital in Manambaro, fifty kilometers down the dirt highway toward Fort Dauphin. Fenistina stood by to attend her sister in Amboasary; the mother-in-law stood by cooking. Everybody dithered but the expectant mother herself, who remained as pretty and calm as ever.

Fenistina began to tell me about customs of childbirth. You do *not* scream.

"I have heard that Western women cry out a lot," I said.

"It is all very well for Western women to scream," answered Fenistina. "You know that you won't die." I confess I was taken aback. I hadn't actually thought of mothers dying.

Before the birth the mother goes everywhere as usual and does all her normal work. Afterward she stays in bed in her house for a minimum of one month or, among the Tandroy, for up to four months. During this time somebody else does the cooking and all other outside work. (The houses are so small you practically have to stay in bed if you are cooped up indoors.) The woman paints her face with a mask of white or yellow paste; if she has to go out, this protects her. Her bed is draped with a kind of tent of cloths, "to keep hot." I asked why. Fenistina answered, "For fear of fever." It makes sense. In a place where most people have latent malaria, a chill brings on all the malarial aches, if not worse complications. If the baby dies during this period, it is not counted as ever having lived and is not given a formal burial. When this time of "keeping hot" is over, the baby is ceremonially named and the mother goes back to work. Among Christians, the naming segues neatly into Christian baptism.

At last the sister's waters broke. Fenistina walked her over to the maternity clinic. Fenistina was worried because far too much fluid came out, maybe two liters or three. It was going to be a "dry birth," without the normal cushion of amniotic fluid to ease and spread the stress of contractions. Fenistina was horrified at the clinic. The rooms were bare, cold concrete. The beds were dirty. One overstressed midwife dealt with three to a dozen women in labor at the same time. The only water was in buckets brought straight from the river and paid for exorbitantly by the patients' families. They boiled it sterile only if they could afford the time and the wood for fuel. As in most African and Malagasy hospitals, all routine feeding and nursing fell to the families.

Fenistina's sister was three nights in labor. During the second night, another woman was carried in in the midst of a breech birth. The midwife looked over all the assembled relatives, decided Fenistina had the steadiest nerves, and demanded her help. The two of them worked over the woman for three hours. At midnight they finally delivered a stillborn child, but they saved the mother's life. Fenistina staggered home in shock to try to sleep a little.

The next day she went back to her own sister, still struggling to deliver the dry fetus. On the third night Fenistina at last lost her temper and shouted at the midwife: "There must be something you can do! I have worked for Europeans! I know that there are injections to hurry labor and injections to relieve pain! You have to help my sister!" The midwife injected something — what? — as Fenistina stood over her. The young woman, with final agonized contractions, managed to give birth.

It was a boy, a fine healthy baby. They named him Andrianamora, "Lord Slowly," or better, "The Lord-Who-Takes-His-Time."

The valley buzzed with excitement about Chantal. For years she had been angling for Georges Dupray, who had come to work for the de Heaulmes some years before, when he was demobilized from service in Indochina. Chantal, in fact, had been delegated to meet him at the airport in her Jeep when he first arrived as a new recruit to the firm. However, he went off to raise sisal near Morondava on the west coast, then transferred to the mica mines at Betanimena and Ambandaniry. This last was actually a mine for thorianite, a radioactive uranium compound found with the mica.

I flew up to the mine site once with Jean de Heaulme, and stood amazed. In this country of more or less, of *mora-mora* — slowly-slowly — there was an open-pit mine running twenty-four hours a day under blazing floodlights. Trucks the size of European houses carried the ore to the crusher — but in true Malagasy fashion, the trucks were loaded by scores of antlike men with shovels. The French rocket industry demanded all the thorianite that Madagascar could produce, and the exporters were happy to comply. They dynamited out the ore, shoveled it up, and crushed it. The heavy grains of thorianite, locally called "metal-stone," were sluiced apart from the powdered rock by rows of women working treadle-operated sieving tables — like placer-washing gold. I asked old Geneviève, now retired at Berenty, if it had been a good job. "Oh, yes!" she said. "It was a job where we were sitting down!"

Geneviève does not remember there being any health precautions for the workers, but some workers did observe them. Michel Randelson, doyen of the de Heaulme chauffeurs, was once a driver for the thorianite mine. He wore a face mask and had a film badge that was checked for radiation weekly. He says that the women at the separator tables also had masks and badges. The hardest regulation to enforce in friendly, transport-poor Androy was that the drivers could never give people lifts in the back of their trucks. The trucks were formally locked when they left for Fort Dauphin. Any driver who let a friend with no film badge even ride in his truck cab was fired on the spot.

As in any mining operation, there were more immediate dangers. Georges Dupray himself was nearly killed when a "mirror" slipped. A sheer interface between slanted layers of mica simply gave way, and a quarter of the mountainside fell into the valley. What saved him — and all the others — was that the bell had just rung for lunch, so they were all out of the pit. There is no way to foresee the presence of a buried mica mirror, no way to tell in advance when it will yield to the strain.

Chantal and Georges saw each other only once a year at the Miner's Ball in Fort Dauphin, so the courtship proceeded slowly, if at all. Then, however, he transferred to Berenty as sisal manager. Very soon the valley was buzzing with news: an April wedding! Furthermore, the couple regarded Berenty as their home and meant to marry there!

Jean decided that he must build them a church. He designed the cruciform Berenty Chapel with a framework of angled beams to hold the high central tower. Behind the altar he set a rose window, a concrete image of the spread leaves of a sisal plant, holding between them wedges of colored glass. The chapel was not actually finished until the night before, so on the great day it still smelled a bit of wet paint and damp cement.

The wedding was splendid. *Le tout* Mandrare Valley attended, all one hundred and fifty Europeans. Chantal had a corps of eight tiny flower girls and boys in white dresses or shorts, with red and blue sashes. The bride walked from her house to the church through a double file of everyone who lived on the plantation. The marriage itself was performed by Père Kieffer, who lived in Manambaro. Père Chevalier from Amboasary officiated at the nuptial Mass, flanked by four Malagasy altar boys. A photo shows the guests beyond the altar boys, sitting on the church benches in their 1963 hats and dresses (not a very becoming hem length that year, just below the knee). Afterward everyone walked from the church to the sisal compound, where the largest garage had been cleared for the occasion and filled with round tables and folding chairs for a festive lunch. To Chantal's total surprise, the schoolchildren did a pageant, a mime of a Tandroy wedding, with various little boys curled up on the ground giggling as they played the obligatory sacrificed bulls. A good time was had by all — except Monsieur and Madame Masson-Néné, who decided to walk from their own plantation, the next one down the river. They got lost in the forest and missed the show.

I missed it too. John Buettner Janusch, the professor who had brought to America the lemurs I studied for my thesis, had come to visit, along with his wife, Vina. I was sorely tempted to stay for Chantal's wedding, but instead I followed duty to take my prof to see the marvelously rich forest of Sakaraha in the west of the island. After two weeks of lemur-watching there, I drove for three days to Tananarive to meet Richard Jolly.

Richard was traveling through four African countries to gather material for his own Ph.D. thesis on the economics of education. He hesitantly asked his professor if he might have $150 extra on his student grant to add a further case study in Madagascar. Professor Lloyd Reynolds, who knew us both and, for that matter, my parents, rapidly agreed. When Richard, jubilant, telephoned my mother, she started to giggle. "No, really, Mrs. Bishop," protested Richard, "it is completely intellectually justified!" At that point Mom simply guffawed.

I drove the two hours out of Tananative to Arivonimamo Airport. The Boeing landed. Nobody I knew got off. I waited half a week for the next Boeing. A horde of very small Malagasy men descended the airplane steps in identical blue blazers, white trousers, and red-and-green striped ties, looking like a musical comedy of the seventy dwarves. The plane had been commandeered to transport the national soccer teams home from an international sports meet. The third plane, four days later, was equally barren. I went home and barricaded myself in my hotel room and bawled into my tea.

Enough of this man. I would go watch lemurs. I traveled with Preston and another Yale student, Jeff, down to Perinet in the rainforest. Indri sang their multipart territorial duets: indri sing the song of the forest as whales sing the song of the sea. After another week, though, I'd had enough. Comparative data from Sakaraha and Perinet were no reason to stay away from real work forever. In fury I headed my Land Rover south to my own proper forest and my own little home.

On the plaid straw tablecloth Fenistina neatly stacked nine unopened blue airmail letters and four increasingly desperate telegrams. In the first letter Richard told me he had a marvelous offer to stay and work for a month in Addis Ababa at the Economic Commission for Africa with his own heroes, Professors Hans Singer and Dudley Seers. He hoped I would not mind a month's delay. The last of the telegrams said that in spite of my silence, and my obvious decision never to speak to him again, he would still come to do his thesis research in Tananarive — arriving the day after next! It was impossible for me to get back that soon, and now we had no way to find each other. Where would he go once he left the airplane?

There was nothing to be done except head back the next day into the forest to pick up my study troops where I had left off. Even that was a horrid disappointment. The ringtails had been just gearing up for their mating season when I left; I expected that they would be reaching a sexual frenzy by now. But one look told me that these wounded, exhausted animals draped over branches had finished their exertions for the year. How could I have guessed that the ringtail mating season is one of the shortest known among mammals? — a two-week orgy, over almost as soon as it starts. I had missed it, in any case. The animals didn't even look happy, just bone-tired.

I trailed back out of the forest and bumped into Jean de Heaulme. "Alison! What on earth is wrong!" he exclaimed when he saw my face.

I poured out my story, ending with "On top of all, if I had only stayed for Chantal's wedding, I would have had the first of those blue letters, and I'd have seen the ringtail mating season, and — and — and

— I could meet Richard tomorrow — and my whole life would be different."

"It just happens that I am flying the Beechcraft to Tana tomorrow," Jean announced. "Would you like to come along?"

What should I give my parents-in-law?" Over dinner Richard asked the *sous-préfet* of Amboasary, the official head of the regional government, for his advice. I was learning fast that it was possible to become totally involved with Malagasy people if you hung out with a cheerful economist with curly red hair and a passion for local life.

Richard did indeed find his intellectual justification for studying Madagascar. The Merina kingdom had passed a law in favor of universal primary education in 1882, a year before France itself did. Before colonization, 160,000 children attended school; after colonization, the number dropped to 40,000. Of course, the French thought their educational system was better, but the pattern of underdevelopment — colonization stifling local initiative — is as clear in Madagascar as it is anywhere in the world. Richard had already spent two years as a community development officer in upcountry Kenya, but Madagascar was a revelation to him. It was the first time he really understood how colonialism attempts to wipe out the civilization of the colonized.

At the moment, though, he had a more immediate problem. "Alison's father and mother are due to arrive, to see her life here before she flies back to England to marry me. I am a bit afraid they won't see how fascinating it all is, when they have to step around the pig and say hello to the church warden on the way to the outhouse. At least I have built a bucket shower in her bathroom, the best thing I could do to make her house more habitable for them. And my own parents have arranged for a wedding reception in the Royal Pavilion in Brighton, a fantastic palace that an English king built to entertain his mistress. We've bought forty pointed straw hats in the market to take home so all the children at the wedding can run around the Royal Pavilion looking like little Tandroy! But is there a present of something truly local, something I can give them as a real engagement present?"

The sous-préfet grinned widely. "There is only one possible gift from a son-in-law. In Androy it must be zebu. In fact, the wedding would hardly be legal without a gift of zebu."

"A capital idea! One should have thought of it oneself!" (Richard can sound very Oxbridge when he isn't careful.) "It's not just that it's local custom. That means Pop Bishop can actually have milk in his morning coffee!"

Three days later Richard became the official owner of a small black cow and her piebald nursing calf. Every morning from then on, the youngest son of the herder walked into town carrying a beer bottle corked with a corncob, holding about a cup of zebu milk or whatever the calf hadn't taken. The milk was almost as thick as canned condensed milk, all minerals and protein with no cream. It was the product of a lean, desert-adapted creature, nothing like the diluted, fatty substance we call milk in the West.

The following week we asked the sous-préfet to dine with us, in turn. "I did it!" boasted Richard. "I bought my father-in-law a zebu!"

"Only one zebu?" The sous-préfet grinned. "You do realize that you have a very cheap wife!"

In 1975 I became a real author, Fenistina became a kind of mother, and Chantal's life split in two. Berenty and its people remained remarkably the same for a decade. The golden age of sisal continued under the First Malagasy Republic. Georges Dupray ran the plantation with smooth efficiency, and Chantal the clinic. I returned for two months in 1964, at Richard's urging, to fill in that blank of the ringtail mating season — an orgy indeed. In 1970 Madagascar held its first-ever international conference on the environment, which gave me another chance to visit Berenty. Mostly, though, we lived in England, where Richard headed the Institute of Development Studies in Sussex. A husband, babies, and a part-time academic career seemed to be everything I asked of life.

Then a letter from Tom Lovejoy of the World Wildlife Fund in Washington dropped through the mail slot of our Sussex front door. Could I suggest someone to write a popular book about conservation in Madagascar? Tom thought a book would tell the outside world that

Madagascar matters. He had wangled funding from WWF for an author and photographer to travel all around the island continent!

"Oh dear," I moaned. "I would so *love* to do that! But four children — who else can I recommend to be the author?"

Richard announced, "The United Nations has declared 1975 International Women's Year. We should celebrate it! You take on the book; I'll stay home to look after the kids. Or perhaps I can find a temporary job in Madagascar? Then we'll go there as a family!" He sent a query to the International Labor Organization in Geneva, which snapped right back with an offer to join Madagascar's planning office. They had actually been looking for an economist with an interest in social issues. How soon could he come?

Richard went into a deep slump for about a week. He curled up in the big brown leather chair in our study and sulked. Then all at once he shot bolt upright out of the depths of the chair. He proclaimed, "Look! If I were a woman, and I were a nurse or a secretary, everyone would say how clever to have a job where I could follow my husband around. Why should I be ashamed of being an international economist, so I am able to follow my wife?"

In early 1975 Madagascar's government was in turmoil. Still, Berenty forest seemed almost insulated from politics. Chantal and Georges were absorbed by their work on the plantation. They had hosted a whole string of other scientists after me. The lemurs flourished, the sisal factory produced its golden fibers, magenta bougainvillea still cascaded round the white plantation houses. The most obvious change for me was that now four Jolly kids, aged three to ten, played tag under the trees. Fenistina rode herd on the smallest ones while I counted lemurs and drafted my book.

Fenistina had not married. She never wished to go through what she saw as the horror of childbirth. But now her youngest sister became pregnant. That sister was epileptic and feeble-minded. The whole extended family turned to Fenistina. The others had their own children. Fenistina was the obvious one to care for the baby born of this calamitous pregnancy. The boy, Solofo, was only a little slow of mind. The retarded mother, though, had to be watched day and night. If she had one of her frequent fits, she fell. Once she fell into the cooking fire, holding her baby. For Fenistina it was like having two children, one of them with adult weight and strength.

Fenistina eventually took a taxi-brousse to the mission hospital at Manambaro. She told the doctor, "You must sterilize my sister. I have lived among Europeans, so I know it can be done. You must sterilize my sister, or she will have another child. I am caring for two helpless people; I cannot care for three."

The mission doctor, just arrived from midwestern America, was a temporary visitor with the arrogant certainty of a person who had never lived outside his own culture. He told Fenistina, "Your sister has sinned. She must learn to sin no more. I will not sterilize her."

All her life Fenestina had believed whatever the missionaries told her. She started for home. As the taxi-brousse stopped for her, she swung around instead of boarding it. She stumped back to the hospital and confronted the American doctor.

"Doctor, what you say is wrong," she declared. "My sister has the mind of a child. The Bible says that children cannot sin. Whatever my sister does cannot be sin. The Bible says so. Only you must make her so she does not have another baby."

When she had the courage to quote the Bible back at him, the doctor agreed. There were no more children. After a few years the epileptic sister died, and Fenistina raised Solofo as her son. He stayed with her and helped her, as she him, for years to come.

Berenty's isolation and prosperity could not protect it from political change. Chantal and Georges left on their annual leave to visit Uncle Alain, long since retired to the Dordogne, in France. On October 15, 1975, just as they were about to board the plane to return home to Madagascar, Uncle Alain received a telegram. Unsigned, it came from Chantal's father and brother, but had been smuggled out via Réunion to escape surveillance.

It read, ABSOLUTELY FORBIDDEN THAT GEORGES AND CHANTAL SET FOOT IN MADAGASCAR.

8

If We Hear They Hurt You, We Will Come Back with Our Spears

Malagasy Socialism, 1971–1979

The worst night of Jean de Heaulme's life, he lay in prison in Fort Dauphin. He wrestled with himself whether to raise revolt in the south. In his pride and rage, he told himself, "They want to riot? Then let them riot!" Then he asked, "Have I the right to shed blood — the blood of the people who work for me?" As the night gave way to dawn, he finally faced the question, "Will I stay or will I leave? In the end, do I accept whatever I must accept to remain in Madagascar?"

That was in 1979, at the end of a turbulent decade. By 1970 President Tsiranana's health was failing. The coalitions he had constructed to forge Madagascar's independence were beginning to unravel. One of the first open breaks came as armed insurrection. Monja Jaona, a Tandroy pastor's son, proclaimed that the south should be free — its own country, beyond the sway of either the French or the tribes of the high plateau. Monja Jaona, like President Tsiranana, and indeed Monsieur Henry de Heaulme, had been one of the architects of independence from France.

Monja Jaona was a man who seized people's souls with a total, almost sexual charisma. He could fire a thousand tribesmen to rampage.

He was a thorn in the side of any ruling government, alternating spells as a leading politician with spells in jail under both colonial and postcolonial regimes. Even as an old man, long out of power and poor — an honest politician, he died poor — he could still impart to each one of a roomful of university students the glowing conviction that they must live their lives for the solidarity of the Tandroy.

In 1971 the south reeled from an anthrax epidemic and from yet another drought. Government tax collectors, mainly civil servants from the plateau, still levied the old French poll taxes and cattle taxes — sometimes demanding payment for zebu that had already died from drought and disease. Monja Jaona had ample grievances to work upon when he urged the southerners to rise up with their spears.

Politics filtered all the way down to Jaona Tsiminono, the Never-Suckled, grandson of Mahafaha, who first gave land to the de Heaulmes. In 1971 Jaona was already over fifty. His days as an aeropousse runner and as a member of the Berenty dancing team were long past. He was now a person of substance, deputy to his older brother, who was a village chief. They belonged to the PSD, the Social Democratic Party. The PSD was the ruling party, Tsiranana's party, the de Heaulmes' party, the respectable party for village headmen. However, Jaona had friends across the Mandrare River in Behara who had fallen under the spell of Monja Jaona's Mouvement National pour l'Indépendence de Madagascar — MONIMA. The friends urged Jaona and his brother, "Come on! Join MONIMA, because MONIMA will win. Then we will seize the houses of the PSD and the French! We will eat our fill, and we will have money and clothing!" Jaona and his brother agreed to join, but almost at once the gendarmes came to Berenty to arrest them. Monsieur de Heaulme's influence kept the police off the plantation itself, but the two brothers made a serious mistake. They panicked and ran and were picked up with other fugitives as soon as they left de Heaulme land.

Jaona grabbed his bony wrists to show me how he was tied. The police dragged him off to Amboasary and threw him and his brother into a jail crammed full with people. The prisoners stayed for two days in the heat and stench of the jail without food or water. Some of them died of thirst — and possibly other police treatment — including the man who had persuaded them to join MONIMA. Fortunately, a local politician who knew Jaona and his brother intervened. He declared that they were not hard-core revolutionaries, only innocents seduced and betrayed by the ringleaders.

Jaona laughed as he told me, "When we left jail, we were horribly hungry, instead of all the fine MONIMA promises of food!" Then, suddenly earnest, he rose to his full six-foot-height. "I am still afraid! For you, this is just a long-ago memory for you to ask about. But I tell you, you, sitting there, you cannot imagine how frightened we were! I am still frightened now, just to think about it. With memories like that, no one wanted to revolt any more. The Creator will judge me and reward me, but demons will punish the so-called friends who betrayed us!"

Jaona did not die, but others did. The greatest "battle" followed a few weeks later at the town of Ampanihy. By then the government had sent troops to the south under the command of a known tough man, the head of the gendarmerie, Colonel Richard Ratsimandrava. MONIMA's revolutionaries attacked the gendarmes. The Tandroy hurled spears and launched stones with the kind of leather-strap slings that David used to slay Goliath. Ratsimandrava told the gendarmes to fire a warning volley over the heads of the mob. That just encouraged the attackers. In the tradition of so many African wars, the Tandroy sorcerers swore that MONIMA amulets turned enemy bullets into water. Now here was the proof: the guns fired, there were bangs and puffs of smoke, and not one attacking Tandroy was hurt. The government bullets were water indeed!

Monja Jaona's warriors triumphantly launched a second charge. This time Ratsimandrava commanded his troops to fire in earnest. The official figures were 45 rebels dead and 847 arrested. Later reports said 1,000 dead. The revolt ended there.

The revolt ended, but the Tandroy's pride did not. They had never been conquered by the plateau peoples, only by the French. Now they had yet another grievance against the Merina of the plateau. Many Tandroy would welcome a chance for revenge.

The Tandroy revolted against the Merina; Merina, against the French.
As usual, hardly anyone outside Madagascar heard of the Tandroy revolt. The world press paid just a bit more attention in 1972, when Tananarive's university and lycée students launched waves of strikes and riots, resulting in a few deaths. A student-led mob burned down the town hall of Tananarive.

The university — Université Charles de Gaulle — was one of the chief symbols of continuing French control. Almost all the professors were French; examinations and degrees were administered by the French Ministry of Education. Even the baccalaureate, the high school–leaving exam required for university entrance, was set by France.

In the government itself about a thousand French "advisers" held senior positions, including two hundred on the staff of the president's office. Historian Mervyn Brown comments: "The French not only continued to run the country, but were seen to be doing so . . . With astonishing lack of tact, the French had retained the residence of the former Governor-General in the center of Antananarivo as their ambassador's residence, a situation without parallel in any other ex-French or indeed ex-British territory, where the governor's residence invariably became the residence of the new Head of State."

University graduates who could replace the French professionals were almost all Merina or Betsileo, the other plateau tribe. President Tsiranana and his coastal ministers resisted demands to "Malgachize" if that meant replacing Frenchmen with people from the plateau. Students had little hope of a career when the upper levels of government were closed to them, not only by the French but by their own countrymen.

In October 1972, after a year of intermittent rioting, the central government fell. Colonel Richard Ratsimandrava was sympathetic to the students' views and also personally seared by his responsibility for the slaughter in Androy. In Tananarive he refused to command his policemen to fire on unarmed rioters. General Ramanantsoa took temporary power. One of the general's chief qualifications was that he did not actually want to be president. He promised to hold elections as soon as the situation quieted down.

New cabinet ministers began to make changes that would reshape government in Madagascar. Colonel Ratsimandrava added the post of minister of the interior to his role as commander of the gendarmes. He completely restructured local government. Now the base of power would be the local *fokon'olona*. The term is usually translated as "commune," to imply that Malagasy socialism was something like that in France, which also has communes, though to Anglo-Saxon ears it sounds as though the new local government resembled the Soviet system.

Ratsimandrava's communes were, in fact, traditional village assemblies: the circles of adult men who met under a tamarind or baobab tree. It was a village assembly that Monsieur de Heaulme had to persuade to allow him to cut the spiny forest, a village assembly that Robert Drury described deciding which side to join in the civil war. Each village now elected its own president, who just coincidentally was the traditional headman. Colonel Ratsimandrava's plan was that the communes, in turn, would elect delegates to higher levels of government, right up to the National Assembly.

The changes hit hard at the lower civil service levels. Officers formerly appointed from Tananarive would now be replaced by people elected from below. Simultaneously, the government began to nationalize companies like the Electricity Board and Air Madagascar. It set up new state companies. The most important one was for marketing agricultural products. The goal was to undercut the Indian and Chinese middlemen who went to remote areas and bought peasants' produce — often at derisory prices with a thumb on the scales. The new central marketing agency was supposed to offer fair prices to the peasants, but too often the state-owned body issued vouchers for payment that were never redeemed. Deprived of middlemen who did at least pay something, many villagers stopped planting crops to sell. The first oil price rise, in 1973, and the beginnings of corruption, made the economy even worse. Ratsimandrava began to investigate state corruption. He soon had enemies at all levels, from French companies threatened by nationalization, to high-placed Malagasy suspected of corruption, right down to those at the bottom of the civil service. Not to mention a few snobs who never forgot that this high-flying, left-wing graduate of Saint-Cyr, the French elite military academy, came from slave ancestry.

A second leader who made his mark was the handsome young foreign minister, Frigate Captain Didier Ratsiraka, the highest-ranking actual Malagasy in the Malagasy navy. He too was socialist in conviction, but more attuned to international Communist theory than to peasant assemblies. He championed the radical wing in the Organization of African States. He canceled trade agreements with South Africa; broke off relations with Israel, South Vietnam, and Taiwan; and opened relations instead with North Korea, China, and the USSR. He called his policy *tous azimuts,* "all compass points," though France quietly continued as the major source of foreign aid.

Ratsiraka saw himself, perhaps, as a Julius Nyerere, whose Tanzanian socialism was so widely praised in the West. In Ethiopia, Guinea, Angola, hard-line dictators also invoked socialist theory. Madagascar thinks of itself as the largest island in the Indian Ocean, not a mere small African country, but Ratsimandrava and Ratsiraka were right in tune with their times when they attempted to blend Western socialism with Malagasy traditions.

A worsening economy, plots, counterplots, the defection of a small part of the armed forces, the arrest of French managers of the leading French export company — it all boiled up together at the beginning of 1975. Colonel Ratsimandrava replaced old General Ramantsoa as president on February 5. Six days later someone efficiently machine-gunned Ratsimandrava's car on a twisty Tananarive street corner as he drove up toward the Queen's Palace with his bodyguard and chauffeur. A few of the dissident army faction apparently carried out the murders. They were tried and convicted — to just five years' hard labor — though the evidence was conflicting. Rumors continue to this day naming a wide variety of possible perpetrators behind the scenes. There were plenty of potential suspects besides the most obvious beneficiary — the next president.

As soon as the show trial ended, the ruling junta chose thirty-eight-year-old Didier Ratsiraka to become president. After his accession on June 15, 1975, Ratsiraka's portrait in his navy uniform stared down from the wall of every post office in Madagascar, gradually yellowing over the next twenty-seven years.

That was the year I agreed to write a book on Malagasy nature for the World Wildlife Fund and Richard took a job in Madagascar's government planning office so he could come with me. We arrived in Tananarive just as Ratsiraka came to power. The town was once again to be called by its proud old name, Antananarivo, the Place of the City of a Thousand. Coastal towns officially changed their names, too. Fort Dauphin took its old Tanosy designation of Taolagnaro, the Bone Place. Tamatave, the country's chief port, became Toamasina. Tulear, on the west coast, was just respelled Toliary, which is pronounced the same way. On the coast, though, people were slow to change — no one except Air Madagascar actually calls Fort Dauphin Taolagnaro.

On Independence Day, June 26, we clambered up with our four kids and a picnic to a little hill near the zoo to watch the entire air force do flyovers in celebration of the holiday and of the new president's inauguration. There were maybe only a dozen planes, but they zoomed around and around over the city. The sky roared, delighting our little boys, as well as all the other little boys in town. A few of the planes were overage MIGS, a present from Madagascar's new friends in the Soviet Union.

During Richard's first week in the planning office, the president announced the nationalization of banks, insurance companies, the port of Tamatave, and all the cinemas. Richard, as the newest staff adviser, tentatively suggested that the planning office send a mission to Tanzania or another socialist country to find out how to accomplish nationalization most effectively. There could be pitfalls. Big international banks tend to have a lot more negotiating savvy and economic clout than the governments of small countries. But Madagascar was not about to seek advice from Black Africa. The government would figure out how to cope as it went along. And it would nationalize whatever else it pleased.

The president demanded back rent on the American satellite tracking station outside of Antananarivo. The U.S. ambassador swiftly departed; the embassy largely closed down.

The French overseas scientific institution, ORSTOM, pulled out. They agreed by contract to leave their buildings and vehicles, but they sent home every spare part for the four-by-fours and sold even their tables and chairs. One of the last to leave was the director of the oceanographic research station on the island of Nosy Be, who told me bitterly, "I am a physical oceanographer! Now my own French government has made me into a secondhand carpet merchant! I have to leave this research station unusable, without even floor coverings. If I comply, ORSTOM will station me somewhere else, like New Caledonia, where I can be an oceanographer again. If not, my own career is finished."

Did the changes mean I had to stop work and go home? Here I had this amazing chance to write what was then a whole new kind of nature book, one that acknowledged human beings as the major influence on "wild" places. (That was all Richard's idea. He told me, "Tell the whole truth — ecology with people, not just your animals!") Foreigners' research visas were now canceled. But Malagasy scientists reassured me. My book would not be science but popularization (the French word is *vulgarisation*). So long as I traveled with Malagasy colleagues and told the outside world about *their* research, that would fit the new laws. The upshot was that the friends Richard and I made then have remained our friends ever since, because in 1975 they had to take care of me.

French businessmen had reason to panic. With some firms, the government simply demanded to be the majority shareholder. Others, like the petroleum companies, in the midst of what they thought were negotiations, came in after lunch on a Friday afternoon to find their offices occupied by soldiers and their bank accounts blocked. Many tried to sell and leave; some just fled. The Jenny family of Fort Dauphin simply boarded an airplane for Switzerland as though they were leaving on holiday. They never returned.

Others were ordered to leave. Aline de Heaulme still has the official letter saying that Georges Dupray's job as manager of Berenty must instantly become a Malagasy post. Hence that urgent telegram, "Absolutely forbidden that Georges and Chantal set foot in Madagascar."

"It is not us who make the laws," Arnaud de Guitaut wrote to his brother Aymar in 1976. "We *can't* plant on the barren hillsides as the government wants us to. I will order a *coupe à mort* of the sisal [harvesting all the plants' leaves at once instead of staggering the cut over three years] to fulfill our obligations." Aymar replied from France, "The shareholders will refuse any agreement . . . as long as they are not sure that you can negotiate in their name in complete liberty, not under threat or as a hostage." He added, "The government cannot distinguish between us and Jean. He has nothing to lose. We have everything to lose." The de Guitauts were heirs to the medieval Château de l'Epoisses in Burgundy, forests and vineyards and a French fortune that they could not allow to be sucked into a country apparently bent on destroying its own economy. The de Guitauts put their sisal plantation under the management of Merina overseers. They closed their pillared house, where troops of chocolate-and-white sifaka — the rare melanistic form — came down to hop across their manicured green lawn. They flew away to France.

The de Heaulmes, however, had nearly all their investments in Madagascar. They could go join Uncle Alain, now retired in France, where he could treat his worsening diabetes. That would mean, though, giving up all they had built, not only wealth and power but their family's pride.

Even before President Ratsiraka's accession, Jean de Heaulme told Aline that they must brace themselves for hard times. They ended the contracts of fifteen French employees — but not Georges Dupray's. In Fort Dauphin people daubed COLONS DEHORS! on the de Heaulmes' garden wall. The local radio broadcast and rebroadcast, "Monsieur de Heaulme, pars en avion avant de partir en cercueil!" (Monsieur de Heaulme, leave in a plane before you leave in a coffin!) Jean tried to persuade his father to leave. Jean would stay and try to carry on the family business, but he could not risk his father's safety.

Henry de Heaulme complained, "Why should I go to live in a country that I hardly know? My boyhood was in Réunion; my manhood and everything I have struggled to build is in Madagascar. Why must I leave to begin again in another country?" But he also was a realist.

One awful evening Monsieur de Heaulme and Jean met me in the salon bar of the Hotel Colbert, Antananarivo's fanciest hotel. The populous front bar is where you go to be seen, to pick up on expatriate gossip — especially among the wildlife gang. The private salon bar — dark, small, with circles of high-backed crimson plush sofas — is where you go to whisper and not be overheard.

The two de Heaulme men floated the idea that the World Wildlife Fund or some other such organization might take over Berenty Reserve, the beautiful forest that they had saved, and guarded, and watched restore itself, the forest where scientists seemed to be perpetually in residence. "Perhaps," Jean said to me, "it is you who will save Berenty, not us."

I had to say that I did not think so. Conservation organizations are rarely strong enough to take on a national government. Even if they were, they would risk it only for a huge area of great conservation significance, like the climate-shaping span of the Amazon. They would not challenge a government for two square kilometers of Madagascar gallery forest, even if it was a tiny paradise. Even if it was a scientific jewel. Even if it was a place I also loved.

I could not believe what I was hearing, anyway. All my experience of the de Heaulmes was as lords of their domain. How could they be thinking that it would be taken away, that they could no longer rule their kingdom? I looked at the two almost identical profiles, the father's face now softened a little with age, the son's firmed by maturity, both silhouetted against the crimson upholstery of the Colbert salon. I simply did not believe that these men would plead for help.

In the midst of Madagascar's paranoia, an Unidentified Flying Object landed in Fort Dauphin's marketplace. Bad timing. The economy was strong enough at the central government level, but on the ground there were shortages: no soap, no cooking oil, no candles, chronic fuel stoppages, and grumbling unrest. In 1978 a wave of xenophobia swept over the country, fueled by a desire to blame the misery on outsiders. Two South Africans were imprisoned on charges of sedition. They somehow escaped, went to the airport, stole a light plane, and flew away home. Newspapers and radio screamed that white mercenaries were poised to take over the country. In the Comoro Islands, just to the north of Madagascar, an alert customs inspector decided that some alighting white men did not look much like the football team they claimed to be. He inspected their gym bags, which were full of semiautomatics and ammunition. The Comoros were chronically occupied by ex-mercenaries from the Congo, but Madagascar would be a considerably richer prize for a gangster government than the Comoros.

The Fort Dauphin incident began with a tragedy. In May of 1978, a young Swiss accountant who worked for the de Heaulmes asked to borrow a sailboat for a Sunday morning outing on the ocean. He went with a much older friend, a man in his sixties. The wind rose and the sea with it. The little sailboat could not beat into the wind and clear the cape. Then the boom swung around and hit the older man's head, knocking him unconscious into the sea. He drowned. The accountant panicked. Local fishermen saved his life. They saw the floundering sailboat, rowed out in their dugout pirogues, and brought the young man back to land.

Afterward he said, "If I'd only had a distress flare, I could have alerted the harbor. They could have sent a boat that perhaps would have saved us both." When the next big ship came in to port, the young man bought from it a few flares, which he duly declared to customs, officially and aboveboard.

What he never should have done was to set one off. It was a Saturday night, a bit of fun, just a test to be sure the flare would work. It arced up from his house on the Miramar ridge and burst into white magnesium light that illuminated all of Fort Dauphin, terrifying the inhabitants. The flare sizzled down straight into the marketplace and burned out in front of Chez Marcial, everyone's favorite grocery shop.

The army moved in. The Swiss man had permits for eighteen flares. He'd set off one — but six were missing. He had given two each to three other people, one of whom was Jean de Heaulme. The soldiers ransacked the suspects' offices and homes.

They found Jean's two flares and, incidentally, the three pistols Aline kept, complete with their official permits. In another suspect's house was a hunting rifle with no serial numbers and a note saying it had been given to him by a friend. In the office of the man who managed the port the soldiers found a minuscule pile of prohibited foreign exchange. An old Frenchman with a calcium deficiency had given it to the manager in hopes that he could buy a bit of cheese from a passing ship. These transgressions served to slap all five Frenchmen into prison. The charge was harboring explosives, possibly to blow up the government or at least to signal treacherously to foreign submarines. Subversion and espionage carried potential sentences of life imprisonment.

Jean, at fifty, was at the height of his personal power. The other men were small fry: Jean was the tarpon.

Jean and Aline's two sons, Henry and Philippe, were due to return to boarding school in France in September 1979, at the end of their summer holidays. Seventeen-year-old Philippe, the more devil-may-care of the two, did not really take the political situation seriously. Driving to Berenty, he was more excited than scared when soldiers stopped the car and shoved their machine guns into it. It was like being in a Western film. He remembers the incongruity that their father was held and questioned at first in a little house on the Miramar ridge. Allowed outside for half an hour a day, Jean would emerge grimly, never saying what went on in the house, then speak with his family on a terrace in bright sun above the sparkling blue sea, as people swam at the beach below.

The family decided that the youngest child, twelve-year-old Claire, must leave with the boys. Monsieur Henry de Heaulme would also go to France. Aline would stay. Bénédicte, in her senior year at the American Lutheran School in Fort Dauphin, also demanded to stay to help her parents. Jean was told that he could go to the airport to say goodbye to his father and his three younger children — but only between two guards with Kalashnikovs. He refused, not wanting the children to see him under guard. The family left for France. Jean was fully interned in the square compound in the middle of Fort Dauphin, the same prison where France kept the suspected rebels of 1947. Jean's view was the wall topped with broken bottles. He could only imagine the sapphire sea beyond.

For Monsieur Henry de Heaulme the blow was shattering. The man whose word had been law in the south was abandoning the empire he had built. He saw his elder son arrested by the nation whose independence Monsieur de Heaulme himself had championed. Henry, his grandson and namesake, recalls bitterly, "From that time, my grandfather became an old man."

Prison was filled with petty humiliations. Jean was stripped naked "so they could measure his height." The five Frenchmen were kept in a slightly separate part of the prison, but their cells were no larger and their beds of bare planks no softer than any others. Prisoners' meals, as still today, were provided by the families. At six A.M., noon, and six P.M., a file of women forms outside the jail gate. In those days Aline stood among them. She saw Jean for five minutes each time, always with a guard watching and listening. As she entered, the guards rooted through everything in her basket, stirring the food all together like a dog's dinner.

It took her a month to figure out how to cope. She says that if you are honest yourself, you lack the imagination to see how to act toward people who are not honest. Eventually she realized that a couple of extra bottles of beer — big ones — and a casual remark that it was a hot day, so the guards might like a bit of beer, would get Jean's dinner through intact, and sometimes a small bottle of beer with it. Soon Aline was feeding not only Jean but fifteen other prisoners who had no families of their own. Otherwise they would have had only the prison rations, a little dried maize porridge with stones in it. No matter what time Aline appeared, first or midway through the queue of other wives, she was always the last one allowed in. That meant waiting forty minutes or an hour every time — and there is no shade by the prison wall to escape from the noonday sun.

Jean had no reading matter, no radio, no other contact with the outside world. His principal pastime was rat hunting. He found a long stick and would wait until a rat ventured onto the cell floor, then test his speed against the rodent's. After a while, though, the rats were either dead or too smart to enter that cell. At least it was not solitary confinement. Every morning the prisoners were let out of their cells into the central courtyard to fill a cup from a single tap for the four hundred inmates. One day a Tandroy with his wrists tied together dropped his cup and splashed a guard's boots. The guard kicked the bound prisoner. Jean saw red, ran across the yard, and knocked the guard to the ground, roaring "You cannot do that! Stop! You cannot kick a man with his hands tied!" In later years a wide variety of Tandroy turned up at the de Heaulme house, seeking his help because they had become friends with Jean in prison. Jean himself was treated, in his word, "correctly." He was not manacled or tortured, only confined and questioned. His main fear was of falling ill. Although Madagascar's government almost never issues an order of execution, people die in prison with terrible suddenness.

The weeks dragged on. At Christmas all the Malagasy prisoners were sent home. Only the five Frenchmen stayed inside over the holiday. Their families were allowed to join them for Christmas dinner. Bénédicte, then in her senior year of high school, remembers as perhaps the most poignant memory of her life eating Christmas dinner with her mother and father in a cell of the Fort Dauphin prison.

All that time Jean actually remained in jail by his own choice. Aline was the local French consul. The French embassy told her, "Say the word. We will have your husband released. We'll fly him to France within the week." Jean stayed in jail for five months, refusing anyone's terms for his release. Jean and Aline supported each other: when one lost heart, the other stood firm and had courage. They each say they could never have won through without the other.

"We cannot leave him in jail! Where is our honor as Tandroy?" Out at Berenty, Madame Sercleux incited her people to action. I remember Madame Sercleux as a barrel-shaped lady with as many gold teeth as He-Who-Cannot-Be-Thrown-to-Earth and a fondness for bright red dresses. She was a true queen, descended from Tandroy kings — far outranking her French husband, the acting plantation manager. When people spoke to her, they did so on bended knee. When she spoke to them, proud Tandroy remembered every slight that the plateau governments had offered the south, from the nineteenth-century invasions, through Monja Jaona's rebellion, right up to the imprisonment of the man who paid their wages.

One evening Aline told Jean that several hundred of his workers wanted him to send trucks to Berenty so they could travel to Fort Dauphin to set him free. If he refused, a small group planned to come anyhow. The Tandroy of Berenty were ready to take matters into their own hands.

Jean de Heaulme tossed and turned on his bare plank bed, thinking of the people who were much more than employees — they were bound to him feudally, for good or ill. Would he send the trucks for them to run riot in Fort Dauphin?

As he explained to me later, "There had already been a revolt in the south, the revolt of Monja Jaona. At Ampanihy [in 1971], Colonel Ratsimandrava fired on the Tandroy, and there were thousands of deaths. They had — they had a certain rancor — how to tell you — a certain courage! So they said, 'We are not afraid of all those people!' . . . That was the period when Monja Jaona was in the south to say, "The South is Free. The South has no bonds!" . . . It was a tribal sentiment — nationalism, actually. More than tribal. It was the People of the South, the People of the South. 'We have no fear of the People of the Plateau!'

"So that emotion played a role. And then, a second emotion, to say, 'Here is someone who is on our side. What did he do wrong? . . . We will go find him, we will get him out, we will not allow him to be a prisoner . . . It was for me, but it was also a rejection of the central power, to say 'People do nothing for the south. The south is an abandoned region.' All mixed up with the emotions of pride and courage.

"All that white night I asked myself, 'What do I do? Do I give them the vehicles? Do I tell them to come and attack Fort Dauphin? Or do I refuse?' You understand, after all, one has a feeling of rage, of fury. At one moment I said, 'After all, if they want to riot, I have only to let them riot!' Then, after I had reflected, I asked myself, 'But what will you do afterward? Afterward, you will be obliged to quit, to leave for Europe, to abandon everything. You cannot make a real revolution, like the Congo, like Zaire, where there were mercenaries and all.

Rioting will lead nowhere. And you have no right to shed blood just for your own pride.' Finally, that thought won, so I refused to send the trucks."

He told Aline his decision at dawn. Then a score of determined leaders decided to go to Fort Dauphin anyhow. Among them were Tsiaketraky, the sisal commander; Alexandre Mosa, foreman of the processing factory; and Say Moy, the plantation's Chinese-Malagasy accountant. Militant Madame Sercleux, the queen, did not go herself — she just told the others to go.

"Were you planning to riot? Did you take your spears?" I asked Alexandre Mosa.

"Oh, no! There were only about fifteen of us, and we were very frightened!" said Alexandre, laughing. "We put on the very cleanest shirts we owned and walked very softly. We wanted to do everything correctly. We informed the Amboasary police of our intentions before we took the bush taxi into Fort Dauphin. They phoned ahead, so the Fort Dauphin police were waiting. They picked us up straightaway. We saw the people from the Deuxième Bureau [Madagascar's CIA or MI5]: three Merina inquisitors who were staying in Fort Dauphin to interrogate Monsieur de Heaulme. Only three of us, Norbert Kambola, Kamaly, and Say Moy, were allowed to actually speak to Monsieur de Heaulme in the police station. He told them, 'Just wait. You see, I am waiting too. It is the government, and that is beyond you. I cannot really give you reasons for all this.'"

The others meanwhile declared to the inquisitors that Jean de Heaulme was innocent of the charges against him. He had no explosives. They had the run of the factory estate. They knew there were no explosives. And while Jean de Heaulme was in jail, Berenty was closed down; the factory was not running, which meant hard times for all the workers. Their most urgent message was that the government not freeze the bank account. The account must stay open for the plantation to function even minimally. And above all, Berenty must not be nationalized. They demanded that Monsieur Jean de Heaulme be allowed to talk with Madame de Heaulme in order to keep the plantation going.

The Merina interrogators assured the men that they had already decided Monsieur de Heaulme could return to Berenty, just not right
away. But could the delegation be sure of that? The fifteen Tandroy
hung around outside the police station, in the public square that looks
out to the blue harbor and the rainforest mountains. The police grew
worried. They decided that only one person could cope with the danger of bringing all Androy like a hornet's nest around their ears. They
went to Jean's cell and asked him, "Monsieur de Heaulme, would you
please calm these people down and tell them to go home?"

Jean emerged from prison for the first time in many months. A
guard with a Kalashnikov stood on either side of him. He met his
workers in front of the post office. Bystanders hurried away to keep out
of trouble. Jean told the delegation, "Go home. Keep Berenty going as
though I were still there. I swear I shall return."

They answered, "Very well. We accept that because it is you who
ask it. You, Monsieur Jean. But if we hear you are hurt, we'll come back
straightaway. And it won't be fifteen of us. It will be five hundred, and
we will come back with our spears."

In that white night, Jean de Heaulme made his own decision. He
would continue to make his life in Madagascar at whatever cost. He
signed the documents the government put before him, abandoning
control of his plantation.

Meanwhile, out at Berenty, Madame Sercleux, the queen, was bitterly disappointed that the workers' delegation did not succeed in freeing him. She turned to other means. The water basin constructed for
the first sisal factory, just below the present restaurant, was now a pit
where baby crocodiles lived in a shallow pool and boa constrictors
twined among rocks and branches. This mini-zoo saved the crocodiles
from being killed by local people; the boas were just for show. The
queen reasoned that the kokolampo, the forest spirits who make their
home in boa constrictors, were angry at their imprisonment. She organized a ritual sacrifice. Several sheep were killed, and a due invocation
performed by a sorcerer. Then the queen let the boa constrictors slither
to freedom in the forest, confident that they would finally lift their
curse and free Jean de Heaulme.

Two weeks later the prison doors opened. The five Frenchmen emerged. Four of them were banished from Madagascar for life, although the old man who had wanted cheese was in the end allowed to stay with his Malagasy wife and children. Only Jean de Heaulme had made his Faustian bargain or, from another point of view, his great-hearted commitment to the land of his birth. His wife drove him the few hundred yards to their home in Fort Dauphin.

He went home, but he hid. He recalls, "When you have spent five months in prison, that — that marks you, after all. I had no more desire to go back to work, I had no desire to do anything. I just stayed there. From the twenty-ninth of February, when I came out of prison, to the twenty-sixth of June I stayed in my house or at Berenty. All the time still waiting for judgment. I have never been tried and judged over that charge of espionage. At any time the government could tell Aline and me to leave Madagascar — we had many sleepless nights, waiting. Then, toward the end of June, the authorities came. And they said to me, 'Monsieur de Heaulme, we invite you to take part in the national holiday June twenty-sixth, to take your place again in the official viewing stand for the Independence Day parade.'

"That was a real second crisis of conscience, after the first one on that night when I asked myself if I should help the Tandroy attack Fort Dauphin. I wanted to refuse their demand. I still held the desire of revenge for injustice, if you will. It was my wife who asked me, 'Well, what will you do? Do you want to stay in Madagascar, or do you want to leave?' . . . And in spite of prison, in spite of all that, I wanted to stay in Madagascar. I have never written an article in a newspaper, never spoken of my case, never made myself out a martyr, because my hope was always to stay in Madagascar . . . But all the same, it was a second crisis of conscience to accept that official invitation. In the end I went.

"And I must tell you, it was magnificent! Everyone applauded me! Everyone! Six months before . . . I could not go out on that same public square without Kalashnikovs on either side. Now, six months after, I stepped up onto the official viewing stand, everyone applauded, and everyone said, 'Wonderful, you are back among us!' as though nothing had happened at all!

"That, if you will, is what gave me confidence. A month later, I was actually called before President Ratsiraka. I had fifty minutes of conversation with Ratsiraka . . . He said to me, 'I do not understand why you, a Frenchman, a colonialist, a complete example of colonialism, you are loved by the Malagasy. As for me, their president, Androy is against me; Androy is against the government. And why did you support Monja Jaona? . . . Why did you support him? Why are you close to him?'

"I said, 'Monsieur le President, my father was always a part of those who voted for the independence of Madagascar. Monja Jaona, Botokeky, Resampa, President Tsiranana were friends of my father's, the people who built the First Republic. So for my part, whatever happens, I cannot reject them. They will remain my own friends.' I added, 'Even Monja Jaona. I do not play politics. I do not want to be involved in politics, but these people were friends of my father's and will stay my own friends.'

"That finished the political point. But on the second point, there I said to him, 'Monsieur le President, as for the south, no one has taken care of it. Sisal was the riches of the south. Today the plantations are closed. People have no more work. The port of Fort Dauphin has lost nearly one hundred percent of its activity. There is nothing in the south. And no one is paying attention to the south. How do you expect those people to support the government?' . . .

"Then the president proposed that I take over not only my own plantation but the entire Mandrare Valley, all the plantations that were closed and abandoned! Fifty-one percent for the Malagasy state, forty-nine percent for me. But I said, 'No. First, I am a capitalist, and forty-nine percent is not enough control to take decisions. Second, I cannot seize the others' plantations.'

Ratsiraka then proposed a fifty-fifty split of returns. And he sent Jean to France to negotiate with the other sisal owners. Two of the owners, Confolent and Gallois, accepted the government's terms. Two others sold instead at a fire-sale price to a Swede named Bertil Akesson. He put it to the government that he was from a socialist country himself and would happily work within the system. For a while, indeed, Jean agreed to manage Akesson's plantations, since in the beginning the Swede knew nothing about growing sisal. But Aline and Bénédicte were not allowed to go to France with Jean; the government held their passports. They were hostages for his return.

When Jean returned home he had to surrender his passport at the airport. He was not trusted to travel for several more years, even to visit his children in France. He threw himself into work instead. He built up the derelict plantations in the face of ever-dwindling supplies of fuel, vehicles, spare parts. There was at least a ready market: the USSR was buying sisal at top market price, though it paid in nonconvertible Malagasy francs. After two more years, the government stunned Jean by unilaterally offering to reduce its ownership share to thirty percent. It was now clearly crucial for political stability in the south to have the sisal industry well run and profitable. Nationalized industries and plantations were just not working, in the south or anywhere else in the country.

Jean's personal crisis was over. He had committed himself to Madagascar, but the country he had chosen was entering economic free fall. Madagascar was essentially bankrupt, in the receivership of the International Monetary Fund (IMF). The government was forced to sign the terms of its own new captors.

9

Our Country Is Committing Suicide

Debt, Conservation, and the Bank, 1980–1992

෮෴෧

*"Would you mind telling me how Madagascar fell into the debt trap —
with a tape recorder beside that teapot?"*

"Why not?" answered Léon Rajaobelina. "It is ancient history by
now." We were having tea at a little white table under a white sun um-
brella on the patio of the Hotel Ibis in Antananarivo, cocooned from
the traffic and beggars of the street. Léon's voice was periodically
drowned out by the hissing cappuccino machine. He spoke in English,
which could not be easily understood by people at the nearby café tables. But then he has the diplomat's knack of being totally frank and
charming without saying a word more than he means to. I first met
Léon when he was Madagascar's ambassador to the United States, at
a time when that meant ambassador to the International Monetary
Fund, the holder of Madagascar's purse strings.

He began, "The debt story starts in 1972 with the revolution. That
was a revolt against the fact that twelve years after independence
the French were still very much in charge, politically, economically,
and culturally. The revolt started with the university students, and it
spread. Basically the revolution was against a regime which was seen as
too too *too* much under the influence of the French . . .

"We belonged to the French Franc Zone . . . The French had a big influence on everything through the French franc. In May of 1973, the decision was taken to leave the French Franc Zone . . . The cabinet could not agree on someone to head the Central Bank, so as a last resort, the military called me and said, "You have been in the IMF; why don't you take over the Central Bank?" . . . The situation was not brilliant, but good, in the sense that we had enough education, public finance was well managed, money was well managed, more or less . . . We didn't have that much debt. We didn't have to use the guarantees that the French brought under the French Franc Zone.

"Between 1973 and 1977–78, we managed to maintain this balance of public finance and external finances . . . But . . . there was no economic growth. The economic growth was not there because we had all this nationalization . . . Primary trading, banks, energy. With all the nationalization, in spite of stability, we did not have growth. And then in 'seventy-eight one of these ministers — one of the ministers who really wanted to have his name in history — sent a letter to the president. A very short letter:

> Mr. President:
>   It seems to me that we don't have enough debt. The time has come to get ourselves into debt.
>   Signed, the Minister

"Four lines! It was that, the debt, with four lines. The president called us to Majunga. And there for one week we had this meeting in Majunga. We looked at whether we should go into *investissement à outrance* [all-out investment]. And the minister of finance and myself, we did manage to moderate it. But at that time we didn't have any arguments . . . Well, the situation was healthy, the public balance was in order, so 'Let's go into debt!' you know.

"At the same time the World Bank said, 'Yeah, we have no problem.' The IMF? 'No problem.' . . .

"We didn't have any plan or systematic approach to any program. Every ministry . . . wanted to go into investment. No coordination at all. Everybody went traveling and signing debt like *mad!* And the minister of finance and myself, we didn't have any control of that. We just had copies of the contracts, and we had to take notes. Utter chaos. Projects, stupid projects, all of them white elephants! None of the projects which were signed at that time survived three or four years. None! . . . There were a lot of new ministers . . . Some of us were in public service before, during the First Republic. We knew the dangers. Some ministers did not, so they wanted to go.

"'Let's go!'

"'Let's go into — soya production!'

"'Where?'

"'We don't know where, but — let's go! We need — what?'

"'Fertilizer!'

"'Fertilizer! My God, let's go!'

"No asking for bids. No studies. No feasibility studies. No more studies at all! I remember very well — the minister of planning and myself had come together. We were meeting in the president's office. There were two ministers, they wanted to have a project . . . We *knew* it was a stupid proposition. And we had to borrow up to *here* for this project." Léon sliced his hand across his throat. "We said, 'No! We cannot approve that! There are no feasibility studies.' And one of the two ministers said (he is still around, actually, he is supposed to be a friend) — he said, 'No, that is a consideration of the past. You are too much with the World Bank and IMF mindset. *Le mouvement se démontre en marche.* We demonstrate movement by moving . . . Let's go!'

"Of course there was a lot of corruption. A lot of crooks came in to sell everything. Like this. You remember that project in Amboasary? The fertilizer in Amboasary? . . . Nobody knew what it was about. A crook from outside came in, and [there was] some naïf or accomplice inside . . . Before 'seventy-nine you did not have that much corruption. It was created because of the debt crisis. We are still living within that . . .

"We had a very naive and very innocent approach . . . And of course, 1981 was one of the best years of increase of production, because of all the investment. That lasted exactly one year — and then — PLOP — the bottom just fell right out."

At that point, Keith Bezanson, the big, bluff Canadian director of

Britain's Institute of Development Studies, blew into the hotel. Léon grabbed Keith's arm in self-defense before Keith could give him a big friendly Canadian whack on the shoulder. Léon said, "Keith! How are you!"

Keith groaned. "Terrible! Exhausted! I have just had a forty-hour journey from Vietnam — missed connections, engine trouble, sitting in Singapore airport —" Keith is the ex-director of the Canadian funding organization for research on Third World economies, and was at another point Canada's ambassador to Peru. What people like that do at the end of a forty-hour air trip is sit down and eagerly join the conversation. So I switched my tape recorder on again, and Léon continued his account:

"We had the second oil crisis. We had to pay more for the price of petrol. At the same time, the debts went bad with the Mexican crisis . . . We continued payment . . . We had borrowed for everything. We borrowed for beer. We borrowed for tea. We borrowed for anything. Mainly for white elephants. Following the Mexican crisis, we were stuck. Couldn't repay. And what happened when we couldn't repay? We had to do many things. The first thing that happened was that because we were in default, we got penalty rates on all commercial loans. Meaning that we borrowed at seven percent. With the interest rate rising to fourteen percent, plus six percent penalty, we were charged *twenty percent interest* on our loans. We were not alone in that. Most African countries were the same — in the eighties that was the big reason for the increase in debt expenditure of most African countries."

Keith exclaimed, "A spread of fourteen percent!"

Léon said, "Spread! Penalty rate *plus* spread! . . . People did not even know what was spread . . . Consequently we could not pay. Consequently we had to go to — mainly to the IMF . . . That's how it started — and ended. So beginning in 'eighty-two and 'eighty-three, we have been under World Bank and IMF programs, right up till now."

Keith could not resist painting the broader picture for me. "But put that in context. That was the ruling international dimension at the time . . . There was surplus capital in the world. The liquidity was enormous."

"Enormous," agreed Léon.

Keith carried on, "And the banks in the U.S. were trying to sop it up, because if they didn't there was going to be a global trade crisis. What happened was that the money went from a surplus in OPEC, via the U.S. banks desperate to get rid of it, desperate European banks, the merchant banks, and everybody saying, 'My God, we can invest in developing countries and we will get high rates of return because you have a quick take-up.' And the result was there was easy money. So when you took the decision, Léon, remember there was naiveté on the other side as well. Huge naiveté. And it came to a crunch in 'eighty-two. When the Mexican crisis hit, it just spread like dominoes."

But Léon refused to turn aside Madagascar's responsibility. "It's very easy for me to say that now. We talk about it. But perhaps I should have yelled more. Screamed more. We knew it would happen. We knew! We knew!"

I asked, for the record, "Is it true what I read, that Madagascar's debt repayments right now are double the budget for health and education together?

"Oh, more than that, more than that!" said Léon.

"I mean, *after* the recent sixty-seven-percent debt relief."

"Oh, *after* sixty-seven percent relief, debt payments are double what we spend on health and education, yeah, yeah, that's right."

Our family moved to the world's richest city so that Richard could fight the world's injustice to poor children. James Grant, executive director of the United Nations Children's Fund (UNICEF), offered my husband the post of deputy executive director. On January 1, 1982, we moved to New York. We found an apartment on Roosevelt Island, in the middle of the East River. From our balcony we watched thunderstorms and sunsets over the pinnacles of the Chrysler Building and the Empire State, the wedge of Citicorp, the green glass slab of the UN itself. Way downtown rose the upright rectangles of the twin towers of the World Trade Center. The children and I learned to live at the top of the world's heap, while Richard raged at its economic stranglehold on the Africa he loves.

When loans go bad for families or firms, they declare bankruptcy and start over. We no longer throw people into debtors' prisons. Countries, though, cannot legally go bankrupt. Instead, the World Bank and the International Monetary Fund take on responsibility for the many countries that share Madagascar's plight.

Mission after mission flew out from Washington to stay in the Madagascar Hilton and tell the country how to reorganize its economy. They promised that if Madagascar became a "good pupil of the World Bank," then it would be able to support the hemorrhage of debt repayments. Madagascar swallowed the Bank's bitter medicine, the financial austerity that was supposed to bring economic good health. That prescription, the same for all faltering economies, was called "structural adjustment." It was based on a free-market view of the advantages of competition. I note that even lemurs and chimpanzees form coalitions to keep a monopoly of territory, so I wonder why free-market economists think that humans are less savvy than lemurs and chimpanzees. Nonetheless, structural adjustment became a Washington religious credo, unfalsifiable by mere experience, even as the losses of many Third World countries grew far worse than those of the 1930s Great Depression in the West.

In 1985 Richard went public with his own views in a lecture called "Adjustment with a Human Face." He followed it up with a book written with his fellow economists Andrea Cornia and Frances Stewart. They argued vehemently that the World Bank and IMF must adopt new policies to safeguard the poor. In the Bank's view, Madagascar was "free" to choose which government programs to cut when it tightened its belt. There, as everywhere, health, education, and other social services were the most vulnerable programs. The services that touch people's lives the most were seen as catering to mere personal consumption, not as productive investments over the short time period that the Bank expected structural adjustment to last.

One small piece of the data that supported Richard's case was the statistics on malnutrition in Madagascar. While the country took its bitter economic medicine, more and more children went hungry. Malagasy friends used to talk with horror about Brazil's child gangs, saying that in Malagasy culture people would never abandon their children. Then it happened. Antananarivo's streets began to swarm with *quat'mies,* orphaned and quasi-orphaned child beggars and thieves.

Richard is fascinated and appalled by poverty and injustice, the way Saint George was fascinated by the dragon. He hates not the mere lack of dollars and cents but the hemming in of human beings until they have no control over their own lives. He never loses his conviction that the monsters can be checked.

He was in a key position to act on that belief. UNICEF led the world in promoting the Child Survival Revolution, which swept forward with the backing of democracies and dictators, priests and mullahs, journalists, film stars, and millions upon millions of health workers and parents. Organizing mass vaccination campaigns, offering oral rehydration salts for diarrhea, encouraging breast feeding, monitoring children's growth with simple "Road to Health" charts that any mother could understand, UNICEF pushed the world at large to deal with the simple, preventable causes of children's dying. Jim Grant, Richard's boss, quoted Arnold Toynbee and Primo Levi over and over, not like a broken record but like a defiant trumpet fanfare: "Our age is the first since the dawn of history in which mankind dared to believe it practical to make the benefits of civilization available to the whole human race" . . . "If we can relieve torment and do not, we become the tormentors."

Richard was in the thick of it, on a perpetual adrenaline rush of excitement. He seemed like a quantum particle with a finite probability of being in any country of the globe at any moment, playing his part to fight the roots of poverty and the senseless death of poor children.

I, on the other hand, see no attraction in poverty, not even a challenge to face. What I like is riches — riches of art and good manners and exuberant biodiversity. To me, Madagascar is one of the richest countries of the world, far more than all the zoos and theaters and museums of New York. I couldn't wait to get back to Berenty.

Tourism saved Berenty. I was furious at the thought of tourists trampling my personal paradise. Jean de Heaulme still teases me about that.

We both know that his gamble on tourism meant survival, with Madagascar's economy collapsing as the government grew ever more rapacious.

Jean seized on the idea even as the socialist revolution began. Jay Russell, a doctoral student at Duke University, wrote home from Berenty in 1974 to the students who had been there the year before:

> Monsieur J. de Heaulme is quite conscious of the fact that [Berenty forest] doesn't stand a snowball's chance in hell of surviving once he is forced to leave Madagascar. In an effort to save Berenty, he is turning the forest and its lemurs into a tourist attraction. A commendable effort which involves great expenditure and effort on his part. However, the influx of tourists mark the end of Berenty as a place where lemurs can be observed by scientists . . . It would be an understatement to say that you'd no longer recognize the place. Gardens have sprung up overnight, and . . . next to the guard's house, a parking lot . . . complete with signs and rope fences . . . There appears to be one area set aside as a picnic ground or perhaps a restaurant-hotel site. Berenty will soon be Tsimbazaza [Antananarivo's zoo] or more appropriately, the Disney World of Southern Madagascar.

It was a totally bootstrap operation. Jean's father had invented a sisal factory. Now Jean and Aline proposed to invent a safari lodge. Aline supervised the catering, which meant that she went to Fort Dauphin market herself to buy fresh vegetables and seafood. The nearer market, in Amboasary, mostly sold sweet potatoes and manioc for the local Tandroy, so tourist supplies had to be trucked in from Fort Dauphin along with the tourists themselves. Say Moy, the plantation accountant, refurbished some of the old houses for tourist accommodations and set up transportation and a guide system. I asked Say Moy how he learned the business. "Well, Monsieur and Madame de Heaulme had actually stayed in hotels before, so they told me very clearly what to do."

I accompanied one of the first tour groups in 1980. Madagascar still gave no research visas. I wanted to recensus the lemurs, so I enlisted as a guide, very unsuccessfully. After the group left, I wrote a draft of a detective story. I murdered the worst of my clients in the first paragraph, and all the rest chapter by chapter, until I got rid of them all. In 1982 I returned to Berenty with the BBC. It was still the era of government censorship: a man from the Ministry of Information proposed to vet every shot.

I first heard of Earthwatch in 1983. It took an hour's explanation to make me understand the setup. Basically, amateurs pay as much as they would for a luxury holiday to visit a field site for two weeks or more. Then they spend their time working like mad. The financial lure is that the "holiday" is tax-deductible, because they are volunteering money and time for scientific research.

I asked the Earthwatch organizers, "Can I really make these people get up at five in the morning to watch lemurs?"

"Of course; they will love it!"

"Will they be afraid of tiger-striped hissing cockroaches?"

"Not if you warn them first."

"Will they actually take standardized data?"

"They are people who mostly run their own affairs at a pretty high level. Taking standard data will be much, much more relaxing and interesting for them than two weeks on a golf course."

So I said, "Whoopee! I have always wanted to know what six different lemur troops are doing at the same time! This could be the answer!"

My bemusement at the idea of volunteer researchers was nothing to the reaction of the Malagasy authorities. Why on earth would twenty Americans spend *two whole weeks* just watching lemurs, followed by another gang of twenty Americans? Were they spies? Mercenaries? If they were scientists, the hard-line Ministry of Culture decided it should check up on them, so it created a brand-new compulsory application for research visas.

This demand came when the first group of volunteers was already on the plane. Bedraggled and bleary after two successive nights in the air, they first had to weather the two hours of incomprehensible bureaucracy that greeted all arriving passengers. Then I broke the news that each of them had to fill in an extra three-page form. In quintuplicate. And the entire country was out of carbon paper. The group turned to the task without complaint. When he reached the section on his education, Hal Pearson of Boston looked at me with a twinkle in his eye and asked, "Do they count honorary doctorates?" I could not believe I was directing these people!

Of course the Earthwatchers loved Berenty. The refurbished houses were not so ragged now, though the beds still sagged. But the Americans had come for the lemurs. When we met the first lump of sifaka cuddling together on a branch, a schoolteacher from North Carolina exclaimed, "This is the *most* exciting thing I have ever done in my life — except have babies!" They faithfully wrote down, every ten minutes, where their own lemur troop was in relation to flagged trees on the paths, what the lemurs were doing — when they howled or yapped or scent-marked — and what led up to every intertroop meeting, describing the encounter from both troops' points of view. One Earthwatcher identified so closely with her animals that when they were beaten in an encounter, she snarled over her shoulder at the opposing team, "We'll be back!"

The government stipulated that I should take Malagasy interns along to learn research techniques. I was so busy trying to adjust to the rather daunting Americans that at first I paid little attention to an intern named Hanta, a smallish, pretty woman, with a surprising command of English.

One afternoon Hanta was on a solo shift with ringtails deep in the greenery of the densest part of the forest. It was November, the opening of the rainy season. A huge thunderhead built above the mountains and sucked itself westward over the river, swinging lightning bolts like a cane. I ran through the woods, calling the watchers to come out. Most of the Americans were on the paths already, heading out fast from under the trees. But I couldn't find Hanta. I zigzagged back and forth through her troop's range, hollering, until I finally heard an answering "Hoo-oo," just as the cloud went that menacing green-black of the last moment before the wind hits and all hell breaks loose.

"Come on! Run!" I shouted. We scooted back together, branches crashing to the ground all around us.

I panted, "Where were you? Didn't you see the sky?"

"Of course," said Hanta, "but you said never to lose our lemur troops, even if it rains."

It occurred to me that I'd met a quite dedicated naturalist.

It was only in 2000, after Hanta had supervised batch after batch of her own students' research at Berenty, that she admitted, "Don't you know why I first came with you? I was a *spy!* Of course I was supposed to learn some science from you, but mostly I had to write a report to the authorities, to say what you were really up to in the woods with all those Americans!"

Rosiane H. Rasamimanana was a thoroughly irritating adolescent. Her mother, looking back, confides, "The problem was, Rosy really wanted to be an only child, not the oldest of seven!" In Malagasy tradition you honor the parents who brought you into the world to see the sun. Rosy's view was that children never asked to be born. Furthermore, girls should not be told constantly how to behave when boys have perfect freedom. She prayed to God to die rather than keep on living with her family — though she never actually considered suicide.

Rosy submitted to her mother's efforts to teach her dressmaking and embroidery. She also took her baccalaureate in science at the Lycée Jules Ferry in 1975 — that first girls' lycée, launched by Governor-General Cayla and named for the educator who announced France's mission to civilize benighted people. She applied for scholarships to study abroad, the farther away from home the better. The offer that came through was from Moscow. A photo taken on the day of her departure from Antananarivo shows a grinning eighteen-year-old in a pleated turquoise minidress, more little-girl than sexy, surrounded by her family. Her mother and her sisters cried, but Rosiane was simply bursting with excitement and impatience to leave.

The plane landed in Moscow. She boarded a train to Krasnodar by the Black Sea for her Russian language course. She sat with a Malagasy boy and a boy and girl from Panama. Rosiane had taken five years of high-school Spanish. As the Panamanians chattered to each other, she tried out her Spanish on them. She felt practically fluent three days later, when the train finally arrived in Krasnodar. She eventually roomed with the Panamanian girl. In the next room was a Nigerian girl who spoke only English. Again the student from Madagascar interpreted. Soon she met Ina, a blond East German who became her best friend, so she sopped up German. Among the assembled Third World students was a group of French-speaking Laotians, including one particularly handsome boy. She singled him out at first sight. The courses were conducted, of course, in scientific Russian. She became the whirligig center of a group of friends, hopping from language to language, laughter to laughter, endless student get-togethers and semiofficial parties, where she sang and danced in Malagasy dress — even on Russian television.

But she wasn't Rosy or Rosiane. She was Hanta. She dropped the French name of her childhood for her Malagasy middle name, Hantanirina. *Hanta* means "capricious," in the sense that the child is so adored that its parents will grant every caprice. In Hantanirina the wish is doubled: "Capricious-Greatly-Desired." Her father chose the name because he so much wanted a girl as his first child. In Russia, Hanta became more Malagasy than she had been at home, as well as becoming a good deal more capricious.

Most of the foreign biology students planned to be veterinarians. "Not me!" declared Hanta. "I detest injections and blood and sicknesses! I am going to do animal husbandry instead!" (She did not confess that she was actually scared of animals — even chickens.) She wound up in Moscow's agricultural university, the only foreigner in a class of Russians. She learned to analyze feedstuffs and to milk cows, and she went off to summer study in Kazakhstan, shearing sheep. No more chance to be afraid.

In the Cold War, both Soviets and Americans expected foreign students to convert to their hosts' ideologies — that was the point of giving them scholarships. Many Third World students were swept up in Communist fervor. Hanta, instead, watched Communism with a critical eye. She noted that workmen constructing houses did not even bother to use a right angle to true up the corners. Farmers could not be bothered to pull the potatoes from the ground before frost. Her class, though, was expected to "volunteer" en masse to help with the late harvest of potatoes and cabbages. Hanta went to the university rector. "When I accepted my scholarship and signed the *protocole d'accord,* it was to study! There is nothing in it about digging potatoes!"

She visited many corners of the Soviet Empire, though not Siberia, which was closed to foreigners. She spent holidays in France and went with Ina to East Germany. A few smuggled pots of Russian caviar would pay for a long European holiday. She was appalled, though, at the scale of smuggling by some of the richer students. One Aeroflot plane bound for Guinea-Bissau had so many solid steel Russian fridges and televisions on board, their weight undeclared by bribed officials, that it fell right out of the sky. The Soviets were all set to develop their own Mafia, given the chance.

At the end of seven years, Hanta faced a hard decision. Would she really return to Madagascar? Her own family by then was in France. In 1978 the family had emigrated and settled in Laon, north of Paris.

Hanta's father hated the freezing French winters. He asked rhetorically, "Why am I in exile here?" He knew the answer, of course. Ratsiraka's government had changed the language used in Madagascar's schools from French to Malagasy. It was an effort to promote democracy, so as not to favor the French-speaking elite. The upshot was even greater inequality. Parents who wanted their offspring to win white-collar jobs pulled the kids out of the public system and put them into Francophone schools. When Hanta's father was offered a job in France, it meant that his children would get a real French education — the path to advancement in either country. In the end, all six of Hanta's younger brothers and sisters remained in France.

Not Hanta. Russia turned her not Communist but nationalist. She didn't dig potatoes, but the experience set her thinking: "The Russian students are proud to work for their own country. Shouldn't I be proud to work for Madagascar?"

She returned home to a country in dire economic straits, with shortages of oil, gas, even rice. She could cope. The shortages had been even worse in Moscow. While her siblings gained French citizenship, she wrote her final Russian essay on zebu hybridization and took a job as an animal nutritionist for Tsimbazaza, Antananarivo's tiny zoo and botanical garden. How odd, after all her training with domestic stock, to be looking after lemurs!

Soon she met the chief of the zoo's garage, a slim, well-born young man named Ratovonirina, or Niry for short. Niry commanded a fleet of four-by-fours that had once carried research expeditions all over Madagascar, and he also repaired what little scientific equipment remained in the zoo-based research institute. In his own way, Niry was as independent-minded as Hanta. He came from a family of doctors and lawyers, but he had chosen a technical education instead. Niry would rather build things than talk about them. That was just as well, because Hanta talked enough for two.

They married. Two years later, when Hanta was assigned to report on my Earthwatch, she was very much annoyed, because by then she was a nursing mother. Fortunately, Niry is one of those self-confident men who will back up his wife in almost anything, even feeding bottles of refrigerated breast milk to six-month-old twin boys while his wife runs around in a forest.

Hanta loved the forest. She already knew that from her very first field assignment, before she married. A Japanese television team came to Madagascar to look for aye-ayes. (Aye-ayes are lemurs with beaver teeth, bat ears, an ostrich-feather tail, and a skeletal finger that taps on wood to locate juicy beetle grubs to eat.) Hanta was chosen as the team's Malagasy scientist and political minder. For their first meeting, in town, she wore dangling earrings, elegant eye makeup, and high heels. The chief of the team stared at her. "You can't wear that in the forest!"

"Of course not!" she snapped. "I don't usually put on high heels in the forest!" In fact, like the overwhelming majority of urban Malagasy, even the best educated, she had never actually seen a forest in Madagascar. It costs money to visit forests.

The Japanese took her to the island of Nosy Mangabé — tall, dark, lowland rainforest, with that moist scent of mold and rampant growth that intoxicates scientists in rainforests the world over. Blue couas squawking, waves lapping the beach, black-and-white ruffed lemurs bellowing, white-fronted lemurs clicking dubiously as they swung their pendulum tails. Hanta loved it all, but she soon figured out that the TV team was dismayed, not just at her makeup but at being saddled with a woman. Then she made sure she walked first and fastest on every slippery trail and carried the heaviest loads. She defiantly wore a pink T-shirt and fuchsia jeans. "The forest is full of orchids!" she announced to the Japanese. "Pink won't scare the lemurs!"

After her stint at Berenty, she returned home to Antananarivo and told her husband she wanted to write a doctoral thesis on ringtailed lemur nutrition. From 1987 to 1989 Hanta and Niry traveled south at every vacation, Christmas and Easter and July and September, bringing their growing twin boys. The de Heaulme family gave them free lodging, as they do for all their researchers, so all Hanta had to find was bush-taxi fare, which she obtained with a minimal grant from the New York Zoological Society (now the Wildlife Conservation Society).

Hanta based her research questions on her background in animal nutrition. She compared females and males in two troops in different parts of the forest, noting mouthful by mouthful what they ate, how long they paused between mouthfuls, how many other animals were feeding within five meters. Then she analyzed the chemical composition of the lemurs' food through the periods of mating, gestation, and birth. Her method was so much more detailed than most other researchers' that two people had to work as a team. Hanta stood beneath the troop, binoculars glued to her current focal animal. Niry stood beside her with stopwatch and notebook, writing down the seconds as the lemur chewed or paused. In those years when foreign aid for field research was still under ponderous governmental restrictions, Hanta and her husband just went out and did it.

"Your country is committing suicide!" exclaimed the Duke of Edinburgh. He came to Madagascar in 1985 as president of the World Wildlife Fund. He presided over a major conference on the country's environment and sustainable development. While the thousand delegates harangued each other, the Duke flew Malagasy ministers above their countryside in his royal plane. It was a bad October. The usual clearing

fires and pasture fires had doubled and trebled because of political unrest; fires were poor people's only way to register a protest at their hard-
ship. The Duke rubbed the ministers' noses in the smoke of their
burning forests.

The 1985 conference was an about-face in policy. Suddenly, Madagascar's environment was no longer just propaganda by foreign lemur-
lovers. The ministers realized that their palms and pandanus and orchids, their chameleons and mongooses, their soulful-eyed lemurs,
were a fantastic fishhook to capture foreign aid.

Madagascar's timing was impeccable. In the West, millions of people had converted to a new religion called Environmentalism. Some
dedicated their lives to the new mission field, hearing the call to go
forth and Save the Rainforest. As in any good religion, there is heart-
stopping awe and ecstasy before the wonders of nature, as well as an
abstract philosophy, the science of ecology — and battles to fight
against evil enemies. Crusading Environmentalists scaled a building in
Washington across the street from the World Bank. They hung out a
huge banner whose dripping red letters proclaimed: THE BANK MUR-
DERS RAINFOREST! The Bank could not deny it. Bank-funded development in the Brazilian Amazon shouted its record of forest destruction to satellites in the sky.

Madagascar was just what the World Bank — and all the other donors — needed. Here was a virgin country where they had had no projects at all, so they had not yet been able to make any environmental
mistakes. Go for biodiversity aid to Madagascar!

At the 1985 conference Kim Jaycox, vice president of the World
Bank, made a speech announcing the economic conditions that would
accompany aid under his direction. He then met with the minister of
finance and flew away as fast as possible. The Duke of Edinburgh,
however, toured the country to see it for himself: he went north all the
way to the Amber Mountain, south as far as Berenty.

Aline de Heaulme turned herself inside out to welcome the royal
guest. The Duke's chamber was Chantal and Georges' old bedroom
in the two-story plantation house, where Chantal used to listen to
brown lemurs thunder over the roof. An elegant French dinner was

served on the formal family china brought out from Fort Dauphin. The Duke was already delighted with his walk through the moonlit forest, where the eyes of mouse lemurs and lepilemurs stared back at him, and white-browed owls barked, and chameleons donned their ghostly night hue. After dinner he retired, asking for breakfast to be served at seven-thirty A.M.

At seven-thirty the next day his aide came downstairs and took the tray that Aline had prepared with the best of everything: jam from raspberries of the rainforest mountains, wild bee honey, fresh bread and croissants rushed at dawn from the Fort Dauphin bakery, a spray of bougainvillea, and of course a finely hand-embroidered tray cloth. The aide disappeared. The rest of the twenty-strong company sat down to breakfast. Half an hour later the Duke descended and asked if he could join in, at the table now covered with croissant crumbs and half-eaten butter pats. The aide had eaten the Duke's breakfast himself! Aline nearly burst into tears. The Duke himself seemed totally oblivious to the lèse majesté. He was enjoying the nature reserves and the relaxed company like any other passionate conservationist.

He then flew north toward Morondava on the west coast, taking Jean de Heaulme along. The Duke indicated that Jean should sit beside him in one of the padded armchairs of the royal plane. Jean suddenly realized that his seat would have been the queen's had she been there.

Their goal was the Great Forest, Analabé. That was the property that Monsieur Henry de Heaulme bought in 1959 as a pledge of faith in Madagascar, on the eve of its independence. "It was the last business that my father launched — his last child," says Jean de Heaulme.

Analabé is a forest like no other on Madagascar. The tallest of all the endemic baobabs rise above the common ruck of trees. They are called *reniala,* mothers of the forest. Their white trunks taper with a gentle entasis, like the Doric columns of the Parthenon. The forest is home to an extraordinary number of wholly local species, including the giant jumping mouse, which could be a poster child for conservation: huge eyes, wiggly rabbitlike ears, and a lifestyle of exemplary monogamy. The father brings up the year's single baby, keeping a watchful eye out for predatory fossas (Madagascar's ocelot-sized predatory mongooses).

When the plane landed, Jean and the Duke found the forest on fire from bottom to top of the white columns of the baobabs. Some local farmer had picked that day to clear a new cornfield next to the airstrip.

The water and forest minister blustered about permits and prisons. Jean de Heaulme countered, "Most of these people came here to work on our sisal. We kept Berenty going, but we have abandoned Analabé since 1975. We cannot expect them to save forest without an economic alternative!" The Duke of Edinburgh turned to the presidential councilor, Rémy Tiandrazana, and said: "Your country is committing suicide!"

Back in Tana the Duke's discourse was to be the last word of the environment and development conference. The British ambassador squirmed with anxiety. The ambassador is supposed to make sure that royalty enters the scene only after everybody else — and that royalty does not say anything too undiplomatic. In this case, with the usual Malagasy confusion, a thousand people milled around for the final session long after the Duke had seated himself on the podium. He obviously did not care. He was concentrating on notes for his speech. I suspect he thought of, and then thought better of, the words about suicide.

He began at last, "I am hesitant to say how astonished I am that an island which depends so much on its forests should be so denuded, and which depends so much on water should let its waters be so polluted by erosion." He ended, "It would be easy to despair after what I have seen, but conservationists share one trait — an almost unlimited optimism. Still, pyromania must stop!"

It remained for Rémy Tiandrazana, the president's councilor, to take the microphone and close the conference. It was Tiandrazana who chose to echo the Duke's own wake-up call for Madagascar: "Sustainable development is our only choice. Otherwise, our country is committing suicide."

I have been on only one World Bank mission, but that one was a lulu. After the 1985 conference, the Missionaries of the Environment went into high gear. Russell Mittermeier of Conservation International and Tom Lovejoy of the World Wildlife Fund pushed hard for funds for

Madagascar. The Alton Jones family provided start-up funding. (The full story of those years of maneuvering may still not be printable.) Some Malagasy officials had kept their own faith and fascination with nature during the lean times. Madame Berthe Rakotosamimanana, the Tiger of Tananarive, was wholly delighted when she could stop vetoing research visas and instead welcome her natural colleagues. Joseph Andriamampianina of the agriculture school actually wept salt tears of joy at the opening of Beza Mahafaly, the first new nature reserve in twenty years.

Eventually, in 1989, representatives of a whole crew of donor agencies met to hammer out a seventy-five-million-dollar package, the Program for Environmental Action, or PAE. I wrote home to Richard in New York:

> Picture us all at one of the meetings to . . . have our in-group confabulation about how the mission is going. We're in the Presidential Suite of the Hilton, sitting (all 20+ of us) round a hollow rectangular table with a white cover and a red frilly skirt. Windows on the long side look out at the Queen's Palace on its hill, gold with sunset.
>
> François Falloux is at the head of the table, in his spade beard and neatly parted moustache, and shirt with wide blue and white stripes. On his right is his right-hand man, Bruno Ribon, an abnormally thin, saturnine Frenchman . . . who explains the Bank's policies of cost calculations to the rest of us, with the aid of felt tip pens and a flip chart. He could play Cardinal Mazarin.
>
> No one but Bruno will sit at the exposed position beside François, so there's a space to François' left. Then, decorously round the corner of the table is Viviane Ralimanga, head of the Support Cell for the PAE. She is about 30, with quick grin and close-cropped hair . . . She turns out to have a mind of her own.
>
> Opposite her, on Bruno's right, sits Daniel Crémont. White hair, erect military carriage, the slight garrulity of the distinguished retiree. He does satellite mapping and surveys. François confided with some awe that Crémont negotiated a $250M loan to Brazil for satellite surveys, so Madagascar is peanuts.
>
> [The rest of us] are higgledy piggledy down the table . . . François says it's the largest mission he has ever worked with. At the end, he said it was the hardest one.

Robert Drury, a fifteen-year-old midshipman from London, was shipwrecked on the coast of Androy in 1703.

Drury became a Tandroy slave and wooed his wife by promising to love her with "as tender a heart as any black man."

Woodcuts from *Madagascar* by Robert Drury, 1729

Tsiaketraky (He-Who-Cannot-Be-Thrown-to-Earth), whose title of respect is "Father-and-Mother," with Tsoloho, the wife he kept when he became a Christian. *Cyril Ruoso*

Rehomaha (Abandoned), who dictated the list of the first 150 workers at Berenty, and his wife Segonde, who wrote down the names. *Colin Radford*

Left: Jaona Tsiminono (the Never-Suckled) in 1964, in traditional dress for the Tandroy Dance Troupe of Berenty. *Original portrait by Paul Richard, photographed by Colin Radford*

Below: Jaona in 2000. *Alison Jolly*

La Basse Terre, the de Heaulme family mansion in Réunion, in the 1800s.
Collection of Jean de Heaulme

Androy in 1905, just after the French conquest. The tall plants are endemic
Aloe vaombe. Collection of Henry de Heaulme

Left: Henry de Heaulme with his fiancée, Marcelle Bellier de Villentroy, in 1925. Her sister is behind them. Archibald Alatari, the American who sent Henry the first truck in the south of Madagascar (a Chevrolet), is on the right. *Collection of Henry de Heaulme*

Below: Henry and Marcelle at their first house in Fort Dauphin, about 1930. *Alain de Heaulme*

Bringing the steam engine to Berenty, 1937. *Collection of Henry de Heaulme*

Jean de Heaulme at eighteen
during his military service in
occupied Germany, 1947.
Collection of Jean de Heaulme

President Tsirinanana decorates Henry de Heaulme with the National Order
of Madagascar, 1960. Henry was vice president of the Constitutional Assembly, which prepared the way for Madagascar's independence. *Collection of Jean de Heaulme*

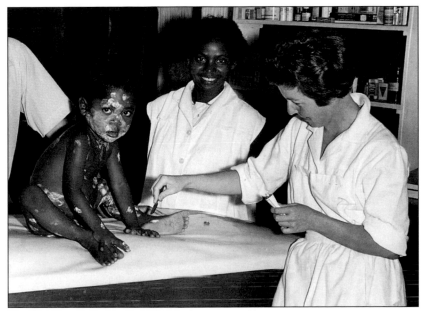

Chantal de Heaulme in her clinic in the 1960s. She and nurse Micheline treat a toddler who fell into a pot of boiling rice water and suffered whole-body burns. *Collection of Chantal Dupray*

Jean and Aline de Heaulme in Jean's office, 2000. The photomural by Paul Richard shows the Tandroy Dance Troupe of Berenty, which danced on Independence Day in 1960. The nearest dancer is Jaona Tsiminono. *Alison Jolly*

Cutting sisal leaves and putting the fibers to dry in the 1960s. Sisal work cannot be mechanized, and the process has changed little today. *Collection of Jean de Heaulme*

The Duke of Edinburgh, as president of the World Wildlife Fund, helped launch modern conservation in Madagascar in 1985. *Left to right:* Joseph Randrianansolo, the minister of water and forests; Russell Mittermeier of Conservation International; the Duke of Edinburgh; Jean de Heaulme; ornithologist Mark Pidgeon. *Sheila M. O'Connor*

Alison Jolly in Berenty forest.
Christopher G. Knight

Fenestina, Alison's maid, chaperone, bodyguard, and friend. *Alison Jolly*

Hantanirina Rasamimanana, prima-tologist, next to octopus trees. *Alison Jolly*

The Village of the Lucky
Baobab at dawn. *Alison Jolly*

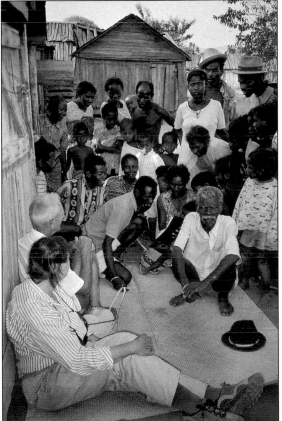

Alison and anthropologist
Georges Heurtebize inter-
view Valiotaky about the
three-month-long prepara-
tions for the funeral of his
older brother at the Village
of the Lucky Baobab.
Eighty people may be
within earshot of speakers
seated on a village mat.
Richard Jolly

The funeral involves days of feasts and dancing, celebrating the family and boasting to members of one's own sex—and the opposite sex. *Alison Jolly*

Tandroy pride and wealth revolve around zebu cattle. Here they stampede past the dead man's house. *Richard Jolly*

Left: The dead man's sons and sons-in-law slaughtered a whole herd of zebu to accompany their Ancestor into the afterlife. *Alison Jolly*

Below: Elaborate tombs ensure the Ancestor's status and also display his family's wealth. Valiotaky's brother was a Christian, so a cross was added to the traditional display of zebu skulls. *Alison Jolly*

After the funeral, relatives of the dead man are finally allowed to wash, shave, and cut their hair. *Alison Jolly*

The next of kin, in new clothes and hats, are now ready to disperse. *Alison Jolly*

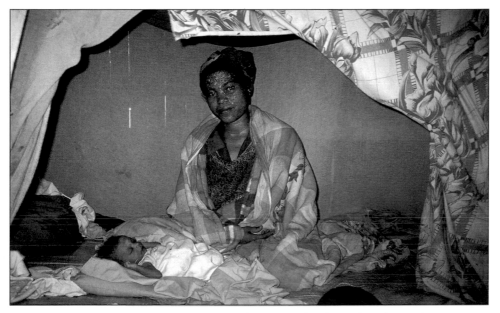

Kazy Elvina "keeping hot" a month after giving birth, with Vola Lendovina, the child she feared would die. *Alison Jolly*

Hope for the future: Kazy with Vola, one year old.
Alison Jolly

I said we were higgledy piggledy. That was in the first two weeks, before our weekend in the rainforest . . . Monday after that weekend of internal presentations . . . the aid donors sat in a grim clump at the far end from François. Tuesday there was an item on the day's agenda, "Rapport Hans Hürni" [of Swiss Aid]. When François called on Hans, Hans just rose with a paper in his hand, walked silently the length of the table, put it down in front of François and walked silently back. Do you remember when the mutinous pirate gang in *Treasure Island* presented Long John Silver with the Black Spot?

The PAE as presently constituted has a gaggle of parts, about ⅓ for Biodiversity . . . Biodiversity gets $21M over 5 years, of which $13M for reserves and protected areas proper, $9M for ecodevelopment round the reserves . . . The Aid Donors' aide-memoir, Hans Hürni's "Black Spot," stressed that Biodiversity is the only coherently worked out section, and the original heart of the plan . . . They suggested cutting everything else down to pilot programs, and mainly concentrating on the Biodiversity aspect which started the whole PAE.

Then the Malagasy counterattacked. Viviane Ralimanga herself wrote an impassioned letter saying if we thought we could just emphasize fauna and flora, we were sadly misjudging the temper of the Malagasy, as well as their needs. Philippe Rajaobelina, Directeur Generale Adjoint the Plan, wrote to say that even within the Biodiversity sector it was unacceptable to have more money allotted to the reserves than to peripheral development around the reserves, because "There are more important primates in Madagascar than lemurs."

A cartoon in Madagascar's morning paper showed a fat fuzzy lemur, its ringed tail wrapped around hundred-dollar bills. Beside it two skeletal humans hold out clawlike hands. "Nothing for you!" sneers the lemur. "You're not an endangered species."

No one made the point that the World Bank estimates Madagascar will get $700M in aid and loans next year. Even supposing $300M of that is fictitious, merely postponing debt interest, it is still churlish to begrudge $2 or $3M a year to nature protection — especially since Malagasy nature is the one good thing which the world at large knows about the country. But passions are high.

The other big chunk is $25M for teledetection, cartography, land surveying, and a land title tribunal, starting off with some $10M worth of equipment. The next step is to sit on two warring agencies in the government, because only one of them can have that equipment. After some institutional surgery, one then trains 500 surveyors (also a few high level people to run the machines). Out of it comes, with luck, a set of base maps, a set of roving land-courts, and enough land titles granted five years hence to equal what would be granted under the present system in eight centuries . . .

"Poppycock!" say the other aid donors. For all Daniel Crémont's august and snowy-haired demeanor, he and François are offering technicians' pipe-dreams. It will all bog down in the Malagasy's deliberate inefficiency. No one wants the land titles clarified except people who don't currently have land titles, and who do you imagine will listen to them?

"You don't understand!" replies François. "There is accelerating land-grabbing now in the west, with the fat cats fattening. On the plateau, much belongs to absentee landlords, farmed by share-croppers on short leases who have no incentive to build dikes, save soil, plant trees. Only rapid registration of titles can save traditional rights to land."

"Fine, register the land!" shouted Hans Hürni, pounding on the table. "But you'll need land courts and adjudication, not fancy maps. Make your judgments on the spot, and put a great big stone at the field corners. Your $10 Million machine would do more good at a field corner with two peasants agreeing on the boundary than it will in Tananarive!"

Looking back on that World Bank mission I uneasily see the recurrent link between fixing land titles and setting land aside for nature. We were replaying the colonial "solutions" of the 1920s, when Madagascar's great reserve system was first established, while driving peasants out of the forest in the name of modernization. To me, Madagascar's great reserves are temples of beauty, awe, and scientific understanding. Still, I recognize that for many Malagasy, to make a living forest into some kind of temple or museum, where you may not touch the exhibits, is total perversion — a betrayal of the gifts left by the Ancestors for future generations.

My letter home ended:

> So what happened?
>
> François has bluffed it out, much as Long John Silver did with the Black Spot. ("This 'ere paper's been tore out of a Bible! What unlucky sailor's gone and spiled a Bible to give me the black spot! I'm afeared fur you, whomever done it.") We staggered on through the week to the final meeting on Friday with a roomful of Malagasy chaired by Philippe Rajaobelina, Adj. Dir. Gen. of the PLAN. We each presented our sections of the PAE. Rajaobelina still said there was too much money for biodiversity. A great silence greeted the $25M land survey plan, except for a kind of dying squawk from the Direction de Patrimoine which didn't get the $10M machine — but someone else still does . . .
>
> After Friday morning's stand and deliver, and the "closing pre-lunch cocktail," and the closing mission meeting, François actually hugged me (not for my wholehearted support — I think I'm just the most huggable mission member) and confessed this has been the worst mission he's ever been through.
>
> So I said, "I've got just one question. Isn't what the Bank is doing the new colonialism?"
>
> He said, "Of course. Exactly."
>
> So I tried another: "In how many countries has the Bank taken over virtually every ministry, like Madagascar?"
>
> "Not many. Ghana, perhaps. It's more partial most places."
>
> "How do you justify it?"
>
> "This time we have to get it right."

"The de Heaulme family has won the J. Paul Getty Prize for Conservation!" The letter arrived in Fort Dauphin in early 1986, to Jean's astonishment and delight. Someone, somewhere, thought that Berenty's conservation over fifty years was truly important. One of the previous Getty Prizes had been won by Jane Goodall. Now the World Wildlife Fund offered to fly family members to Washington to receive a

$50,000 check from Gordon Getty in honor of their work in Madagascar.

It was a delicate diplomatic situation on all sides. WWF wanted to raise Madagascar's profile and could not think, at that time, of anyone else in Madagascar who had done so much for conservation. Proud as he was of the prize, Jean was immediately afraid of the jealousy it would arouse within the country. He publicized it as little as possible in Madagascar — not exactly what the Getty donors imagined as a result of their generosity, which was supposed to set an example for others to follow. He also stipulated that at the ceremony in Washington the prize should be presented as an award for the country itself, through the Malagasy ambassador. The ambassador accepted that role. The ambassador was Léon Rajaobelina, who later told me how Madagascar fell into debt.

By this time the de Heaulme family had once again reaffirmed its commitment to Madagascar. Bénédicte, the eldest daughter, had never left. She established her own life in Fort Dauphin, running a French-language nursery school. The other three, though, had stayed in France throughout their school years. Jean's passport was not returned for years after his release from prison, so he could not travel to see them. Now, as his children were graduating, which country would they choose? Henry, the oldest son, declared, "Papa, nobody but you believes in Madagascar." It took him another decade to change his mind and bring his own family back to his natal land. Philippe and Claire, though, the two youngest, wanted to come straight home after their studies.

In 1984 their father offered them a magnificent adventure: an overland trip home from France along with several college friends and Jean himself. The expedition crossed Africa in two white Toyota Land Cruisers, lettered FRANCE–MADAGASCAR along the sides in red. A ferry from Gibraltar to Morocco, then Algeria, Chad, down through the Central African Republic, across northeastern Zaire to Kenya, and thence by ship to Madagascar. Predictably, they were held up by assorted bandits in Zaire, but they made it through. By the 1980s Africa was far poorer and far more dangerous than when Jean drove his Land Rover from Cape Town to Cairo in the 1950s.

At the end of the trip, Claire continued south, to offer her mother much-needed help with the ever-growing hotel business. One of the friends who shared the adventure, Didier Foulon, turned out to have a surprisingly persistent interest in staying. Eventually, he and Claire were married. He settled to work in marketing and export in Fort Dauphin. Thus, when the Getty letter arrived, the next generation was already committed to carrying on in Madagascar.

Jean and Aline packed their bags to fly off to the prize ceremony. It was Jean's first trip to America since fetching the Beechcraft, and the first ever for Aline. They marveled at the opulence of New York's Bronx Zoo: so strange to see an artfully sculpted indoor jungle, with heating and air conditioning, artificial thunderstorms and waterfalls. They relaxed in the Duke University Primate Center, where lemurs frolic with squirrels and raccoons among North Carolina's pine trees. What riches the United States lavishes on its own conservation, while saving a real forest in Madagascar seems to be such hard work!

In Washington, Léon Rajaobelina introduced them at the ceremony with exactly the right speech about the honor being given not just to specific people but to the biological riches and importance of Madagascar. It was extraordinary to the de Heaulmes to be openly admired for what they had done, not treated with distrust for being richer than those around them and for following their own idiosyncratic ideas of saving forest.

The next day Jean and Aline went to see the National Geographic Society and its museum. I had written about Madagascar in the *National Geographic.* Berenty even made it onto the cover, with a photo by Frans Lanting of two white sifaka with long dangling legs, each animal tucked into a crotch of an enormous tamarind tree. Another photo, even more spectacular, was a portrait of Rekanoky (the forest guardian who told me, "They took our land and all they gave us was a few zebu for a party"). Rekanoky stands in front of dark spiny forest, cradling an *Aepyornis* egg bathed in golden light. What Jean and Aline wanted most to see at the Geographic was another *Aepyornis* egg, the highlight of an article on Madagascar written by editor Louis Marsden twenty-five years earlier. It stood as the centerpiece of the little museum that greeted visitors to the magazine, backed by an x-ray photograph some eight feet high, showing the near-hatched chick entombed inside its two-gallon eggshell. Jean and Aline laughed in recognition. That egg had been a present to the magazine from Jean's father.

Henry and Alain de Heaulme, old and frail, were too ill to travel to Washington to receive the prize. Monsieur de Heaulme had left Madagascar in 1975 and moved to the Dordogne, to a house near his brother, Alain. Chantal and Georges also settled nearby, after receiving that telegram forbidding them to return to Madagascar. They still live there in a little stone farmhouse. Malagasy statues and family photographs crowd the sideboard. Slabs of black, silver, and gold mica stand upright on the hearth. On the walls hang a hawksbill turtle's shell and a display of Tandroy spears, in a sitting room rimmed with never-unpacked boxes.

Chantal says, "The country of my birth chose to exile me. I do not forgive. I have never returned."

Chantal's sister and brother, Huguette and Jacques, also moved to France. Both eventually died from Parkinson's disease. Huguette was nursed for many years by her husband, the pilot-novelist Jacques Lalut. Chantal, with her background as a nurse, shouldered all the rest of the family care: the final illnesses of her father, uncle, and younger brother.

Monsieur de Heaulme aged rapidly after leaving Berenty, the physical and human creation that was the flywheel of his life. He visited Madagascar for the last time in 1984 to see Berenty enter its new incarnation as a tourist destination. When he returned to France he brought his sister with him, the redoubtable Soeur Gabrielle, after her lifetime of service in Madagascar.

Chantal said it gave her the fright of her life to see them. "Two people getting off the Paris–Bordeaux airplane after a flight from Madagascar, each holding up the other, and each as tottery as the other. I don't know whether you know the old Bordeaux airport, but you had to climb a staircase to get there. I told myself, 'They are sure to tumble down it,' but you could not go in to help them. I spent a quarter of an hour saying, 'They are coming, they aren't coming, they won't make it,' and finally there was Papa bringing his sister the nun. She lived on in

France for another ten years. Oh, but she was cosseted! She was in a convent, the Sisters of Saint Vincent de Paul at Montaulieu, actually a magnificent place, luxurious. She was adored by the sisters until her death."

Monsieur de Heaulme, exhausted, staggered up the steps of his home and was an invalid thereafter. His mind wandered, though he did know of the Getty Prize and his family's pride at the accolade from far-off America. In late November of 1986 he suffered an aneurysm and fell into a coma. For one last week he looked young again, peaceful and handsome. Then he quietly slipped away, on November 29, at five P.M.

His year-younger brother, Alain, finally succumbed to diabetes. When the doctors told him they had to amputate one leg, Alain said, "No, wait twenty-four hours, I have time." The next morning at five A.M., Alain died in his sleep. It was November 28, 1987, one day less than a year after Henry's death. Chantal could not think how to break the news to her mother. Her mother consoled her, "Your father could not leave Alain to live with just one leg. He came to fetch his brother."

Monsieur de Heaulme did not live to see his son restored to honor within Madagascar. In 1989 Jean was awarded knighthood in the National Order of Madagascar, the same order that Henry himself had joined in the year of independence. Jean's award was signed by the president who had thrown him in jail ten years earlier. The medal was pinned on his chest by an old family friend, Prince Pierre Ramahatra, who now held the rank of the order's grand chancellor. The grand chancellor had not forgotten, though, the days when he was a young police inspector in Fort Dauphin, when the de Heaulmes helped send him to Tananarive to blow the whistle on French rapes and tortures, way back in the War of Independence in 1947.

10

SOS: Save Our South!

Famine, 1991–1992

꙳ꙮꙴꙵ

"If the sisal shuts down, a child will die in every family." I kept a diary in the field season of 1991. It somehow eased my anger to write what I heard and saw. Apparently no one in the capital, no one in the rudderless government, cared that there was drought in Androy. Perhaps they did not even know.

September 20, 1991

I confronted the sisal manager, Christophe Lemonier.

Me: Christophe, I've watched your face, yours and Monsieur de Heaulme's when he is not being courtly and smiling at me and the Earthwatchers. I'm here being spoiled like a tourist, and so ignorant. Tell me, what happens if the sisal shuts down until it rains?

Christophe: What happens? If these people go two months without salary, a child will die in every family.

Me: How many people live in Berenty village?

Christophe: A thousand sisal workers and their families — say five thousand people or more. But it's an artificial place, a plantation town. Since we've been running on quarter time, many have left already to go to their own villages. Of course in the villages still more people depend on each Berenty salary.

Photo, four-thirty P.M. The sun dead center, low, like an orange eye. The sweep of the wide flat riverbed, with a curve of dark forest on either bank. In the photo you won't be able to see the difference between Berenty's bank, rich with birds, lemurs, and undergrowth, and the far shore: a canopy of trees with zebu grazing on packed earth below. They are just two dark crescents converging as they curve around a quarter-mile width of sand. The riverbed is dry. It is like a piece of the Sahara, where a river should flow. Its yellow surface is pocked with the hoofprints of zebu, led to drink at the one last stagnant puddle in the center. Also with pits where people have dug for their own water. Walking up the riverbed, toward the sun, the silhouettes of two tiny figures: a man and a woman trudging northward. The woman bears a three-foot pile of their goods on her head.

Hanta and the Earthwatchers and I arrived in Berenty full of glee. We were amazed at our temerity in going south while a quasi-revolution was going on in the capital. I had gone to one antigovernment demonstration on Tana's Avenue de l'Indépendence with my friends Helen Crowley and Caroline Harcourt. Foreigners! Cameras! Do come straight down front to take pictures of our leaders! Oh, but you will be hot in the sun, you seem to be turning pink already. Let us give you three foreign women some sisal hats, and then you will look like the rest of us, supporters of the revolutionary Forces Vives! (Imagine a revolution dressed in pink and purple candy-striped sunhats!)

At noon the tens of thousands of demonstrators dispersed, so that people could go to their afternoon jobs, where they actually earned money. They still drew their civil service salaries, of course, but by that time nobody could make an honest living on a government wage.

There was just one day of bloodshed. On August 10, 1991, a crowd of protesters marched toward the president's bunkered palace outside of town. The country's two helicopters took off from the palace. Soldiers threw grenades from the helicopters onto the advancing men, women, and children. About a hundred died, though the exact number was never known. The president controlled the radio; the Forces Vives controlled the newspapers, so people believed neither one. Mostly they listened to rumors, like the rumor that the president had hired a corps of Tandroy with slings and spears to terrorize the capital. Aged Monja Jaona, who had incited the Tandroy revolt twenty years before, went on television to say that if the government attacked Androy, he would raise his people to kill Merina families living in the south.

Even Hanta was concerned about going to the south in 1991. Then she decided that in Berenty she was known as a person, not as a generic person-from-the-plateau, so she would be safe. Many American Earth-watch volunteers canceled their trips, but about half promised to come anyhow, led by the indomitable John Walker. A single violent day demolished most of Madagascar's tourism for that year, but Hanta and I decided to go ahead.

We arrived at Berenty to find that the tourist restaurant was running. Everyone was glad to see us. We thought we were home. Little by little, we understood that Androy faced a crisis far deeper than any political games: an El Niño year of drought combined with government stagnation. I wrote:

Sept. 23, 1991

Jean de Heaulme: "We have lived through three revolutions, 'forty-seven, 'seventy-two, and now this! In 'forty-seven there were many deaths, in 'seventy-two far fewer. Now there have been practically none except for the idiocy of August tenth. My wife and I are beginning to get the habit! *But* — each time we are older. It grows harder. If it grows too bad we could always leave. We could go to France — half our family is in France. My son Henry says to me, 'Papa, I would never bear what you have borne, submit to what you did, just for the love of Madagascar.' "

This he says standing up, under one of the white-posted, thatch-roofed kiosks outside the restaurant building at Berenty. Bougainvillea flames in the background. Claude, the head waiter, has brought Monsieur's tray of café au lait, his breakfast of fresh French bread, butter on its little dish, plum jam. The chairs are painted white, with tropical-striped red and green cushions. Behind the reed fence is a vista of the grass airstrip and its hangar holding two ancient mothballed Chipmunks, with a wave of red bougainvillea breaking over the hangar roof. A group of four white sifaka dance out of the forest. In single file they leap over the sand, bound one by one to a white-painted kiosk post, then on to the fence top and their favorite feeding tree.

Monsieur de Heaulme pauses to smile at the creatures an arm's length away, but continues his tirade: "The officials care nothing at all for their people. The port is on strike. We find one official who will put his signature to a loading permit — but he wants forty thousand francs a lot when the normal fee is one thousand. So if we load fifty lots in a small shipload he pockets two million francs. His salary is probably fifty thousand a month — for one shipment he clears almost four years' salary. He, and none of them, cares what happens in this valley if the sisal shuts down. And every warehouse is stuffed full — we have to export or stop the machines."

Helen Crowley is there. She is a magnificently red-haired zoologist from Australia, just signing on as the scientific reserve manager, supported jointly by Wildlife Preservation Trust International and by de Heaulme himself. He turns to her: "Helen, you must study the effects of clearing the invading cissus vine, what you do yourself and the places where I have cleared two years and four years ago. And start up a kily nursery. I'll make sure your two-year contract is ready soon, but with trees you must think in decades . . ."

Me: You're planting trees! You couldn't really abandon this, leave for France.

Jean: No, no, of course not. Don't take what I said *au serieux.* But recognize I was not being cynical, just realistic.

Sept. 26

Aline: Could you tell your Earthwatchers to take their tour of the sisal factory today or tomorrow? It's decided. We close down on Saturday.

Jean: There is no choice. No export — and no water. Aline needs a holiday. I'll send her to France, where our first grandchild is due to be born. I'll have a month's holiday too . . . but not just yet, there are still too many things to do.

Sept. 27

Delta Greene, Earthwatcher: Well, we went to see the sisal factory, and it really was interesting. So simple! Just squashing the leaves to make fibers and slushing it down with water. But they didn't let us stay very long. They were just about to shut it down, so I'd have missed the *whole thing* in another half hour!

Sept. 30

Aline: It could rain!

Me: But it never rains in September!

Aline: Look at those clouds! Clouds like that give me hope — the weather is all upside down this year — it could rain!

Jean: Did you see the sisal as you came in? Even the sisal plants are dying. Think what it takes to kill sisal!

Oct. 2

Photo: After the shower, a foot-long planarian, sinuous and shiny black, like wet patent leather, crawls on the clay path of the forest. It lifts its hoe-shaped head to test its course, a child's biology animal stretched to tropical proportions. *Photo:* The geometric rows of freshly washed sisal, stretching toward cloud-capped mountains where the river begins. *Photos:* The river still dry. It takes more than one day's sprinkle to wet the ground. A group of eight women, with buckets and gourds on their heads, trudge toward the pit in the center that their men have dug. The women climbed the steep riverbank, and our group of camera-hung white Earthwatchers asked if they would mind their pictures taken. *So click at* the row of eight standing stiff and formal in African picture pose, each with a bucket or gourd on her head, topped with a tuft of green leaves to keep it from sloshing. *Close-up:* A girl of perhaps fifteen, probably with only one or two children so far, smooth chestnut-colored cheeks, hair in elaborately bunched braids behind each ear, a round brown calabash on her head, the same color as the dirt-dun rags she wears as a dress. *Close-up:* The end woman, short, almost a dwarf, in a loud pink dress torn on both shoulders and a bright blue water bucket. She grins hugely and strikes a pose, hands on hips and one foot forward. The oldest receives 5,000 francs (about two dollars) to share among all. They seem delighted, and turn to the 5 km. trek home.

"We've known since April there would be famine in the south," John Davidson of the United States Agency for International Development (USAID) told me. He said that when I went to Antananarivo for three days in early October I should ask friends what their agencies were doing for the south. He continued, "Médecins Sans Frontières gave the alert back then. So we have acted long ago. A shipment of fifteen thousand tons of rice is due in Tulear harbor in the second week of October. We will mainly rely on the Catholic and Lutheran church groups. Their networks go to the most remote areas, and they know who is really in need. Besides, there is a problem in working through government officials . . . One reason that all this aid is coming to the south, and not elsewhere, is that five thousand tons of AID rice disappeared in Tana not long ago.

C. J. Rushin-Bell, USAID: "This is the most corrupt country I've ever worked in. Africa, West Africa, is nothing compared to this. I'm not talking about the business interests of the president's wife. I mean everyone, at every level. Every single thing you want done involves a bribe. Exporting lemurs? Exporting day geckos? Permission to set up a factory? Whatever you want done at all, you'll find officials on the take — and nothing happens at all without it."

Lisa Gaylord, USAID: "It didn't use to be like this. I've lived here ten years, and I'm married to a Malagasy. Don't you confirm my feeling that this country used to be relatively honest, ten years ago?"

Bob Freitas, WWF: "You want to know what went wrong with the UNICEF project in Fort Dauphin? There was no supervisor on the spot from UNICEF. The budget was all in the hands of a local person paid less than a hundred dollars a month. The temptation was too much. I'm in no position to lay blame. I know my paycheck will come on time from WWF and my trip back to the U.S. when I need it.

David Fletcher, United Nations World Food Program: "I would prefer to have drinks in your room, not the Colbert bar. It's more private . . . This is a very large project. World Food Program is coordinating, but there are eight donors in all. USAID is the major one, with its fifteen thousand tons of rice, but there are Germans, Swiss, UNDP. UNICEF is coming in on the transport costs. It isn't very sexy for UNICEF to do transport, but that is what we need.

"I have hopes of the World Bank coming in, too, but José Bronfmann is not at all convinced. In fact he read me the riot act about food aid skewing local markets. He'd be reconciled only if it were food for work. I'm all for food-for-work projects, but the south has been so neglected in development, and the crisis is so imminent that we can't hold off to identify and set up work schemes unless there are obvious ones to hand. I don't happen to share the Bank philosophy.

"And the local markets are skewed anyway. This year twenty-three thousand tons of maize and nine thousand tons of manioc were exported from the port of Tulear. A colleague discovered in February that fifteen hundred tons of manioc were waiting in Tulear for export to France — for animal feed! We tried to get a European Community loan to buy it back for the starving people, but it took so long that the manioc was exported anyhow."

> *Me:* So some people are getting rich even in the drought.
> *David:* A few people are getting *very* rich. Now, how well do you
> know Jean de Heaulme?
> *Me:* Well, um — well.
> *David:* What is he like? I have never met him.
> *Me:* Courteous. No, courtly. Devoted to the south. Why?
> *David:* The reason I wanted privacy is that I just learned yesterday
> there is a problem with the fifteen-thousand-ton shipment of
> rice. You can imagine that that quantity is coming on a very big
> boat indeed. Well, it's too big to get into Tulear harbor past the

coral reef. We've calculated that if we can offload forty-five hundred tons it will lighten the ship enough to fit at Tulear. So it seems the first port of call will be Fort Dauphin — this week.

Me: Wonderful! But how can such a huge ship fit in Fort Dauphin?

David: They load the sisal with lighters. They can unload rice the same way, however far out the ship needs to anchor. But the port warehouses at Fort Dauphin have the last World Food Project food rotting in them now. I need to jump those warehouses and move this rice quickly — and intact. We need real mobilization. De Heaulme is obviously influential. In short, do you think it would be appropriate to enlist his help?

Me: Okay. Of course, he's a businessman, and I don't know what he needs to do to operate in this country. But I do know that he has an extraordinary commitment to the south — people and land. He is sick at shutting down the sisal this month, not so much because it is money out of his pocket, but because of what it does to his workers. The de Heaulmes are really more feudal lords than capitalists. Feudalism obviously has its downside, but the upside is obligation to others. If you really want my opinion, Monsieur de Heaulme is a prince among men.

SOS: Save Our South! David Fletcher went on the national news program with a video he took with his own little camcorder: skeletal people and blasted crops. The rest of Madagascar watched. Plateau people dug into their own slim pockets to fund a national organization with an English name: Save Our South, SOS. Malagasy medical students and nurses banded together as ASOS, a nongovernmental agency (NGO) for emergency relief. I had been wrong. The people of the capital did care, once they knew what the south was suffering.

The aid community swung into action. Swiss logistics experts sorted out how the trucks of Fort Dauphin could switch over from carrying sisal to hauling sacks of rice and manioc to distant villages. That allowed people to stay at home and preserve their social order rather than trek to handout centers in the towns. Japanese aid workers built a huge underground water cistern by the Mandrare River. The Japanese and UNICEF provided cistern trucks to provision thirsty towns and villages. A host of foreign NGOs, like Aide Contre la Faim and Médecins Sans Frontières, arrived with earnest European volunteers to run shelters and feeding programs. The center of the program was the de Heaulme warehouses and trucks and drivers. Mobilization needed something to mobilize, and the de Heaulme empire was the only organization capable of responding.

Jean de Heaulme notes with great pride that more than ninety-five percent of the donated food that his people handled actually reached its destination. In most famines, aid agencies are proud if half of it is delivered as promised to remote rural areas.

Still the crisis deepened. The rains failed for a second year. People began to call it the Drought of the Century. In 1992 I traveled far from Berenty with UNICEF, to village food distribution centers, to hospices for mothers with toddlers in every stage of malnutrition, to a village that once owned five hundred zebu and now had twenty. (Prices of cattle on the hoof plummet in famine time, even as prices of any kind of food skyrocket.) Most of the time I was at Berenty with the Earthwatchers, eating lobster and roast beef, with cheese omelets for the vegetarians. As economist Amartya Sen trumpets to the world, there is always food for those who can pay. Famines are not about drought but about entitlement. Even in Androy, people did not die because there was no food available; they died because they could not afford to buy it.

In 1992 half a dozen doctors and nurses happened to join one Earthwatch team. We went to see the hospital at Amboasary. The doctor in charge of the hospital showed us around filthy wards, the glass long since gone from the windows. He picked up a two-year-old in his arms, unconscious, flaccid as a tiny rag doll.

"We will save this child," said the doctor. "I want to show him to you because he has just been brought in. This is starvation. But even in this condition we can save him, with feeding little by little. What we cannot do is change the surrounding state of the countryside, or the state of Amboasary town. I was trained in France; I have an education like yours. It has taken me two years to realize that my one medical goal in this town is to persuade the people to use latrines. Nothing of the fancy medicine I learned, the medicine I would like to practice. Latrines. If we succeed, we may, we may just, avoid the epidemics that follow famine."

That same day we saw a family walk in totally naked to the soup kitchen run by the Daughters of Charity, the successors of Soeur Gabrielle. Three of the Earthwatch medical people, who had never been in a developing country before, were too shocked to even speak for the rest of the day. Jim Sellers, another Earthwatcher, seemed strangely confident as he strode among the temporary straw huts in the famine camp. He went away and helped set up an NGO called Starfish, to provide medical volunteers and supplies for Madagascar.

At Berenty itself, a child did *not* die in every family. The World Food Program fed malnourished children there as it did elsewhere. For those who were not so badly off, the plantation manager and his wife, Monsieur and Madame Rakotomalala, bought rice and corn and manioc in town at wholesale prices and resold it at cost, avoiding the many-hundred-percent markup for merchants' grain sold by the Nestlé tinful. When I asked the Rakotomalalas what their best memory had been of their decades in Berenty, they immediately said it was getting food to distribute at cost, first in the famine, then in the lean season in later years, so that people could afford to buy.

Helen Crowley, meanwhile, with her long red hair swinging and masses of Tandroy silver bracelets jingling on her wrist, was deep into her project of managing Berenty forest. Jean de Heaulme says frankly that she saved the forest, if only in her work to conquer the invading cissus vine. Cissus is an African plant that had buried the trees in haystacklike heaps of succulent stems. Helen supervised work gangs that cut and hauled the stuff off physically, armed with gardening gloves imported from the outer world, because cissus is filled with spicules like poisonous fiberglass. Helen also planted nurseries of young tamarinds. She organized visiting researchers and began the task — still unfinished — of coordinating scientific knowledge.

The overseas famine volunteers congregated in Fort Dauphin every weekend. All week they spooned gruel into dying babies, comforted emaciated mothers, fought the breakdown of recalcitrant food trucks, checked tallies to guard the food from going astray. Many were shocked to learn that when village families distributed food, it went first to men, then to women, then to healthy children, not to the smallest or the sickest ones. This is the power hierarchy, of course, but in the harsh Darwinian calculus, breeding adults are the most valuable survivors. Rephrased in cultural terms, it is the clan that must live. Volunteers who had crossed continents to save seal-eyed suffering children dealt all week long with the knowledge that in some ways the clan's cattle mattered even more. On Saturdays the Aid Gang danced all night long at the Panorama Disco of Fort Dauphin to recover.

Helen remembers being amazed by the way people who are far from home and under stress can abandon every rule of their own culture. The Aid Gang swapped partners in a kind of frenzy. Everybody knew all about everyone else's affairs to boot. The Antananarivo plane on Sunday brought in fresh potential mates and swept others away to the sound of jealous screams and breaking hearts. Not to mention hair-pulling, eye-gouging fights outside the Panorama Disco. Social life in Fort Dauphin had never been so *interesting*.

Finally, in October of 1992 the rains returned. People went back to their villages to plant crops, though many needed to be given hoes to break the soil — they had sold everything to survive.

The World Food Program had an intense internal debate about whether to pull out when the crisis ended. Were they mandated to do just emergency relief, or could they take on long-term development? David Fletcher convinced WFP that Androy was a region under perpetual threat of famine. He saw both a moral and a practical obligation to continue WFP aid through food-for-work projects chosen from proposals made by villagers themselves for initiatives like local irrigation or cooperatives to market crops. Such projects might encourage an increase in the food supply of the entire region. UNICEF agreed and set up a program of drilling bore-holes for deep wells. In the villages around the great reserve of Andohahela, which straddles the rainfall line between rainforest and spiny desert, the World Wildlife Fund had to become almost a development agency rather than one simply for wildlife conservation. Other NGOs also settled in for the long haul, particularly the Japanese Southern Cross, which replants areas of spiny forest that have been cut for planks and charcoal.

At the end of the drought and famine of 1991–92, Androy was less isolated than ever before — practically a part of the modern world.

11

Here the Children Inherit

Berenty, 2000

☙

By the year 2000 Madagascar was one of the poorest countries in the world. Cyclones, droughts, Western trade barriers to agricultural goods, debt payments, and World Bank–IMF restrictions all reinforced the internal plague of mismanagement and corruption. An average Malagasy lived like an American earning $766 per year, a third lower than their standard in 1975. Nobody is average, of course. Two-thirds of the population got by on less than a dollar a day. A few profited handsomely. It seemed a miracle that Madagascar could be so poor and yet so peaceful. The Malagasy family remained strong and still remains the center of most people's universe. Life expectancy and children's education were better than the income statistic would suggest. Child survival improved little by little even while incomes fell.

One pinpoint area did flourish. A free trade zone in Antananarivo, physically just a couple of square kilometers of factories, offered a hundred thousand jobs. The workers mostly made textiles and clothing for foreign companies like the Gap and Victoria's Secret. A hundred thousand jobs is a lot of hard cash for a city of two million, even at a minimum wage of about twenty-three dollars a month. The cash boosted everything, from house construction to more piles of oranges sold by the roadside.

"With globalization, countries like France don't know what is hitting them," announced Jean de Heaulme. We were driving north of Tulear on the west coast, where he wanted to show me his latest investment, a little seaside hotel convenient to one of the world's great barrier reefs. The sun blazed down on white beach and cerulean sea to our left, with remnants of the western version of spiny forest poking up beside us on the inland side. Jean was proudly taking me on the rounds of his new projects — expansion in Fort Dauphin and Tulear, and even a dream of bringing tourism to Analabé, the baobab forest near Morondava. The four members of the next de Heaulme generation were all settled in Madagascar, running branches of the family businesses, looking to the future.

Jean hurled the four-by-four at the rutted sand that called itself a road, then slowed to his usual car-conserving pace. He shouted over the motor noise, "Globalization changes everything! Look at France! Its workers make more and more demands for social security and shorter hours, so industry flees to places like Madagascar. Even Michelin Tires has closed its factory. Practically a symbol of France, and they moved to where wages are cheaper. Did you know the first Michelin tires were made out of euphorbia rubber from the south of Madagascar? After almost a hundred years, now Michelin leaves France."

"Well," I thought to myself, "we all grow more and more conservative as we grow older. A man in his seventies should be allowed to grumble."

But Jean went right on. "Madagascar doesn't know what can hit it, either. My son Henry has come back to Madagascar with his whole family. Henry does electrical construction and installation for the firms in the free trade zone. One of his jobs was to set up a blue-jeans factory. Heavy equipment, big steel cutting tables, industrial sewing machines. His brief was to construct it in such a way that all that equipment could be packed into containers in forty-eight hours. The owners want to be able to move their investment out in a hurry. Those firms don't buy their buildings, either. They rent, even at high prices. The first whiff of political unrest, or simply more profits opening up in another country, and in two days the whole factory sails away."

"Well," I thought, "I guess Jean is right! Globalization is very, very frightening."

I also thought how very different from Berenty and the other de Heaulme enterprises! Feudalism, as I had said to David Fletcher, has its obvious downside. Still, it involves a long-term commitment — owners bound to land and to their employees generation after generation, even if the lion's share of profits goes to the rich. The lion's share from that blue-jeans factory goes to the rich as well — but those rich are in another country.

I also thought how different Berenty is from the efforts of major conservation agencies in Madagascar. They have done a great deal to challenge the degradation of the land. The large reserves of rainforest and dry western forest, a legacy of the colonial era, are administered by ANGAP, a quasi-governmental organization set up by that multidonor World Bank mission. USAID and other donors made Madagascar the target of their biggest biodiversity program. Conservation organizations worked with the donors: the World Wildlife Fund, Conservation International, Stony Brook, Wildlife Conservation Society, Durrell Wildlife Conservation Trust, Missouri Botanical Garden, Peregrine Fund — and on and on. Development groups like CARE and Cornell Agriculture labored alongside the biologists to bring benefits directly to the rural people of each region.

Did it work? Pretty well. Not well enough. The conservation enterprise slowed the pace of forest destruction in protected areas, but destruction accelerated elsewhere. The reserves themselves, with their injections of Western cash, were bright spots in Madagascar's economy, like the free trade zone. The most durable gain may be that a generation of young Malagasy biologists has grown up with Western training and support and a passion for addressing the environmental needs of their own country.

The big reserves play host to the tourist trade. Hotels have been built and guides trained to take people lemur-spotting. In some years tourism has been Madagascar's single greatest source of foreign exchange. Tourism looks so good because producer prices for coffee and tea have fallen and fallen, so agriculture in Third World countries has to run three times as hard just to stay in the same place. Here tourism essentially means ecotourism, with lemurs as a trump card; few visitors will travel that far just to find a beach. Ecotourists pay for the unspoiled beauty of the forest itself, not for what can be taken out of the forest and sold, so well-managed tourism is a major goal.

The grand, important government reserves still look at Berenty a little enviously. Berenty is so small that it should be totally irrelevant in the much larger picture of emerging conservation in Madagascar, except for one thing. It works.

The de Heaulmes charge high prices, limit the visitors to forty-four a night, and get away with it. Undemocratic? Of course. Berenty is beyond the reach of backpackers, though Malagasy schoolchildren are not charged at all. Good business? Of course. It rakes in money. Berenty is too tame for purist tourists, who think wide human paths don't look natural, even when a troop of ringtails saunters down the path on their daily rounds, let alone when the creatures come and scent-mark the restaurant bougainvillea. Yes, much too tame. All the same, Berenty remains the high point of Madagascar for many visitors. They appreciate being able to relax in the knowledge that their car will not break down, their beds will be ready, the shower runs water, and, above all, lemurs will reliably fill the photo frame.

Guests arriving from abroad are taken in charge at the de Heaulme–owned hotel in Fort Dauphin. Chauffeurs and guides are de Heaulme employees. The itinerary for one or two or three days is planned to make the most of the little reserve. There are bird walks at dawn, lemur walks in the afternoon, the sisal factory and the Museum of Androy when the animals are sleeping, and the magical moonlit walk in the spiny forest, where the tiny eyes of mouse lemurs and lepilemurs blaze back at the flashlights of the guides. Never mind that the strip of spiny forest looks insignificant by daylight, or that the distant adventure is a short amble from the main gate if you happen to know the way. Whenever I want to see mouse lemurs now, I join the tourists and the sharp-eyed guides in the forest, where moonlight and flashlight conspire to turn the spires of fantiolotse into a world surreal beyond all imaginings.

"Please do not feed the lemurs!" proclaims a new placard by the thatched kiosk where the tourist buses unload. The guides explain, in French, English, German, Japanese: "Bananas are bad for lemurs! They nourish themselves better from the forest. You might even be scratched or bitten yourself." Wild lemurs are very polite toward people, but I am afraid that some visitor — worse, some child — will grab one around the middle and scare it into raking a canine through the skin of a person who traveled around the world for the experience.

The Science Tribe has watched the population of Tourist Front ringtails and brown lemurs grow and grow and grow. Ever-available water and scraps and, till recently, bananas, mean that their infants have been buffered against dying in bad years, while troops only fifty yards back in the woods are still subject to more natural checks and balances. The high level of aggression by Frightful Fan and her ilk does have something to do with the tourists' bounty.

It is hard to explain to visitors why they can't feed the lemurs. They know that in the past people came here with bunches of bananas and were rewarded with photographs of lemurs on their shoulders and the feel of soft lemur fur against their ears. It would even be hard to explain to Frightful Fan and Shadow. They just loved bananas. Now they feel the pinch.

The banana ban is also hard on the guides. Unhappy tourists don't tip. Guides, mostly Tanosy from Fort Dauphin, are the new elite. They are chosen for their language skills, then they learn from each other how to see the animals. Sylvestre Mbola, the only one who grew up in Berenty itself, honed his English by talking to American university students, jotting earnest phrases in his little notebook. On the rare occasions when I did not look busy, he would corner me with impossible questions. "When is it correct to use the present continuous to indicate the future, as in 'I am going to meet your group again after lunch'? In what circumstances would you actually *say*, 'A woman needs a man like a fish needs a bicycle'?"

"What is the worst thing about being a guide?" I asked Benoît Damy, resplendent in his white windbreaker and dark dark glasses.

"Oh, the worst thing is if the group have slightly different treatment. If some are in new bungalows and some in the older houses, they always grumble out of jealousy. The next worse thing is if you have to combine groups. Germans and Swiss and English want to be out in the forest all the time, from five A.M. bird watching until late at night for nocturnal lemurs. French want to eat on time, and Japanese just want to take each other's pictures. With two lots in a single car, one of them inevitably wants to go home earlier! Each alone is fine — but it is very hard work to deal with two different groups at once.

"All the same," added Benoît, "I like it, because I like people. Before doing this, I was the English and science teacher at the Fort Dauphin lycée. Guiding ecotourists is a kind of teaching. Except that unlike school pupils, they come here very eager to learn! I have two small sons. Here there is a tradition that sons follow fathers in the same job. Monsieur de Heaulme even keeps on old people here, when they are retired — basically a charitable deed. My own sons can do whatever they want in life, but I would be happy if they want to be guides."

"Suddenly there was a huge noise, like an approaching car, VROOOM, *and the big wind hit us!"* Théophile Zafison told me, "It was October 2, 1999. I was here guiding a party of nineteen French people. They arrived in time for the afternoon walk at three P.M. Fortunately they complained that it was too hot, so they wanted to leave the forest quickly — even though it was not really hot, only October. So they were all drinking at the cafeteria when it began. First, about four P.M., the sky just began to cloud up — before that it was blue. Then around four-thirty a little wind came up from the south, kicking up big, twirling dust devils. Then VROOOM, the wind hit us. Everybody ran for cover: the tourists to their rooms, myself to the guides' house. Soon the roofs came off Bungalows seven and eight, which happened to hold two elderly couples. The tourists hid under their beds. They must have had to lie very flat!

"It only lasted about two hours. Then people emerged. We four guides went down to the restaurant to see about feeding the clients. But the roof was gone!"

Clément, the headwaiter, and his crew were walking from Berenty village toward the restaurant just as the storm hit. They bent over double against the wind — fortunately no one was on a bicycle. A few of them clawed their way to shelter in the airplane hangar, while Clément and four others huddled against a wall beside the restaurant porch. They stayed there for two hours, listening to the storm tear huge strips of corrugated iron off the restaurant roof, while the thatched picnic pavilion collapsed on its support posts. When the wind stopped, guides came to find cooks and waiters surveying the wreckage in a decapitated restaurant full of cement dust.

Fortunately, the basics of dinner are cooked at lunchtime. The chef made cold chicken sandwiches for everyone. Berenty was absolutely full — forty-four overnight visitors. A contingent of Germans and Swiss had arrived exactly as the storm hit. They did not dare move away from the bungalows. They ate sandwiches and soda and beer served by their guides in their tour bus, under the bus roof lights — the only working electric lights on the plantation. They cheered up when they had had enough beer. Zafison's French group wanted proper dinner in the restaurant, true to national form, but they had to eat by flashlight, since it was still too windy to keep candles alight in a roofless building.

After the storm, tourism just carried on. It was high season, with sixty to seventy people a day, counting the ones who came only for lunch. Nobody canceled. There was a long waiting list to stay at Berenty. It took a week to restore the electricity and water. The tourists bought expensive bottled water to wash in and flushed the toilets with buckets of river water. Meanwhile the kitchen staff cooked and washed up for seventy using just water buckets. Monsieur Rakotomalala, the plantation manager, and his team of mechanics, carpenters, and electricians had to repair and rebuild. They cleared forest paths and uncovered wells so that the tractor could deliver water to the house reservoirs. Not to mention rebuilding houses in Berenty village, where people had huddled twenty to a room in the buildings made of ce-

ment; wooden houses blew away. In a place like Berenty, there's no re-
pairman to call if the work can't be done on the spot.

Randry, Tahiry, and Dina, three of Hanta's students, were studying
ringtails with Ethan Pride, a doctoral student from Princeton. In the
cement student house it was so dark during the storm that they could
not see, only hear, the trees lashing back and forth in the forest and rat-
tling against each other. They had no idea of the damage till the next
day. Ethan said, "When we went out in the morning, we couldn't even
find the forest paths. We scrambled over fallen tree trunks until we located our lemur troops. Tough beasts. They were all still there — every
individual. The only casualty I saw was one sifaka, sitting curled up
with its arms over its head. I do not know whether it was wounded or
simply shocked. As far as the ringtails are concerned, they just have a
new set of paths to follow along fallen trunks, and a new set of twigs to
scent-mark."

Finally the students reached the house of Filomana and his wife,
Ndaisoa. Filomana was a forest guardian, much photographed because
he usually sported not only a spear but a goatskin hat with a fringe of
long black hair, which he wore with great panache. One of his small
sons played the valiha, its haunting chords totally in keeping with the
forest bird songs, well worth the occasional tourist tip.

Filomana lived with his wife and their three youngest children in a
little hut at the bottom of Banyan Trail, next to the cattle drove. I admired them greatly. Ndaisoa said she liked living in the forest. She
could always walk the couple of kilometers to Berenty village if she
wanted to see her friends. When she was about to give birth, Monsieur
Rakotomalala, the plantation manager, would drive her all the way to
the maternity clinic in Amboasary. Filomana also boasted that he liked
staying away from the backbiting and rumors of the village. "In the
forest I am king!" he proclaimed. At one point they tried to give Hanta
and me a live duck for our courtesy in visiting them. Hanta protested
that we absolutely could not take the duck home on the airplane next
day. "That's your problem!" retorted Filomana.

On the evening of the storm, it happened that the older children
from Filomana's previous marriages were all visiting for the weekend.

The two parents and ten kids clung to each other in the tiny wooden hut as the wind roared around it. The house stood in a grove of majestic acacia trees. It turns out that acacias are the most vulnerable trees of all. That night a quarter of the acacias broke off short or had their roots torn out of the ground. All around the little house, trees crashed to earth — sixty-foot-tall trees with trunks three feet in diameter.

No trees fell on the house. In the morning Filomana and Ndaisoa and all the children emerged unscathed.

"Matthew's parable says, go work in the vineyard: go help build Berenty's school!" With Berenty's new prosperity, and the influx of educated guides and waiters from Fort Dauphin, it was clear that the school must reopen. The old plantation school had closed when its operations were suspended under Malagasy socialism. The government school that succeeded it closed after the teachers' salaries went unpaid for years.

Hanta and I went to hear Pierre-Robson, the Catholic catechist, exhort his congregation in the church that Jean had built for Chantal's wedding. The catechist, who looked to be in his early thirties, was short, with a mustache and a little sticky-out goatee. That meant he was in mourning, for otherwise it is rare here to dare a beard, or even to be able to grow one. Tanosy and Tandroy are, like Jacob, smooth men. The congregation sang like mad, led by a soprano with green headscarf, purple pleated skirt, a baby tucked in her lap, and an actual hymnbook, shared with another soprano, for the words. Their voices carried, perhaps, into the next county. The rest of the women sang harmony; the baritones and tenors, antiphony. Hallelujah!

Pierre-Robson launched into his sermon — pure, magical oratory. He pulled every trick of crescendo and pause, fixing on the assembly and sweeping them into a serious whisper, then dropping into a colloquial joke and back around the gamut again. In half an hour he did not once shift his feet, but did it all with voice and eyes and a few pointings of the hand. I was transfixed. Hanta, who actually understood what he was saying, said the text was from Matthew, the parable of the son who claimed that he would labor in the field and did not, as against the son who said he would not work but did. Which is the better Christian? Indeed, if there are people in Berenty who say they are not Christian, but actually come to help build the new school, are they not better than those who merely stand and sing in church?

Pierre-Robson has children, and he wants them to be educated. He asked his congregation some time ago if they wanted their own kids to go to school. Yes, they did. They really, really did. What should they do then to get a teacher? Ask Monsieur de Heaulme, they said, to pay for a teacher's salary. And to repair the derelict school? Ask Monsieur de Heaulme, they said, to rebuild the school. So the catechist asked Monsieur de Heaulme — who said yes. Yes, but on condition that the parents contribute. By the time the government school collapsed, some years before, parents literally would not buy their kids so much as a pencil. When Hanta visited the school in its last days, she found all the children sharing a single pencil, which they passed around in turn to learn to write.

The sermon galvanized people to clean up a big lumber shed and get it ready for Monsieur de Heaulme to put in windowpanes and blackboard and benches. Parents must pay fifteen hundred francs a month in fees, all of twenty-four cents. The twenty-year-old teacher, Prospère Sambiavy, had already arrived, freshly graduated from Catholic high school and looking absolutely terrified.

Two weeks later Hanta and I went to see Prospère register his first class. It is wise for any project to start small in Madagascar. Only twenty of the two hundred or so Berenty kids aged seven to thirteen would be accepted in the first first grade. A dozen mothers waited on benches, each nursing the latest baby. The woman beside me had borne ten children, including two sets of twins. Six of them lived, four had died. Oddly, all the twins survived. Her infant, maybe five months old, sucked my knuckle trustingly and looked at me with eyes like pools of chocolate from under a frilly white cap, his main apparel.

She showed me the precious birth certificate for the schoolchild she was registering. It was a long document typed in duplicate on something that had the consistency of rice paper, brownish and much folded, finished off with a red stamp. Hanta says that to get the certificate you have to go to the official center, in this case Amboasary town, and commonly bribe an official — a chicken for a girl, sometimes as much as a pig for a boy. Without the certificate, it is impossible to enter school. The women's organization Soroptimist International is now running campaigns to register children en masse, with the volunteers supervising officials to see that they don't take bribes. I crossed my fingers in hope that Berenty's school will continue and expand until the chocolate-eyed baby can attend in his turn.

A year later, Hanta and John Walker and I returned to the school bearing the photographs we had taken of the entering class. Prospère had coped so well that his first class actually stayed on instead of dropping out, as so many Third World kids do, confronted with the apparent pointlessness of school. Now he was teaching second grade as well as a new first grade. The pupils showed off for the visitors, greeting us with a chorus of "Bon-JOUR, Mon-sieur." The stars of the second grade presented a mini-skit: "Bonjour, Monsieur. Bonjour, Madame. Ça va? Ça va, et vous?" shaking hands with each other formally in front of the chalky blackboard. They ended with the round that first-year French students sing all over the world, "Le coq est mort." I chimed in, which reduced the class to hysteria.

Hanta asked them, "Why do you go to school?" The children looked at each other, then one bright spark gave the obvious answer: "To learn French." The others all nodded in agreement. At Berenty, as throughout Madagascar, the way forward is to learn French. And soon, English. Ex-colonies have spent all of the past century gearing up toward globalization.

I asked, in every way I could think of, if Berenty's workers were content. Of course, as the boss's friend, I would never get an impolite answer. Plenty of people were eager to tell me that they would like higher wages. Several people said they wanted a bigger school, with enough grades and teachers to give the children a real future. I was surprised that no one raised what would have been my first priorities: pumped water and decent latrines. It seems that they accept traditional village conditions in that regard, even in the year 2000.

Berenty still came as a shock to many tourists who had never seen a real village. The traditional north-south alignment of the Tandroy houses, their traditional small size, and the workers' names stenciled by the doors made the plantation village look to Westerners like the worst kind of factory town. But the workers uniformly agreed that there was no real labor unrest. On other plantations, yes, but at Berenty, no. Why not, if their wages are so low?

Over and over, I heard the same phrase: "Here the sons inherit from the fathers." (I prefer to say, "Here the children inherit," because it is true for women too.) Field crew bosses, factory workers, women sisal sorters, Lahivano the chauffeur, Alexandre the factory commander, and Tsiaketraky, the Father-and-Mother, all used the same phrase. They see a future for their families. They repeated, almost as often, "We have confidence in Monsieur de Heaulme."

Berenty village in 1999 held 2,876 people, over half of them under fifteen, according to the careful tally of Alexandre Mosa, who was both the factory commander and the elected village secretary. That population was much lower than the numbers before the 1992 famine, and much, much lower than in the golden age of the 1950s and '60s. The sisal industry carries on in large part because of the interplay of wage earning with traditional life. Sisal cutters leave after work at nine or ten A.M. to return to their own fields, cattle, and children. For families living in Berenty village who came from elsewhere and so had no traditional land, Monsieur de Heaulme allocated plots for vegetables and grazing for their cattle. Salaries were never meant to cover everything.

Of course there had been friction. In the '92 famine, nonlocal Berenty employees turned to eating wild prickly pear fruit, which was also the local fallback food in times of famine. The village split into two rival communes: the employees and the nonemployed. That rift eventually died down. By 2000 the elected commune presidents and their secretaries were all brothers-in-law.

Voting in both local and national elections sounds potentially fair. In one room, people take a sheaf of colored ballots and a single envelope. Then, in an inner room, they put the ballot of their choice into the envelope, and the envelope into the voting box. Envelopes and col-

ored ballots are counted in public by at least four officials, plus delegates from all the parties, on a table in the open market where the entire populace is free to watch. Of course, peer pressure sways the vote,
not to mention other inducements.

Disputes between people within the village are judged by a panel of
four respected elders, including, of course, the grandest of all, Tsiaketraky, He-Who-Cannot-Be-Thrown-to-Earth. The fine for theft, such
as stealing a bicycle, is a chicken and thirty thousand francs in cash
(about five dollars), paid to the victim in compensation. The judgments are conducted in public. The whole community knows the
thief's identity and the fine to be paid. As of 2000, the community
was calm. But it was calm in a time of fairly good rains and of steady
employment.

*Richard and I met Henry de Heaulme in the Colbert salon bar in
Antananarivo.* This was the same quiet room with crimson plush sofas
where Henry's father, Jean, and his grandfather, Monsieur Henry de
Heaulme, had once asked me whether WWF might take over Berenty
Reserve, when the family feared they could not save it. We settled
down to gin-and-tonics, though I held out for Madagascar's lychee-
fruit vermouth, with its overtone of herbs that rises to perfume the
back of your nose.

Henry was the last of Jean and Aline's children to return to Madagascar, after attending one of the prestigious French *grand écoles* and
starting a first career in France. In a coincidence that would seem far
too contrived in fiction, when Henry committed himself to Madagascar, his wife, Pascale, had to give up her work as a doctor of pharmacy
— in the Hospital of the Salpêtrière in Paris! It was the Salpêtrière that
sent out the Daughters of the King to Louis XIV's farflung colonies,
including Françoise Châtelain, the pink girl who was the first de
Heaulme ancestor in Fort Dauphin.

Hanta and her husband came to join us, Ratovonirina silent and
strong and smiling as usual, Hanta gaily talkative as usual, done up in
fawn jersey with a heavy, heavy, cream silk lamba around her shoulders,
gold earrings swinging from her ears. We all asked Henry about the future of Berenty.

"The future of Berenty? Widen the horizon. The sisal is not *rentable* — not profitable. A cold capitalist would say, cut off the dead limb. Tourism is profitable, but at Berenty it cannot expand without killing the forest. Tourism employs few people — only two hundred and fifty, counting Fort Dauphin, very few of them Tandroy of the region. Sisal, in contrast, employs many — still around six hundred. But surely the workers realize that there is no reinvestment, no renewal of machinery, no expansion of fields. Surely they realize that lack of maintenance is equivalent to a slow stop."

"They *don't* realize it is stopping!" Hanta challenged him in her usual forthright style. "What about the son of Tsiaketraky? I asked him that directly, and he said he had faith in the sisal and in the de Heaulmes. He is settled there, he thinks for life, with his two wives and his children in school."

"Yes, but he is a sisal commander, isn't he? His father is practically king, so of course he expects to go right on being king."

"Well, what are you planning to do about it?"

"Well, a capitalist would say shut it down."

I chimed in, "But it isn't capitalism. It is a feudal domain. And that is why it works at all."

"That," said Henry, "is just the problem. It *is* a feudal domain. We have, supposedly, the rights of *usus* and *fructus* and *abusus*." (I grimaced at his deftly sarcastic link between the de Heaulmes' usufruct of land with the capitalists' power to abuse people.) "But when you come down to it, Tsiaketraky has full right to pasture his cattle and grow his crops on land that is also in some sense ours, and all the people who plant corn between the rows of sisal have their rights, and much of the land is set aside for gardens for the people who have none — and all the moral obligation to find them jobs if the sisal closes . . . The rights and wrongs are so tangled up that it is impossible to know what to do."

"So what will you do?"

"I don't know. Any ideas?"

What future for the children's children? The sisal machinery has not been replaced since the 1950s. Sisal at the turn of the millennium made just enough money to break even. There were some new markets:

China and, amazingly, Mexico, where the plant evolved. Mexican wages had risen too high to make harvesting sisal profitable in their own country; an effective machine has never been invented to do the job of cutting. So Mexican spinning factories wanted Madagascar's sisal to keep their own wheels turning.

Tourism is the moneymaker, but it does not provide jobs for the unskilled — Tandroy who would otherwise be field or factory workers. What other possibilities might there be for future diversification? One is livestock. Worked-out sisal fields are turned one by one into pasture. Madagascar's population is growing, and even growing richer. People will want beef. Before World War II, Androy exported at least ten thousand head of cattle a year to Tamatave, Réunion, and Mauritius, along with two thousand sheep and goats. The animals used to be hoisted alive, kicking and bawling, with a great strap under their bellies, from lighters into the transport ship. Why not export beef again, this time humanely, with improved stock and using a local abattoir and freezer? Another possibility is ostriches. The African cousins of Madagascar's extinct elephant birds are ideally suited to the climate of Androy. In a little experimental pen at Berenty, young ostriches stare down from their huge, fringed eyes at astonished tourists. Though the land is semidesert, Androy was always the powerhouse of the region's economy: hungry in famine years, but a place that exported food in the years of plenty.

Much depends on Fort Dauphin and on hopes for a new port. That in turn depends on government approval of a proposed mine to extract titanium sand from the fossil dunes around Fort Dauphin. That is another whole story for another book someday. It's enough to say here that *if* the mine is approved, and *if* the World Bank sees fit to back the construction of a large, safe port for Fort Dauphin, the whole region's economy could change. Of course, development does not necessarily make poor people richer; honest politics and bargaining power are needed in order for the poor to share in any of the wealth.

Meanwhile, an AIDS epidemic hangs over Madagascar like a tidal wave about to crash onto the shore. Only a few hundred cases are known so far, which means there are actually many more. Very few people in Madagascar have any idea what the epidemic will mean. They have only to look next door to South Africa and Zimbabwe to see countries where forty percent of adults are infected. Uninhibited sexual mores and the already wide spread of gonorrhea and syphilis set Madagascar up to be the next place where most adults die young.

The population cannot continue to grow as fast as it has been growing. But only prosperity — not poverty, and certainly not AIDS — will curb it. As long as children are the only bulwark against uncertain fate, you cannot expect people to limit family size. The birth rate will fall only after improvements are made in health and schooling and material wealth, not before.

Lahivano the chauffeur asked us to his home. He had driven me around and also listened to all the interviews — occasionally pointing out something else that was important for me to ask, like asking Jaona the Never-Suckled about being imprisoned during the Tandroy revolt of '71. In 1999 Hanta and I went to meet Lahivano's wife, Georgette, who works as a sisal sorter. All eight children and the grandchildren crowded into the tiny floor space of one of their houses to welcome us, an unbelievable mass of small-sized humanity.

Hanta lit into Lahivano later about his oldest daughter. "Don't you think Kazy Elvina should hold off? She has three children already — what is she, eighteen now? And her lover still can't afford a cow so he can marry her and adopt their children into his own clan. They are all still your responsibility! Those kids will never eat their fill; they'll never go to school."

Lahivano explained, "You just don't see it the way we do. We love children! Children are always welcome, and grandparents are glad to feed them."

"Do you know about birth control?"

"Of course. Everybody knows about birth control. It's unhealthy, with all those chemicals."

"Why not count days?" persisted Hanta.

"Hey, get serious," chuckled Lahivano. "It's hard to go without sex for a whole week — even for a woman."

So the next year when we went back, we visited nineteen-year-old

Kazy Elvina and her fourth baby. She was being "kept hot" inside the house. A tent of bright cloths was draped over the bed, like a regal four-poster, to keep away evil spirits and the chills that bring out malarial fever. Kazy Elvina's face mask — the yellow aloe paste that protects her from harm and restores her beauty after childbirth — was flaking off in patches.

The baby, already eighteen days old, was either premature or just small, a tiny scrap named Vola Lendovina (*vola* means silver, or money). She lay in a comalike sleep, curling and uncurling pink-palmed hands, sucking a little in her sleep with purplish lips. Her mother's milk had still not come in. At first Kazy Elvina cried and cried that she had so little milk, but now, two and a half weeks after giving birth, she was just numb.

Hanta asked if there were no local remedies to make the milk rise (they say rise, not let down). Mothers drink a concoction made from leaves of the strychnine tree after childbirth to shrink the uterus and discharge toxins, but they have nothing to induce milk. I desperately wanted to offer Western-style advice, but Kazy Elvina had borne four children, as many as I had, and her mother, Georgette, had borne eight. If they did not think that tinned milk mixed with Mandrare River water was something to feed a newborn, who was I to say differently, now that they had gone so far toward physical and emotional acceptance that the child was doomed? All I could offer was some paltry francs for habobo yogurt to build up the mother's own strength.

I almost could not bear to go back to see them. A month later, Lahivano told me the baby was still alive. There sat Kazy Elvina in her yellow face mask, still keeping hot in the bed. And there was Vola Lendovina, already with one little earring, plumped up like a balloon since we last saw her and swigging away at Kazy's balloonlike breast. When the baby was totally filled up, Kazy Elvina turned her daughter around to show us huge, huge eyes looking out at the world between curly lashes, in a round and smiling face. Six weeks old, out of immediate danger, with the whole family delighted to welcome yet another child.

The price of a return to the past, when rural people were stewards of their own land, treading lightly, would be too high to pay. How could population and consumption fall back to the levels of Robert Drury's time, before the intrusion of the outside world? AIDS, economic starvation, resurgence of clan war are not effective limits to population growth. People's numbers recover rapidly from such disasters. An actual return to past conditions would mean leaving the south prey to recurrent famines, which the outside world would know nothing of and care less about. Also, there would be no alternatives — no sisal or tourism, no livestock export, charcoal burning, titanium, or emigration to a place with jobs. No birth control, no birth clinic, no medicine for malaria. In a world where everyone is year by year more closely linked to everyone else, the outside world will not go away. The south may be poor, but it will never again be left alone. We must go forward, since we cannot go back.

If, as I hope, Androy is ready to change for the better, little Vola Lendovina may be the first of Kazy Elvina's children to go to school.

"You only accomplish something here if you build for decades or for generations," declared Jean de Heaulme. Richard and I had gone to see him in Fort Dauphin, at six P.M. in the last light of an evening when the town generator had been struck by lightning, soon after the turn of the new millennium.

Aline popped in from her office, where she had stayed late to do the accounts for Berenty's tourist business. Both Aline and Jean still work eight or ten hours a day, at an age when many other people are glad to retire. I eyed Aline's pale blue tailored dress with its ruffle of white lace at the low neckline. I ruefully realized that some people will always be chic. It was not just at that first luncheon, when I turned up in crumpled khakis, but over a lifetime that she has set the standard of elegance in Fort Dauphin.

Jean stood up from behind his formal desk, with the huge photomural above it of the Tandroy dance troupe with Jaona Tsiminono the Never-Suckled: men in loincloths and muscles and spears, kneeling women beating their drums — the same mural that hangs in Berenty's restaurant. From the next wall the stern visages of his father and his uncle Alain stared down at us. Nearby hung Jean's framed certificates of the French Legion of Honor and the National Order of Madagascar.

Jean motioned us to comfortable chairs, while darkness took possession of his office and the town. "Do you think," Richard asked him, "that your father could ever have imagined Berenty now? Did he have a vision of it with tourists, scientists, cinematographers?"

"Oh, no!" exclaimed Jean. "He would never have imagined that. What he did see was the need for conservation — not only the forest and the landscape, but the traditions. He would say, 'This place was so *formidable* [fantastic! grand! exciting!] that I want to preserve the image of what I found when I arrived. I am changing it myself, with the sisal, but there must be some witness that remains to what I found when I first came.' No, he welcomed you, Alison, and later Jean-Jacques Petter and other scientists, but he did not foresee that in saving some parts of Berenty for their beauty and their scientific fascination that the forest could later be commercially useful . . .

"My father was totally fascinated with every aspect of Madagascar. But even more, he created structures of society. He believed he was building to last. That was true at the national level, when he was vice president of the National Assembly that wrote the independence constitution. At Berenty he built the place where he expected to die.

"So 'seventy-five was a rupture, a breakage. Newspaper articles announced, 'De Heaulme, pack your bags! Leave in an airplane before you leave in a coffin!' For him it was unthinkable. But even when I was in jail then, I could not blame the Malagasy as a people. I remembered too well that the French had jailed other Frenchmen during World War II. I remembered that Malagasy abused Malagasy during the revolution of 'forty-seven. I could never see what Malagasy did to me in racial terms . . .

"My family have deep roots here. My next project is to build a museum for Fort Dauphin like the one at Berenty for Androy. A museum to show one thousand years of history of the Tanosy! Then tourists can learn that here we do have a history. Of course, it is my family's history as well. But much, much more important, townspeople can come to see the history of their own ancestors."

We left the deep darkness of the office for what seemed to be a film set: a thumping generator and brilliant white light projected from a spotlight. Eight or ten dark figures were silhouetted in front of the light as they labored to install a new transformer: a machine with bulbous ceramic towers like a modernist version of the *alo-alo* sculptures that Tandroy place on their tombs. The electricians were working on the hill slope beside the de Heaulme offices, on the same platform where Jean's friend Bernard Astraud first installed an electrical system. All very well to talk of history — the modern town is also a legacy of the de Heaulmes. I kept thinking over and over of Jean's conclusion:

"You only accomplish something here if you expect to remain for decades or for generations, to build for your children and grandchildren. That is what is wrong with conservationists, for all their ideals, and even the aid agencies that bring development. They do good work, but in the end, their work cannot last unless they are committed to Madagascar."

12

"This Is Anything But Idiot. This Is Whole"

Funeral at the Lucky Baobab, 2000

෯෩෩ච

"Please, I want to attend a funeral . . . I don't quite know how to say this," I said to Tsiaketraky, He-Who-Cannot-Be-Thrown-to-Earth.

"Tsiaketraky, you told me at the standing stone how to begin my book. I have written about the past, your story of King A-Thousand-Cannot-Lift-Him, Mahafaha the ferryman, and the coming of the de Heaulmes. I have written about famines and revolutions, even the Time of Bones of your own childhood. I have told about sisal workers and scientists and tourist guides, and about children going to the new school. I have written why Monsieur and Madame de Heaulme and their children remain in Madagascar. Now I want to end the story by saying Tandroy traditions are still strong, even in the modern world. That means I want to go to a funeral. Only — I've been talking to so many elderly people here to ask for their memories, and the last thing I want is for anyone to die!"

I felt uncomfortable asking him. I was embarrassed even beforehand. Tsiaketraky had seated me and Hanta on his two handmade wooden chairs on the porch of his village president's office at the northern end of Berenty estate. My discomfort was that sitting in the chair put my head higher than Tsiaketraky's as he squatted on the porch. When messengers came to speak to him, they crouched on bended knee to stay lower than their lord.

Tsiaketraky announced obliquely, "Everything I have now I owe to the French, from the day I came to work for Monsieur de Heaulme in 1951, at the age of eighteen." He rose to his full height and commandeered Lahivano the chauffeur with the same decisiveness as when he first took us to see the standing stone. They drove off together.

"I think he means that he will help," said Hanta. "He includes you and me with the French."

They soon reappeared, accompanied by a man in a vaguely military gray raincoat with brass buttons, a very dirty white shirt, and a grizzled beard. Tsiaketraky introduced him. "This is my friend Valiotaky [Troubled-by-Others'-Talk]. He is president of the adjoining village, Anjamahavelo [At the Lucky Baobab]. He is preparing to bury his older brother. I think he will invite you to the funeral."

"There will be two funerals," explained Valiotaky. "One is for just the intimate family, and then a public one for all of our friends, two weeks later. We should be ready for the first in about three weeks, when we know the auspicious day. If you really want to see Tandroy customs we will invite you to both funerals, even the one for just the family."

"When did your brother die?"

"A month ago." Well, that explained Valiotaky's appearance. It was taboo for him to wash his clothes or shave until his brother was buried. But even with the backing of Tsiaketraky, the Father-and-Mother, I was troubled. Was I really going to be a horrible paparazza, intruding on a family of strangers in their mourning?

At the moment Valiotaky's brother died, they killed a fine bull. Its breath mingled with the breath of the dying man and carried the spirit toward the place of the Ancestors. Then specialists — a particular clan whose task this is — sealed the body into an airtight coffin made of two corrugated iron roofing sheets welded together. (Even this first coffin costs as much as a zebu.) The coffin waited now in the dead man's house, watched day and night by two mourners, either two women or two men together.

In olden times people were buried within three days. This was partly because of disease and odor, but mainly because clan raids were so frequent that everyone feared an enemy clan would come and attack the family at this moment of distraction, and — horror of horrors — prevent the burial of the corpse. Now, however, the body is kept, not for a year or two, as in the neighboring Mahafaly tribe, but for a few weeks or a month. A diviner places magic beans on a mat to choose an auspicious day for the funeral. Meanwhile, the family is in a furor of preparation.

I read up about funerals. The one thing that stood out was that many guests have to give the dead man's family a zebu. Giving the equivalent in cash is all right, if it is defined as a zebu in an envelope. It depends, of course, on what kind of guest you are. I was a senior member of the plantation's Science Tribe, invited rather particularly. I felt I had to do something. I sealed 300,000 Madagascar francs (about fifty dollars) in an envelope, which I was told was the price of a not-very-large zebu, like the cow Richard had presented to my parents. A bull can cost as much as 500,000 francs. But prices have dropped this year (again, little rain), so my envelope might even hold a biggish cow.

The Village of the Lucky Baobab looked typically Tandroy. Some twenty wooden houses, a few with tin roofs, stood on bare earth. The corrals were to the east. Valiotaky's house was rather substantial, with a front porch and two separate rooms. The bed, table, bright cloths, and the radio playing the local station, Kaleta, meant that he was indeed a rich man. Valiotaky received his envelope graciously. I said, in what I hoped sounded like an official orating voice, that I did not know the customs and I did not own a zebu, so I would like to give him merely this envelope. Tsiaketraky beamed approval with all his gold teeth. He announced that this was obviously a zebu. I said, "Only a little one." I couldn't remember if you are supposed to boast that you are giving a great big present or sound deprecating.

Valiotaky's eldest daughter, Claudine Sana, hugged me, saying that she had nine children and *lots* of grandchildren.

"I have four children of my own!" I countered proudly.

"Only four? Well, I guess some people study and some have kids. But it is wonderful that you will come and take lots of photos, and we will have lots of dancing!"

At the intimate family funeral? Really?

At least I would have moral support. Richard had just retired after twenty years at the United Nations. He was coming for an actual *holiday* in Madagascar. I greeted him at the airplane: "Wonderful you're here! Now we can go to a funeral together!"

We arrived at the village on the chosen auspicious day, October 4, 2000, along with Philibert Tsimamandro, the anthropologist. Valiotaky and his daughter seated the three of us on a mat in a scrap of shade, our backs to a house just across from the dead man's house, where the coffin lay. The air erupted with gunfire as a herd of fifty zebu careered out of the distance, apparently stampeding straight at us. Young men ran behind, firing blank cartridges into the air. Others careered along beside the herd, whacking the beasts with sticks to make them gallop even faster. On either side of the village's main street some three hundred people stood lined up with their backs to the house walls, whooping and cheering as the herd thundered past. This was the intimate family — so far. As each branch of the clan arrived, they stampeded their own zebus through the village. Nine different times — some seven hundred animals. The gristle and fat of the humps were the highest points, then the tangle of horns and rolling eyes and hooves thundering in the dust. One toddler strayed into the dusty street. Its mother streaked out, snatched it up, sprinted back to safety, and slapped the child soundly in her relief, as another seventy animals, centering on an enormous rufous-red bull, hurtled by. This time Valiotaky himself, in his antique gray coat, ran too, whacking the beasts with all the vigor of a young man despite his seventy years.

"Isn't it marvelous!" exulted Philibert. "This is the dance of the cattle! They circle around the dead man's house so that everyone can admire them."

Richard exclaimed, "Running the bulls at Pamplona isn't a patch on this!"

When the cattle ended their "dance," women sitting at the doors of the low house where the dead man lay in his coffin smiled across at us and waved. Other women began to light fires for the cauldrons of maize meal to be cooked for the festive lunch, pouring in water from bright lavender and orange plastic buckets. Women clustered against the houses in the scant late morning shade began to chatter and laugh. A row of men sat under a temporary line of dry trees that had been cut and planted for shade. Most of them wore an ancient, faded dark jacket and hat over a shirt of sorts and either shorts or an embroidered loincloth. Formal dress in every country reflects past fashions. At English weddings men wear frock coats; at Tandroy funerals men wear loincloths. They sagely commented to each other on the size of the herds and the stature of the biggest bulls.

Valiotaky and another of the dead man's brothers danced a boasting dance before the row of men. Valiotaky stamped his heels and thudded his spear butt on the ground, chanting about the prowess of his herd, the number of his grandchildren, and the splendor of the funeral he was giving his dead brother. Dance-oratory-boastings are hugely appreciated and finely judged, because everyone knows how many cattle you actually do have.

On our side, another temporary stick marquee shaded most of the women relatives. Everyone wore her best white plastic pretend-straw hat with a fringe of plastic lace and a bright red rose, a pink or blue Save the Seals or Amoco Oil T-shirt, a wrap skirt of emerald or scarlet or magenta or saffron or canary yellow, and bare feet. They stood shoulder to shoulder, chanting, as Valiotaky arrived to dance in the sun before them, knees up to his chest with each step, stamping the ground with his rawhide sandals. A woman came forward to answer his dance. Her bottom stuck out and her back bent in an S-curve, hands at shoulder height, palms fluttering suggestively — at least the sound of the laughter suggested that it was exceedingly suggestive.

A gang of women broke loose to dance before Philibert.

"It would be very, very shameful not to return the dance," he said. A woman put her hat down on the ground; Philibert put a banknote in it. He got up and danced before the women, while they cheered and clapped.

The dancing went on for maybe three hours of the morning. Philibert explained that each branch of the family, besides showing off its zebus, must give a zebu to the host. A son-in-law is particularly obligated to give a zebu at such a ceremony. In fact, funerals transfer wealth from the young and poor to the old and rich. If the son-in-law does not have a zebu, he loses his wife. The father-in-law takes his daughter's hand and announces publicly that the marriage is broken, because the son-in-law is unworthy. The woman is now on offer to anyone willing to pay what she is worth. In zebus.

"Besides just losing his wife," added Philibert, "it is very, very shameful for a Tandroy to be humiliated in public."

"Wait a minute — that can't be what really happens! Wouldn't it be better just not to come?"

"It would be very, very dangerous not to come. The son-in-law would offend his father-in-law, who is more powerful. And of course it would be very, very shameful."

"So what happens if the son-in-law is actually poor?"

"Then he can go first to his father-in-law in private. A kind father-in-law may lend a zebu, which can then be given back to him, and the son-in-law will pay later when he has savings. Or else he can work to help prepare the funeral. The poor son-in-law will be sent to walk fifteen or twenty kilometers to market and then back again carrying a fifty-kilo sack of rice to feed the guests. You must understand that funerals are the most important means of uniting the family. Tonight, when all the cousins are together, if a boy and girl cousin are here without their spouses, they expect to sleep with each other. If one wants to and the other does not, he or she has to pay the cousin money as a forfeit. I think I may stay the night."

"Are you a cousin?"

"In Androy, everyone is related somehow."

As the sun reached noon, the hour when a man stands on his own shadow, the massive luncheon of goat meat and rice and cornmeal was nearly ready. Three professional, or at least habitual, musicians took over in the shade of the stick awning. The leader, in green sateen shorts, a loincloth over his shorts, and the little conical Tandroy straw hat, bent almost double while his feet pounded the ground. In his mouth a silver police whistle shrieked the rhythm as he breathed in time with the pounding feet. His two henchmen played violins. That is, their instruments had all the pieces of violins: a bow strung with sisal fiber, box, bridge, neck, tuning pegs, three strings each. Each piece was hand-carved from square pieces of dusty gray fantiolotse wood. The bows themselves were made of some springy stem that could have fired arrows. The musicians improvised praise songs to everybody in sight, at least everybody who would respond appropriately by giving them money.

Richard rose to the occasion. Literally. He took the stick and the spear out of the leader's two hands and danced to him, making Tugan (a Kenyan tribe) straight-bodied leaps into the air over and over, using the tendons as springs. So there was the parrot-green horizontal whistling Tandroy, about as black as a person can be, and a white-haired, white-shirted Englishman, driving straight up and down, and by that time and in that sun about as pink as people get. A couple of hundred members of Valiotaky's family cheered and whooped and congratulated Richard. He did admit that Valiotaky, a still older man, had him beat. It looked as though Valiotaky was planning to dance all day and on into the night.

Before we left, we paid our respects to the dead. The coffin lay in the house where it had been for the past six weeks. The family offered lambas to cover the coffin, and more cloths were hung on a kind of clothesline above it. Mostly these were *lambamena,* "red cloths." They are actually a traditional chestnut brown with thin stripes of white, yellow, and turquoise. Inside the coffin, people say, is now only earth, only the body. The spirit of the dead man has already started its journey toward the Ancestors.

"I missed the taok'omby, the hecatomb, the spearing of the cattle!" We rolled into the village to find Philibert loudly upset. "I missed it!" he exclaimed as soon as he saw us. "It happened at the first light of dawn!" That meant Richard and I had missed it too. I tried to be chagrined amid the rush of relief. Valiotaky walked us a quarter of a mile up the sand track and very proudly announced that twenty-three zebu had been sacrificed. Indeed, among the bushes lay twenty-three large dead oxen.

As I did not see the hecatomb, let me quote one who has — the administrator and anthropologist Marcel Guérin, who fell in love with Androy. He left in 1961, just two years before I first came. At a village perhaps ten miles north of the Lucky Baobab, he wrote:

> In the dawn, about thirty zebu are ranged in a circle around the tomb. They are not restrained, but simply held at the end of a long cord. In the splendor of the rising sun, several young men, almost nude and beautiful as gods, advance spear in hand. They are the sons and sons-in-law of the dead man. In perfect synchrony, they stop several meters from the animals. Thrown suddenly, with the precision of Athenian javelins, the Antandroy spear passes the ribs to reach the heart. Mortally wounded beasts fall without a cry. Men rush forward to cut their throats. Unforgettable scene of savage and exultant grandeur, repeated so long as there is an animal left standing. The hand, repeating the gesture of famous ancestors, is still as sure. Each time, death comes in less than thirty seconds.

Something like that happened here. Each animal lay as if sleeping, with a small hole in its left side, felled with a single spear thrust and no marks of struggle in the sand.

This was at the end of the public funeral, two weeks after the family meeting with the dance of the cattle. The village space was filled with brush shelters erected for the thousand people in attendance. Newly built corrals held the guests' offerings of zebu, including the beautiful red bull. In among them milled a herd of goats, because Valiotaky had to give a counter-present of a goat for each zebu received. I had watched one goat being slaughtered, its head held down over a basin to catch the scarlet jugular blood, the spear thrust so quick that its yellow eyes had time to look only slightly surprised before they went fixed and still.

About seven A.M. the road filled with a parade of people, greeting each other cheerily after the long night of dancing. Tsiaketraky was stunning in a black pseudo-silk blouson jacket and a Western black felt hat. Madame Tsoloho, his wife, wore a gold necklace with a filigree gold cross, made by an Indian jeweler, over her black blouse inset with openwork lace and a shawl around her shoulders. She had gold teeth, though not as many as her husband, and a demure smile. Gold used to be the prerogative of the Tandroy royal clan, bringing evil to any commoner who wore it, but Tsiaketraky has the right to it, being of noble birth. Philibert homed in with his camcorder. "How modern! How modern! I must film them to show how the Tandroy can change!" he breathed. He-Who-Cannot-Be-Thrown-to-Earth magisterially chatted with the other old men, giving out assurance and advice. I suddenly saw him as the Mother-and-Father morphed into an august Supreme Court judge, his silky black jacket a black gown — still, of course, with his glorious golden smile.

The sun already beat hotly on men clustered around each zebu carcass. They stripped the hide so that the body shone in its sheath of white connective tissue. Then they took axes to parcel out chunks of flesh and bone into the guests' waiting baskets. It was like a fairground, with a prize for everyone: beef to take home, as people thanked their hosts for a splendid funeral.

The family members themselves may not eat the meat of the sacrificed cattle, which belong to the dead man. He now takes them as his own herd, to be rich and proud in the land of the Ancestors. I could not watch the decapitations, when the severed heads were tossed on top of each other in an untidy pile of staring eyes and curved horns, each neck a cross section of dreadful red with a protruding spine. The heads would be offered up at the Ancestors' tomb.

Interlude: a village awakes. The next morning the red sun slipped above the horizon, bathing the silvery gray planks of the little leaning houses in pink. A little girl wrapped in a lamba tiptoed between the houses, carrying a glowing brand from an early fire to start the fire in her own house. Her house stood right by the lucky baobab, an old tree with an almost hollow trunk, hung with charms, and a colony of yellow Sakalava weaverbirds beginning to chatter in its branches.

Women rose. They set out mortars and began to pound the corn. "There are so many people, and so calm!" Richard mused. Four corn mortars were pounded in turn by women and little girls, usually with two women in an alternating rhythm of thudding pestles. Richard counted forty people standing quietly around the mortars, almost all of them children.

"Remember our life in New York?" he asked me. "Hurry, hurry, HURRY! Eat up your breakfast, you'll be late for school, Dad is going to be late for the office, you shouldn't have stayed up watching TV if you are going to be late, don't forget your homework GOODBYE."

Here nobody hurried. The breakfast was cooked in common cauldrons, then the cornmeal mush with some sort of gravy was spooned into large enamel bowls. Ten people or so sat around each bowl, each eating with his own spoon. Sexes were segregated, men and boys together, women together, and one bowl with a whole lot of little toddlers somewhat supervised by the women. "Don't you think you would be a whole different person if you grew up with other children always around, not as an only child?" asked Richard.

"I'd have hated it," I growled. "I always think I would have survived village life only if I could be the witch doctor."

Much was being done, with no fuss, almost no noise. Men and women began to dismantle the rows of temporary shelters left from the feast. They piled the brushy shade trees on a *charetty*, an ox cart, to be stored outside the village to the west for firewood. The support poles, tall dried sisal-flower stalks, went in the other direction, where they would be built into new cattle corrals. No materials from the celebration were wasted.

The Puritan ethic might have judged all those people-days spent working on the funeral as wasted. Should the energy have been spent on productive labor, and all that wealth invested in something with a high rate of return? The people of the Lucky Baobab have invested instead in social solidarity — and their Ancestor's afterlife.

Cattle lowed from the corrals on the east side of the village, the sacred side. Young men were taking the cows out to pasture — a huge herd, easily two hundred head, making their way in the direction of the river. The sun, now yellow, gleamed amid the dust rising from their hooves. Next the goats emerged, in two herds, and were sent another way, and finally the fat-tailed sheep. A toddler, maybe two and a half years old, in a little dirty turquoise shirt down to the middle of his fat tummy and nothing else at all, staggered toward the goats brandishing a long whippy stick. He tapped the nearest ones with it and succeeded in starting about twenty of them plodding off in the wrong direction. An eight-year-old boy in yellow shorts laughed and picked up a stick and brought them to a stop, in spite of the macho toddler's furious efforts to be a real herder and keep them going. Then the eight-year-old started to play tag to distract the two-year-old, in total good humor.

Older children began to dress for school. The Lucky Baobab has a real school, with eighty children enrolled from there and from Tsiaketraky's adjoining village. Philibert organized its building when he was local representative of the International Labor Orgnization, as part of the development program after the famine of '92. Tsiaketraky and Valiotaky, as village presidents, made sure their villages and their grandchildren got a school. Valiotaky, too, had been a sisal commander — not in the fields but in the factory. They knew the value of education.

A visiting nurse arrived that morning on her regular rounds. She set up a mother-and-baby clinic under a tree, a shady one, not the twisted baobab, its dappled light falling on her smooth face and the rough wood table that was her consulting room. She weighed the babies in a baby-trouser swing hung from a tree branch. Then she plotted each one's growth on a Road to Health chart: red, yellow, and green bands rising to show the baby's optimal weight at each stage. Each mother keeps her child's chart and turns up proudly at clinic visits with chart and child. After the exam the nurse dosed the babies with polio vaccine.

Strange to think that the ex–deputy director of UNICEF was watching her. When Richard and I lived in Zambia, thirty-some years before, we tested out a prototype Road to Health chart with our own first child. When we lived in New York, Richard helped launch the worldwide move to growth charts, oral rehydration for diarrhea, and vaccination for childhood diseases. At the United Nations Summit for Children of 1990, seventy-one heads of state pledged to bring the Child Survival Revolution to every village. And now we happened to be here on a morning when a health worker gave out polio vaccine by the lucky baobab.

The village knew what it could mean to vanquish polio. A bright-eyed boy, Valiotaky's grandson, Joseph Fagnazogna, hopped around on a homemade crutch with a crossbar on which he could rest the foot of his withered right leg. He was in school, in fourth grade, ready to make his way with his brains. The boy's Malagasy name means "He-Who-Knows-How-to-Hold-On."

UNICEF has graphed, country by country and region by region, how the death rate drops and then, ten or twenty years later, the birth rate drops as people gain hope that their children will survive. Not only survive but succeed. It is not war and famine that change people's lives, it is quiet, reassuring prosperity. To me the Village of the Lucky Baobab seemed on the cusp of that change.

Richard beamed in all directions. "It would be easy to idealize this," he admitted. "But I keep thinking about Marx's phrase 'the idiocy of rural life.' This is anything but idiot. This is whole."

"No foreigners have ever had permission before to visit the cemetery." By foreigners Valiotaky meant anyone outside of the family clan.

Later that morning he came to invite us, wearing a new shirt! Black-and-white zebra stripes! Crisp and clean! Could we take formal photographs of the mourning family? The other men, in their own clean shirts, grinned and leaned on each other like a barbershop chorus of twenty. The women sported new white straw hats with black bands. Men sat and shaved each other's heads, round and round in circular furrows. Women did their hair in beautiful new coiffures of piled and knotted braids. Within the circles of the white mourning hats, the women became a shifting geometry of black and white. One teenager nearly missed the group photo. She rushed up, wrapping herself in a lamba printed with an enormous pink 25,000-franc note, her mourning hat square on her head like an Edwardian skimmer, and her smile the cat-in-the-cream delight of the girl who knows she is the village beauty. Now just why was she so long in bed?

The cemetery stood two kilometers away, not in one of those dense sacred thickets left among the sisal but in a patch of scrub forest where cattle graze unchecked. This sort of place can trap an unwary visitor. Anyone who approached its precincts would wind up owing the family ancestors another zebu.

We met the *mpisoro,* the spiritual leader of the clan, by definition the oldest man of the oldest generation. He looked much younger than Valiotaky. In a place where men can marry women thirty years younger, kinship is classed by paternal generation, with a huge spread of actual ages. (How anyone ever thought that tribal people have "primitive" minds is a mystery to me. In Androy it would take all my brainpower just to remember who to avoid incest with.)

The mpisoro palpably disapproved of Richard and me. He set off in silence, a stick over his shoulder. From it dangled a whole heart from one of the sacrificed zebu, tied to the stick by the aorta. He stopped beyond the new tomb to cook the heart in strips over embers. He would place it on or at the *hazomanga*, the sacred pointed pole that is the clan's center. Phallic, of course. These patriarchal people do not need Freud to point that out to them. The mpisoro forbade us to approach the hazomanga, which was right. It was already a huge concession to allow us near the graves at all. We did not need to intrude on what they still wished to keep sacred and private. I could hardly fail to notice that among the two dozen people at the cemetery, I was the only woman.

Many tombs in the south of Madagascar are huge constructions, rectangles of stone or cement with sculptures of airplanes, zebu, or other powerful objects. These "exposed" tombs are open to public view, often near roads. In Valiotaky's clan, tombs are hidden in the forest. They are called *tseke,* which means "wooden palisade." Valiotaky's brother's tseke, made of breast-high pointed poles, measured about twenty-five feet on each side. The poles were trunks of termite-resistant trees brought all the way from the rainforest: more than a hundred poles on each of the four sides. In the northeast corner of the tseke stood the tomb proper, a little larger than the coffin. The family were now mixing cement to roof it over. Later they would take whitewash and red paint to make it look like a house. A Western house, with windows.

Valiotaky gave us a tour of the cemetery. The oldest and to my eye the grandest tseke held male and female standing stones at the palisade's head and foot, the male one a slab some three meters high. Not so grand as the stone Monsieur de Heaulme put up to commemorate the founding of Berenty plantation, but still a huge jagged finger pointing at the sky. Valiotaky, however, was more impressed with the next tomb. It also had standing stones, but each was a beam of reinforced concrete, the steel rods protruding skyward from the ends. Valiotaky said that only a very rich person could afford concrete memorial posts — and it was Monsieur Jean de Heaulme who gave concrete for the tombs of Valiotaky's parents.

Two ox carts drew up. The first one held the twenty-three severed zebu heads from yesterday's slaughter. They were already clean bone, white skull fronts with horns attached, what anthropologists call a bucrane. Men nailed them one by one onto tall poles inside the tseke palisade. The back of each bucrane showed the round, curly imprint of the steer's brain — in size somewhere between a softball and a hardball, not much for an animal of that bulk. The zebu pulling the cart did not seem perturbed, or rather the black one with white spots didn't, while the white one with black spots fought even being brought to be yoked. Shows how placid animals of little brain can be.

The other cart's load was contrastingly Western: an oil drum full of water, painted bright green with a bright yellow top, a thirty-pound bag of cement, and a lovely lavender bucket for mixing it all up. Also a premade cement cross — it turns out the dead man was actually Christian! His was the kind of restrained funeral you might expect for a Christian, one in which they did not slaughter his *whole* herd.

When the tomb is at last complete, the family will leave the cemetery in single file without looking backward toward death. The Ancestor enters into his final home. He will take care of the family forever after.

Epilogue

2002, 2003

༄༅

July 4, 2002: Since February Antananarivo has been under siege. On December 16, 2001, Madagascar elected a new president, Marc Ravalo-manana. He is a self-made millionaire, founder of the largest Mala-gasy-owned enterprise in the country. His Tiko brand of dairy prod-ucts and soft drinks can be found even in the smallest towns that boast a refrigerator. His aging rival, President Ratsiraka, who ruled for most of the time after 1975, soured over the years; the idealistic young frigate captain who was first elected turned into a venal old admiral. The ad-miral's ruling party bought and commandeered votes in every election — practices that no longer merit comment. Even so, official counts placed the new man, the Yogurt King, ahead in five of the six prov-inces. Madagascar has the French electoral system, in which many can-didates compete in a first round, then the two front-runners in a sec-ond election, until one gains more than half of the votes. The old president expected to win the second round by the usual means. The challenger claimed that a fair electoral count would show he already had fifty-two percent, an absolute majority. He should be declared president.

The Yogurt King's supporters came out in force. For two solid months, the main avenue of Antananarivo filled with cheering crowds:

first fifty thousand, then a hundred thousand, then two hundred thousand. Some days the town was declared "Dead City"; no shops or offices opened and no traffic moved. In the tradition of the pink sunhat revolt ten years before, people made speeches and sang all morning, then went home for lunch. There was no looting, no rioting, no violence. No policemen or soldiers. Policemen came to the rallies, but out of uniform, bringing their families. And the crowds actually cleaned up the avenue before they went home!

Ravalomanana proclaimed Christian nonviolence and democracy as his platform. He promised to turn the country toward efficiency, honesty, and even cleanliness, like his own yogurt business, like Antananarivo itself in the years when he was mayor of the town. The people of the capital cheered and cheered. On May 6, 2002, he inaugurated his official presidency in the great soccer stadium of Mahamasina, where de Gaulle long ago promised Madagascar independence.

Admiral Ratsiraka, the outgoing ruler, did not give up, however. He retreated to his home base, the port of Toamasina. The governors of the other coastal provinces supported him. His men blew up bridges and set up barricades on all roads leading to the capital. All seven roads. That meant no goods and, above all, no gas for cars or diesel fuel for machinery could reach Antananarivo.

Traffic stopped. The modern economy stopped. At least eighty thousand of the hundred thousand jobs in Antananarivo's free trade zone disappeared. Tourism evaporated. The only people making money were Ratsiraka's militia manning the road barricades. They charged a "tax" for transporting fuel past the barricades. At the most precarious bridges, the ones with no detour through the riverbed, porters carried liter bottles of gasoline across rickety planks to trucks waiting on the other side. Over and over, at each bridge. In the West we have forgotten what "highway robbery" meant originally. Fuel did begin to arrive in the capital, at three, five, even ten times its price at the ports. The people of Antananarivo walked everywhere and made jokes about how pleasant it was to be free of traffic jams, trying not to let the coastal people think they could be crushed. Neighborhood watches went on guard in the capital. Hanta's twin sons, who were six-month-old babies when I first met her, are now nineteen. Their aikido martial arts class volunteered, along with many others, to help guard their president against assassination.

The new president finally realized that he would have to use force to retake the provinces. Town after town fell to his soldiers almost without a shot being fired. The populace, after all, did vote for him. In almost any other country there would have been a bloodbath. Madagascar counted less than a hundred violent deaths over six months, in all the separate skirmishes. In one battle Ravalomanana's forces seized a hilltop on the road to Antseranana (Diego Suarez) defended by two machine guns. After eight fatalities on one side and four on the other, and one woman bystander shot, the defenders ran away. Make no mistake, however; this was real civil war, with generals who went to school together fighting on opposite sides — but that was the biggest battle.

The real toll is not counted, nor does it make the newspapers. There are no medicines. Prices for staple foods skyrocket. On both sides, family income disappears. Casualties in this war have little to do with guns and soldiers. A strain of flu broke out in a rural part of the plateau, with hundreds of reported deaths. "MYSTERY KILLER VIRUS" one headline in England announced, over a snippet of news. I called the Institut Pasteur to ask about the flu, which was actually a well-known strain. Anyone in the West who got a flu shot in recent years was already immunized against it. The killer's identity is no mystery. It is poverty, lethal when combined with any passing germ.

Foreign powers have a great deal to answer for. The outside world delayed and delayed recognizing Ravalomanana's new-broom government. Last week, on Madagascar's Independence Day, June 26, the United States and several other nations did recognize him. (One piece of foreign policy that makes me proud of my country!) Among African leaders, Abdoulaye Wade, president of Senegal, was outspoken in saying that Ravalomanana is the democratically elected leader. However, the Organization of African Unity would not abandon its old friend Ratsiraka, one of its longest-standing members. Neither would the French government, up till yesterday, July 3. This in spite of the fact that Ratsiraka split his country playing the race card of coastal people against the plateau, that he ruined the economy by hanging on long after he lost the physical battle as well as the moral one, and that he made himself ridiculous, as well as hated, by hiring a dozen notorious French mercenaries to try to bolster his sagging troops. The mercenaries were notorious enough that France was already watching their leader. France ordered their plane to return before it ever reached Madagascar.

Ex-president Ratsiraka is still holed up in Toamasina. His daughter Sophie goes about in a camouflage suit paying off his militia, while Ravalomanana's soldiers close in. But yesterday the French minister of foreign affairs flew to Madagascar to sign economic agreements. He addressed Marc Ravalomanana as "Monsieur le Président." That is the final bastion: the ex-colonial power says yes. A strange world.

July 5, 2002: He's gone! Ratsiraka has left! Today the ex-president flew away with all of his cronies who could cram themselves into one small airplane. He is heading off to asylum at his home in the fashionable Parisian suburb of Neuilly.

Now all the new president has to do is rebuild his country.

July 6, 2002: Last Friday I had a wonderful long phone conversation with Jean and Aline de Heaulme. They are in France, visiting Aline's mother in Périgord. I confess that when I heard they were in France, I felt a pang of fear. After telling the story of their lives as commitment to Madagascar, telling that story not just to me, but to themselves, had they been driven away finally by the crisis of the two presidents? Berenty — oh, what will become of Berenty? No, they tell me, they have not gone into exile. Monsieur will return to Madagascar in ten days, and Madame after a month with her eighty-nine-year-old mother.

They report that there has been no violence in Fort Dauphin. Indeed there was remarkably little violence elsewhere. Newspapers tell us news only when there are deaths and do not report how much of life has carried on. The de Heaulmes say that the Malagasy are even sweeter than usual toward Europeans, knowing that the eventual reconstruction of the country will need foreign help.

The sisal industry has kept going. World prices have risen since 2000, so it is again making a profit. The port of Fort Dauphin stayed open during the crisis. It has its own hinterland, so its fuel and exports did not suffer. Tourism, of course, has fallen to zero, a catastrophic year with no income at all. Still, the de Heaulmes have managed to keep on half their tourist staff, all the core people, awaiting better times. Their daughters, Bénédicte and Claire, who are solidly involved in the tourist business, are also waiting out the crisis. Henry and Philippe both work to equip the modern economy, so they have been hit even harder. But that sector should revive under a government promising business efficiency.

The de Heaulmes' adventure was in getting to France! With just a single flight per week to Réunion and from there to Paris, they had to arrive in Antananarivo in time for the flight they'd booked. Flights within the country had been canceled for lack of fuel, so they loaded up their four-by-four with extra jerry cans and set off north from Fort Dauphin. It took them twenty-two hours to drive the first two hundred kilometers, the reverse of the journey Jean de Heaulme first made as a six-month-old baby in the sidecar of his father's Harley-Davidson.

The delay was not caused by violence. The holdup was the terrible roads. Oh, yes, they had to show their papers to the police as they entered and left each town, along with a very modest banknote. But no threats, no aggravation — instead, the unquenchable smiles and courtesy of Madagascar. Oh, yes, some bridges were out. But it was the dry season. No problem for a couple in their seventies to steer their four-by-four through riverbeds. In fact, they took along two Canadians who had been stranded in Fort Dauphin. In Tana the Canadians went straight to their tour agency to say they'd recommend the overland trip, with its glorious scenery and its lovely Malagasy welcome, to any future travelers.

Goodbye, I said to Jean and Aline. Goodbye! See you in September, for the lemur birth season!

October 12, 2003: After a year in office, the businessman-president rides a wave of optimism. Ravalomanana has clamped down on corruption. All government accounts are now inspected, which led to some high-profile firings. The names of dead people have been taken off the voters' rolls. The president's new policies support all kinds of business investment. The World Bank underwrites his ambitious program to pave the roads. A new port might even revitalize the whole region of Fort Dauphin! A government school like many, many other new schools has already been built in Berenty — a shining white school with bright blue doors. Little by little, educated Malagasy are returning from abroad, to bring their talents and their energy back to their own home.

The president announced a month ago that Madagascar will triple its protected forest estate, from 1.7 million to 6 million hectares. That is ten percent of Madagascar, practically all that remains in indigenous forest. It is one of the most stunning single efforts a country has ever made for conservation. Ravalomanana is farsighted enough to see that forests are the infrastructure of his people's well-being, just as much as roads and schools.

And now even tiny Berenty has a new regime. Philippe de Heaulme is gradually taking over its management from his father, Jean. I sense that Jean is feeling a little of the shock he gave his own father with plans for improved business efficiency. Of course, this time the technology is computers, not adding machines.

Philippe is very conscious that a business must make a profit to survive. He also shares his family's archaic code of responsibility. Berenty's profits are not a faceless balance sheet. They represent wealth, and the de Heaulmes' power to invest — and also a future for hundreds of other families who proclaim, "Here the children inherit."

The de Heaulmes and the Tandroy inherit Berenty from their ancestors; so do the lemurs. There have been four generations of Madagascar de Heaulmes, four centuries of Tandroy. Lemurs can claim at least forty million years, perhaps a hundred million. Theirs is the prior claim. Tandroy tell stories that the lemurs' ancestors were once people. In Western science, our ancestors were once lemurs. In the longest view, we are one.

Berenty is a microcosm. It is a forest fragment, vulnerable to any change — to windstorms and fire and epidemics, to inbreeding after population crash, which in turn increases vulnerability. Scientifically, it is a scale model of the great national reserves of Madagascar or of the world. Even large reserves are becoming islands of natural habitat, under threat from forces far beyond themselves. At Berenty the forest is drying out. We do not know if the drying comes from local causes or from worldwide climate change or from deforestation around the headwaters of the Mandrare River. The days when the river ran two and three meters deep throughout the wet season are over. There are almost no crocodiles left, to most people's relief, but also none of the huge marbled eels that gave Berenty its name. Flood crests on the Mandrare that used to stretch over days now pass Berenty in hours. Still, a little of the forest remains as I first saw it.

Berenty is also a microcosm of people's relationship to nature in a world where salaries and economic opportunity are replacing the old ways. As the south moves toward greater prosperity, so that people can invest in health and schooling for their families, Berenty shows one way that even salaried people may live beside a forest and its denizens. Berenty is a place where local traditions, a modern economy, the struggles between Madagascar's presidents — and even aid and recognition from Paris and Washington — impinge on the lives of all.

But as far as the descendants of Frightful Fan and Cream Puff are concerned, each day is a day. In the bitter season when their babies are born, they claim space as their own, each in her own way. Fan the ringtail marks the scent-posts of her troop's inherited territory; Cream Puff the brown lemur muscles others out of the particular feeding tree she happens to be in. Cream Puff is still her group's alpha female; Fan's sister Finch, also an alpha, is raising twins. They nurse their babies from their own energy and from the season-end fruit of the tamarind trees.

In mid-September the tamarinds turn yellow-gold — autumn color in a tropical forest's springtime. The trees blaze bright in the sun. Then a wind springs up. The golden rain has come. Tiny yellow tamarind leaves fill the air, swirling as they fall. Now the branches are bare for two or three weeks.

Tree by tree, and soon over all the reserve, new leaves peek through. New leaves are pink, like a rosy veil flung over the ancient gnarled branches. At last the lemurs eat their fill of protein-rich rose-pink leaves, and of nectared flowers that spring on the *Crataeva* trees and on the barbed vines of the lover-of-men. Troop warfare slows. There is enough for all.

Month-old ringtail babies totter off their mothers. They begin to play at hop-and-pop all through siesta time, while their parents doze and groom. They do not look to past or future, only to the warm afternoon, their playmates, and their mothers' milk, in the enchanted forest.

APPENDIX

NOTES

INDEX

Appendix

Scientists Who Have Worked at Berenty

ᏫᎢᎥᎥᏯ

This is a partial list. For many of the scientists, Berenty was their first field work, which led on to other research interests. Current students are not included.

Blumenfeld-Jones, Katherine, University of Arizona
Budnitz, Norman, Duke University
Charles-Dominique, Pierre, Muséum National d'Histoire Naturelle, Paris
Crawford, Graham, San Francisco Zoological Society
Crowley, Helen, Wildlife Conservation Society, U.S.
Durrell, Lee, Durrell Wildlife Conservation Trust, U.K.
Harcourt, Caroline, Oxford Brookes University
Gould, Lisa, University of Victoria
Hirai, Hirohisa, Kyoto University
Hladik, Marcel, Muséum National d'Histoire Naturelle, Paris
Hood, Laura, Defenders of Wildlife
Jolly, Alison, University of Sussex
Hiraiwa-Hasegawa, Mariko, Senshu University
Kilbourn, Annaliese, Wildlife Conservation Society, U.S.
Klopfer, Peter, Duke University
Koyama, Naoki, Kyoto University
Long, Emma, Hong Kong University

Martin, Robert, Field Museum, Chicago
Mertl-Millhollen, Anne, Kansas State University
Mulder, Raoul, Australian National University
Nakamichi, Masayuki, Osaka University
Nussbaum, Ronald, University of Michigan
Oda, Ryo, University of Tokyo
O'Connor, Sheila, World Wildlife Fund, Switzerland
Pereira, Michael, Latin School of Chicago
Petter, Jean-Jacques, Zoological Gardens, Paris
Pigeon, Mark, Muséum National d'Histoire Naturelle, Paris
Pride, Ethan, Princeton University
Racey, Paul, Aberdeen University
Rakotoarisoa, Soava, Cornell University
Rakototiana, Lys, University of Madagascar
Rasamimanana, Hantanirina, University of Madagascar
Richard, Alison, Cambridge University
Russell, Jay, Coton de Tulear Club of America
Saito, Chiemi, Miyagi University
Simmen, Bruno, Muséum National d'Histoire Naturelle, Paris
Sussman, Robert, Washington University
Ward, Philip, Harvard University
Wood, Gwendolyn, Rockefeller University

Notes

⟨ɔɯɯɔ⟩

This book is based on my own memories, letters, and diaries, on conversations, and on formal interviews. I consulted historical texts where possible, but most of the book relies on individual testimony, and people do rearrange their memories.

Information from other people is credited in the notes. "Pers. comm.," personal communication, indicates that the conversation was casual, though I often summarized it in writing shortly afterward. Interviews were formal inquiries. I opened each interview by explaining that I was asking questions in order to write this book and then requested permission to publish the material. If the interview was tape-recorded, I recorded the permission. I did not usually ask for a signature; many of the people I interviewed have a well-founded distrust of signing papers. Local speech uses the same word for "paper" and for "government form." All interviews except those with the de Heaulme, Marcou, and Ramahatra families were conducted in public places. (Eighty people can be in earshot of a speaker seated on a village mat, if the children crowd tight enough.) Anything said was meant to be public, not secret or confidential.

Where I have presented personal communications as quoted speech, it is the gist of the speech as I understood it, not the speaker's actual words. All translations from French are my own. I do not speak Malagasy. Interviews with non-French speakers were conducted through interpreters — a kind of three-way conversation — Hanta Rasamimanana (a university lecturer); Benoît Damy, Andreas Miha, and Sylvestre Mbola (Berenty guides); and Georges Heurtebize and Philibert Tsimamandro (anthropologists). Some interviews were tape-recorded, but because that can be inhibiting, many were not. I circled back to important subjects as a partial check on interpreters' overinterpretation. I have condensed and excerpted interviews for this text. I took extensive written notes as people talked, but obviously I cannot capture the style of Malagasy speech. English speakers can get some of the flavor of this most metaphorical language from the paean of praise to Malagasy in Tyson, P. (2000), *The Eighth Continent* (New York: HarperCollins), 240–52.

I have avoided worrying about the ongoing anthropological controversies over the roles of anthropologist, translator, and informant, and the influence of their personal stances. I hope that those roles become clear from the text. The form of the book emerged from the picture I wanted to paint of a multicultural, multispecies society rather than from self-reflective anthropologizing.

1. Lemurs Just Behind Their Houses

4   My continuing thanks to the Lanier and Essig families for their friendship as well as for their attempts to teach me French French.

5   tamarinds, which Malagasy call *kily: Tamarindus indica.*

5   acacia: *benono; Acacia rovumae.*

6   marbled eel: *renty; Anguilla marmorata.* Behavioral information from Paul Loiselle, curator of fishes, New York Aquarium, pers. comm.

6   Madagascar flying fox: *fanihy; Pteropus rufus.*

6   white sifaka: *sifaka; Propithecus verreauxi verreauxi.*

7   ringtailed lemurs: *maky, Lemur catta.*

8   boa constrictor: Madagascar ground boa, *dô; Acrantophis madagascariensis.*

2. Meow! Sifaka! Pig-Grunt-Grunt-Grunt-Grunt

9   mouse lemurs: *Tsitsiky; Microcebus murinus, Microcebus griseorufus.* Lepilemurs: *tsididy; Lepilemur leucopus.* Red-fronted brown lemurs: *gidro; Eulemur fulvus rufus.* Collared brown lemurs: *Eulemur fulvus collaris,* sometimes given specific status as *Eulemur collaris.*

10 easiest place to film: Wildlife films shot entirely at Berenty include the story of Sapphire, the albino infant ringtail in Warren, A. (1997a), *A Lemur's Tale* (Bristol, U.K.: Partridge Films); Warren, A. (1997b), *The Dance of the Sifaka* (Bristol, U.K.: Partridge Films); Rees, D. (2002), *Gangland Lemurs* (Bristol, U.K.: BBC); Salisbury, M. (1985), *Spirits of the Forest* (Bristol, U.K.: BBC). Films based in part at Berenty include most documentaries on Madagascar, for example, Attenborough, D. (1979), *Life on Earth,* primates episode; *Life of the Mammals* (2003), arboreal episode. There are also Japanese, German, Chilean, Italian, and French films, notably Hulot, N. (1993), *Madagascar* (Paris: Okavango). The Disney publicity film was Hecx, D. (2000), *Madagascar, les Derniers Lémuriens* (Paris: VM Productions).

11 photomural: The photographer was Paul Richard, 1964.

12 Museum of Androy: The museum was created by Georges Heurtebize of the Musée d'Art et d'Archéologie, Antananarivo, and Sarah Fee, Smithsonian Institution, Washington, with Jean-Aimé Rakotoarisoa, director of the Musée d'Art et d'Archéologie.

12   Dina, Takayō, and Erica: Dina Felantsoa, École Normale Supérieur, Antananarivo; Takayō Soma, Kyoto University; and Erica Moret, University of Sussex.

14   West Side Gang: Rees, *Gangland Lemurs.*

14   boundaries seem to be fixed: Jolly, A., and E. Pride (1999), "Troop Histories and Range Inertia of *Lemur catta* at Berenty: a 33-year perspective," *International Journal of Primatology* 20: 359–73; Mertl-Millhollen, A. S. (2000), "Tradition in *Lemur catta* Behavior at Berenty Reserve, Madagascar." *International Journal of Primatology* 21: 287–98.

14   which bitch: I give here just one sample of ringtailed lemur behavior. A fuller account would give equal weight to findings from Beza Mahafaly Special Reserve, where the ringtails live at lower population density and are less clearly territorial. The best overall summary is Sauther, M. L., et al. (1999), "The Socioecology of the Ringtailed Lemur: Thirty-five Years of Research," *Evolutionary Anthropology* 8: 120–32. Most research on white sifaka comes from Beza. However, that area has different ecology, a different Malagasy tribe, and a different political background. I hope that someday Joel Ratsirarson of the University of Antananarivo; Robert and Linda Sussman, of Washington University, St. Louis; and Alison Richard, ex-provost of Yale, now vice-chancellor of Cambridge University, will write their own Beza memoirs.

16   A-Team civil war: Hood, L. C., and A. Jolly (1995), "Troop Fission in Female *Lemur catta* at Berenty Reserve, Madagascar," *International Journal of Primatology* 16: 997–1016. Students who have studied the A-Team and parallel troops in birth seasons from 1989 to 2000 include Scott Bizily, Marisa Braun, Tracy Dubovick, Dina Felantsoa, Shea Gardner, Danika Harris, Katherin Heavers, Laura Hood, Alice LaTrobe Bateman, Oliver Maxwell, Christopher Mills, Erica Moret, Hee-Joo Park, Ethan Pride, Doris Rabenandrasana, Hanitraniala Ramanantsoa, Clovis Randriambelona, Tahirina Randriamboavonjy, Teresa Williamson, and Gwendolyn Wood.

17   "zip up wounds": Michael Pereira, pers. comm.

19   Geek's infanticide: Hood, L. C. (1994), "Infanticide among Ringtailed Lemurs (*Lemur catta*) at Berenty Reserve, Madagascar," *American Journal of Primatology* 33: 65–69; Pereira, M. E., and M. L. Weiss (1991), "Female Mate Choice, Male Migration, and the Threat of Infanticide in Ringtailed Lemurs," *Behavioural Ecology and Sociobiology* 28: 141–52; Jolly, A., et al. (2000), "Infant Killing, Wounding, and Predation in *Eulemur* and *Lemur*." *International Journal of Primatology* 21: 21–40.

21   "targeted subordinate": See Vick, L. G., and M. E. Pereira, (1989), "Episodic Targeted Aggression and the Histories of Lemur Social Groups," *Behavioural Ecology and Sociobiology* 25: 3–12.

23   inhibition of the ringtail males: Jolly, A. (1966), *Lemur Behavior* (Chicago: University of Chicago Press); Kappeler, P. M. (1990), "Female Dominance in *Lemur catta:* More Than Just Female Feeding Priority?" *Folia primatologica* 55: 92–95.

24   stress hormones: Cavigelli, S. (1999), "Behavioural Patterns Associated with

Faecal Cortisol Levels in Free-ranging Ring-tailed Lemurs, *Lemur catta*," *Animal Behaviour* 57: 935–44.; Ethan Pride, pers. comm.

25 as old as fifteen: Record lemur life span in captivity is thirty-three years, at Duke University Primate Center. The difference in longevity between cosseted captives and their wild cousins is like the difference in lifespan between humans of the first and third worlds.

25 Some eighty-eight million: Storey, M., et al. (1995), "Timing of Hot Spot–Related Volcanism and the Breakup of Madagascar and India," *Science* 267: 852–55; Djordje Grujic, Halifax University, pers. comm.

26 titanothere dinosaurs: Flynn, J., and D. W. Krause (2000), "Monsters of Madagascar," *National Geographic* 198 (Aug.): 44–57; Rogers, K. C., and C. A. Forster (2001), "The Last of the Dinosaur Titans: A New Sauropod from Madagascar," *Nature* 412: 530–34.

27 lemurs in the north: Fleagle, J. G. (1988), *Primate Adaptation and Evolution* (San Diego: Academic Press); Krause, D. W., et al. (1997), "Cosmopolitanism among Late Cretaceous Mammals," *Nature* 390: 504–7.

27 on Madagascar itself: Martin, R. D. (2000), "Origins, Diversity and Relationships of Lemurs," *International Journal of Primatology* 21: 1021–50; Sussman, R. W. (1995), How Primates Invented the Rainforest and Vice Versa," in *Creatures of the Dark: The Nocturnal Prosimians,* ed. L. Alterman, G. A. Doyle, and M. K. Izard (New York: Plenum), 1–10; Masters, J. C., et al. (1995), "Pattern and Process in Strepsirhine Phylogeny," in ibid., 31–44; Bearder, S. K. (1999), "Physical and Social Diversity among Nocturnal Primates: A New View Based on Long-Term Research," *Primates* 40: 267–82.

28 last giant lemur: Flacourt, E. de (1661), *Histoire de la Grande Ile de Madagascar* (Troyes: Nicolas Oudot), as quoted in Tattersall, I. (1982), *The Primates of Madagascar* (New York: Columbia University Press), 207.

28 wondering if she'd gone deaf: Chantal de Heaulme Dupray, pers. comm.

28 red-fronted brown lemurs: *gidro: Eulemur fulvus rufus.*

29 magpie robin: *Copsychus albospecularis;* toulou bird: Madagascar coucal, *Centropus toulou;* hook-billed vanga: *Vanga curvirostris.*

30 Fort Dauphin subspecies: *gidro; Eulemur fulvus collaris* or *Eulemur collaris.*

31 Brown lemurs have: Overdorff, D. J. (1996), "Ecological Correlates to Social Structure in Two Lemur Species in Madagascar," *American Journal of Physical Anthropology* 100: 487–506; Pereira, M. E., and P. M. Kappeler (1997), "Divergent Systems of Agonistic Behavior in Lemurid Primates," *Behaviour* 134: 225–74; Pereira, M. E., and C. A. McGlynn (1997), "Special Relationships Instead of Female Dominance for Redfronted Lemurs, *Eulemur fulvus rufus,*" *American Journal of Primatology* 43: 239–58; Overdorff, D. J. (1998), "Are *Eulemur* Species Pairbonded? Social Organization and Mating Strategies in *Eulemur fulvus rufus* from 1988 to 1995 in Southeast Madagascar," *American Journal of Physical Anthropology* 105: 153–67.

31 song for the browns:

Allons les troupes d'*Eulemur fulvus!*
Emparons-nous de la forêt!

Contre nous les preux *Lemur catta:*
L'êtandard annelé est levé!
L'êtandard annelé est levé!
Entendez-vous du haut de la branche
Mugir l'élégant sifaká?
Il saute jusque sur nos pas!
Vienne l'heure de notre revanche!
Grognons, compagnons!
Grognons comme des cochons!
Mangeons, mangeons
Feuilles, fruits, et fleurs!
Pissons sur les chercheurs!

31 "It's got to be": S. Pinkus, interview Oct. 2000.
32 serial killer: Pitts, A. (1995), "Predation by *Eulemur fulvus rufus* on an Infant *Lemur catta* at Berenty, Madagascar," *Folia primatologica* 65: 169–71.
34 forest survey of 1972: Budnitz, N., and K. Dainis (1975), "*Lemur catta:* Ecology and Behavior," in *Lemur Biology,* ed. I. Tattersall and R. W. Sussman (New York, Plenum), 219–36; Mertl-Millhollen, A. S., et al. (1979), "Population and Territory Stability of the *Lemur catta* at Berenty, Madagascar," *Folia primatologica* 31: 106–22.

3. He Wanted the Whole Forest!

36 "Madame, if you want": Tsiaketraky, interview Sept. 9, 1999.
36 thornbush: *roy; Mimosa delicatula.*
37 crocodiles: *voay; Crocodilus niloticus.* Jean de Heaulme, interview Sept. 8, 1999; Geneviève, guardienne of Naturaliste House, pers. comm.
39 "My grandfather said": Jaona Tsiminono, interview Sept. 18, 1999.
41 what were the sanctions: Rehomaha, interview Sept. 15, 1999.
41 "They took our land": Rekanoky, interview Sept. 25, 1999.
42 "Kokolampo are not Ancestors": Tsiaketraky, interview Sept. 9, 1999. See also Tsimamandro, P. (1998), "Le Kokolampo: essai d'interpretation d'une phénomène de possession dans la région Est de l'Androy," unpublished paper, Anthropology Department, University of Tulear, Tulear, Madagascar.
43 Fort Dauphin began: My account is mainly from Guët, I. (1888). *Les Origines de l'Île Bourbon et la Colonisation Française à Madagascar* (Paris: Charles Bayle); and Souchu de Rennefort, U. (1688 [1988]), *Histoire des Indes Orientales* (Sainte-Clothilde, Réunion: ARS Terres Créoles). Isidore Guët quotes every ship captain's letter of the time. He lists the twenty-one survivors of the Fort Dauphin massacre who reached Réunion together. De Rennefort was sent in 1664 to establish Louis XIV's Grand Compagnie des Indes Orientales in Madagascar, confronting the fractious inhabitants of the fort. I adopt his opinions of Dian Manangue (Lord Manangue) and La Case, as well as his account of the reasons for the massacre. De Rennefort was an accomplished travel writer, de-

lighting in what he saw. Many later administrators (including modern aid donors) have echoed his pleas for reliable logistical support, competent officials,
and close attention to local politics. His final prescription for a successful colony is less often echoed: marry local women and settle down.

43 "extremely large trees": Souchu de Rennefort, *Histoire des Indes Orientales,* 62.

44 Sieur Etienne: Flacourt, E. de (1661), *Histoire de la Grande Île de Madagascar*
(Troyes: Nicolas Oudot); Flacourt, E. de (1661 [1995]), *Histoire de la Grande
Île de Madagascar,* edition annotée et présentée par Claude Allibert (Paris:
INALCO: Karthala).

47 Jean Roland: Jean de Heaulme married Jeanne Mélanie Bourdois in the late
1600s. Their daughter Jeanne de Heaulme married Henry Boutsocq at La
Romagne in the Ardennes in 1704. Henry's son Jean Roland Boutsocq de
Heaulme, born in La Romagne in 1705, emigrated to Réunion in 1729, became
officer of the Grand Compagnie des Indes in 1732, and died about 1773. See
http://www.le-coultre.org.

48 Françoise Châtelain de Cressy: Henry de Heaulme, Jr., pers. comm.

48 *mainty,* blacks: The most moving account of Malagasy racial relations that I
have read is a novel by the poet Rabearivelo, which to me ranks with Faulkner's
novels of the American south. It shows how Merina pride was wounded all
the more because they had always looked down on their own black slaves, until they in turn were reduced to a kind of slavery by the French conquest.
Rabearivelo (1927; 1987), *L'Interférence* (Paris: Hatier).

49 last Merina queen: Barrier, M.-F. (1996), *Ranavalo, Dernière Reine de Madagascar* (Paris: Éditions Balland).

49 French expeditionary force: Knight, E. F. (1896), *Madagascar in War Time: The
"Times" Special Correspondent's Experiences among the Hovas During the French
Invasion of 1895* (London: Longmans, Green); Ellis, S. (1985), *The Rising of the
Red Shawls: A Revolt in Madagascar* (Cambridge: Cambridge University Press);
Brown, M. (1995), *A History of Madagascar* (London: Damien Tunnicliffe).

50 she gave the filanzana: The filanzana that took the queen from Antananarivo to
the port at Tamatave had a specially constructed palanquin cover so that people
could not see her, probably over a basket-shaped seat commonly used by
women. The one she gave Mme. de Villentroy was a simpler version for town
use.

51 A photograph captured them: Chantal de Heaulme Dupray, interview Jan. 5,
2000.

51 decision to leave Réunion: Henry de Heaulme, Sr., pers. comm.

52 Soeur Gabrielle: Jean de Heaulme, interview Sept. 27, 1999; Chantal Dupray,
interview Jan. 5, 2000.

53 children must stay silent: Henry de Heaulme, Jr., remarked after reading this
manuscript: "Your conception of my grandfather is not what mine is, but you
knew him before I did — and when you met, you were already old enough to
speak at table."

53 Marie-Céleste Bellier: Chantal Dupray, pers. comm.

54 confiscated twelve thousand firearms: Verin, P. (1990), *Madagascar,* 3rd ed.
(Paris: Karthala).

55 a wonderful solution: Jolly, A. (1980), *A World Like Our Own: Man and Nature in Madagascar* (New Haven: Yale University Press).

55 Raymond Decary: Decary, R. (1930), *L'Androy* (Paris: Société d'Éditions Géographiques, Maritimes, et Coloniales); Decary, R. (1969), *Souvenirs et Croquis de la Terre Malgache* (Paris: Éditions Maritimes et d'Outre-Mer).

55 Middleton argues: Middleton, K. (1999), "Who Killed 'Malagasy Cactus'? Science, Environment and Colonialism in Southern Madagascar (1924–1930)," *Journal of Southern African Studies* 25: 215–48. Middleton identifies the prickly pear as *Opuntia dillenii*, or *O. vulgaris = O. monacantha.* She surmises that the cochineal was a wild strain, not the more benign *Dactylopius coccus,* which produces a sustainable crop of commercial red dye.

56 windscreen apparently drenched: Mme. Kurt Jenny, pers. comm.

57 Tandroy began to migrate: Guerin, M. (1969), *Les Transformations Socio-Economique de l'Androy (Extrème-Sud de Madagascar)* (Tananarive: Université de Madagascar). Official recruiters came from the sugar fields of Nosy Be, at the other end of the island, offering laborers signup gifts of five meters of cloth, one thousand francs, and a blanket.

57 Madame de Heaulme settled: Henry de Heaulme, Jr., pers. comm.

58 *fantiolotse: Alluaudia procera* and *A. ascendens.*

58 Rehomaha: interview, Sept. 15, 1999.

60 *katrafay: Cedrelopsis grevei.*

61 forced labor: Middleton, "Who Killed 'Malagasy Cactus'?"; Brown, *History of Madagascar.* The French did not invent forced labor in Madagascar. Andrianampoinimerina, the king who united the Merina people from 1797 on, built irrigation canals and roads using a *corvée* system called *fanompoana,* which continued until the end of the monarchy.

61 "concessions": The rules are described in de Guitaut, A. (undated) "Souvenirs des Guitaut à Madagascar," unpublished manuscript, kindly loaned by Bertrand de Guitaut.

62 Jules Ferry: Ferry (1832–93) had promoted democratic unification of France, both regionally and between social classes, through education. When he inaugurated compulsory primary education, many rural French children spoke only a local patois. Colonial education in standardized, official French was an extension of the prescription Ferry offered for France itself. I thank Isabelle Essig for pointing this out to me.

62 Cayla "imposed": Martin du Gard, M. (1949), *La Carte Impériale: Histoire de la France Outre-Mer, 1940–1945* (Paris: Éditions André Bonne), 262.

63 Jaona Tsiminono: Interview Sept. 18, 1999.

64 *Sasavy: Salvadora angustifolia.*

64 *Filo-filo: Azima tetracantha.*

64 *tehalahy: Capparis sp.*

64 official minimum wage: In 2000 it was 125,000 Malagasy francs per month. The dollar equivalent varies from about $19 to $24.

65 German steam engine: Its plaque reads No. 8905–10 ATM 1928, AKT. GES. TH. FLOETHER, GASSEN.

66 "so termite-ridden": de Guitaut, "Souvenirs des Guitaut."

66 sisal: *Agave sisalana* or *A. rigida.*
67 villages on higher ground: Jean de Heaulme, interview Sept. 26, 2000.
67 Baobabs: *za; Adansonia za.* Elephant's-foot trees: *Pachypodium lemeri, P. geayi.* Tenrec: *tandraka; Tenrec ecaudatus.*
68 their tractor driver: Toliha, pers. comm.
68 Three-cornered palm: *Neodypsis decaryi* has a native range of only about ten square miles.
68 Rosy periwinkles: *Catharanthus roseus.* The first specimens were sent by Flacourt from Fort Dauphin as a present for Louis XIV's garden at Versailles. The plant was sent to the Chelsea Physic Garden, thence to Kew, and out to the French and English empires. Linneaus's type specimen reposed for a while in the botanical collection of Jean-Jacques Rousseau. Now local healers all over the world use it for everything from stomachaches to abortions. In Western medicine, its chemicals are the chief line of defense against childhood leukemia and related blood cancers. Allorges-Boiteau, L., pers. comm.; Jolly, *A World Like Our Own.*
69 "as a young man dancing": Jaona Tsiminono, interview Sept. 1999.

4. *I Licked His Feet Very Heartily*

72 Kotomahasolo: interview Sept. 26, 1999.
74 prime modern account: Heurtebize, G. (1986), *Histoire des Afomarolahy Extrême-sud de Madagascar* (Paris: CNRS); Heurtebize, G. (1997), *Marriage et Deuil dans l'Extrême-sud de Madagascar* (Paris: L'Harmattan).
75 ostracized from the paternal clan: Guérin, M. (1977), *Le Defi: L'Androy et l'appel à la vie* (Fianarantsoa, Madagascar: Librairie Ambozontany).
75 women do not act submissive: Dreo, P. (1976), *Pélandrova . . .* (Montvilliers, France: Éditions du CEDS); Heurtebize (1997), *Marriage et Deuil;* Fee, S. (2000), "Note introductive sur le genre à Madagascar," *Taloha (Revue du Musée d'Art et d'Archéologie de Madagascar),* Repenser "la femme malgache," numéro spéciale: 13–39; Middleton, K. (2000), "The Rights and Wrongs of Loin-washing," ibid.: 63–99. Karen Godden (pers. comm.) suggested the importance of being raised by a stepmother.
76 "Better that a child's": Sarah Fee, pers. comm.
77 vertical chain of descent: For information about the vertebrae as well as about captives' narratives in general, I thank George Macdonald, director of the National Museum of Man in Ottawa. He and his wife, Joanne, came on this trip, as did John Walker of the Berenty lemur project and student Oliver Maxwell.
77 oldest Tandroy style: Heurtebize, G. (1992), *L'Habitat Traditionelle Tandroy* (Antananarivo: Centre d'Information et de Documentation Technique), available from the National Museum of Man, Ottawa, Canada. The Tandroy adoption of the Sakalava spirit cult is explained at the Museum of Androy, Berenty.
78 King Kirindra: In Drury's original account of his time with the Tandroy, Malagasy names are Cockneyfied. He prefixes nobles' names with *Deaan,* equivalent to the modern *Andriana,* or Lord. I use translations from Molet-Sauvaget, with

modern spellings from Parker Pearson and Godden. Of more than a hundred names recorded by Drury, I mention only:

> King Kirindra: Deaan Crindo, Roandriankirindra (King Stubborn), death name probably Roandriamanajoma (King Friday)
> Lord Miavaro: Deaan Mevarrow, Andrianamiavaro (Lord Magnanimous)
> Lord Sambo: Deaan Sambo, Andrianasambo (Lord Ship, a sign of the zodiac)

The two principal women in Drury's life, his wife and his mistress, are never named.

78 "seem to have been planted": Drury, R. (1729), *Madagascar, or Robert Drury's Journal during Fifteen Years' Captivity on that Island* (London, W. Meadow); Drury, R. (1890), *Madagascar, or Robert Drury's Journal, during Fifteen Years Captivity on that Island, Edited with an Introduction and Notes by Capt. Pasfield Oliver, R.A.* (London, T. Fisher Unwin).

80 Drury's "Transcriber": The transcriber's preface declares that the book is not "such another Romance as *Robinson Crusoe* . . . It is nothing else but a plain, honest Narrative of Matter of Fact." *Robinson Crusoe* starts with the same claim! The case for Defoe as transcriber is made by Moore, J. R. (1939), *Defoe in the Pillory and Other Studies* (Bloomington: Indiana University Press); Defoe, D. (1992), *Madagascar, ou le Journal de Robert Drury,* traduction critique par Anne Molet-Sauvaget (Paris: Éditions l'Harmattan). For the case against Defoe, see Baine, R. M. (1974), "Daniel Defoe and Robert Drury's Journal," *Texas Studies in Literature and Language* 16: 497–91; Furbank, P. N., and W. R. Owens (1988), *The Canonization of Daniel Defoe* (New Haven: Yale University Press); Furbank, P. N., and W. R. Owens (1998), *A Critical Bibliography of Daniel Defoe* (London: Pickering and Chatto).

80 parish records: A. W. Secord verified much of Drury's account by finding tax records, parish records, the crew list, Benbow's squadron logbook, the deposition of John Benbow, and John Drury's will. Secord, A. W. (1961), *Robert Drury's Journal and Other Studies* (Urbana: University of Illinois Press).

84 Only Robin and three other: People through the ages have made slaves of women and youngsters but put adult men to the sword, thinking them too hard to tame. See Oliver, R. (1999), *The African Experience* (London: Phoenix Press). Up to the account of the massacre, Drury's tale is confirmed by the "Deposition of John Benbow, made to the Authorities of the Cape of Good Hope" after his rescue from Fort Dauphin in 1607. See Leibbrandt, H.C.V. (1896), *Précis of the Archives of the Cape of Good Hope, 1696–1708* (Cape Town, South Africa).

85 *milela-padia:* Defoe (1992), *Madagascar, ou le Journal de Robert Drury.*

85 noble and ignoble directions: In Androy, east is spiritual, west secular, south noble, north ignoble. In the rest of Madagascar, north prevails over south, and the northeast corner of a house is reserved for the Ancestors. In Androy, south is most important, so the master of the house sleeps with his head to the southeast. Georges Heurtebize, pers. comm.

86   tenrecs may have more: These Malagasy insectivores resemble hedgehogs. On
      their litter size, see Eisenberg, J. F. (1981), *The Mammalian Radiations* (Chicago:
      University of Chicago Press).

87   Sambo is still: Sambo Clément, professor of sociology, University of Tulear,
      Madagascar, pers. comm.

90   Mike Parker Pearson: See Parker-Pearson, M. (1996), "Reassessing *Robert
      Drury's Journal* as a Historical Source for Southern Madagascar," *History in Af-
      rica* 23: 1–23; Parker-Pearson, M., and K. Godden (2002), *The Red Slave* (Phoe-
      nix Mill, Stroud, Gloucestershire: Sutton Publishing).

92   landscape history: Burney, D. A. (1997), "Theories and Facts Regarding Holo-
      cene Environmental Change Before and After Human Colonization," in *Natu-
      ral Change and Human Impact in Madagascar*, ed. S. M. Goodman and B. D.
      Patterson (Washington: Smithsonian Institution Press), 75–92; Leach, M., and
      J. Fairhead (2000), "Challenging Neo-Malthusian Deforestation Analyses in
      West Africa's Dynamic Forest Landscapes," *Population and Development Review*
      26: 17–43.

92   apparently from foreign parts: Flacourt and Drury both describe the kings'
      light coloring. The royal clan may have been Arab or Indian. Both the Maha-
      faly and the Tandroy say that their first kings were brothers. The brothers
      apparently quarreled over the cooking of a wild boar. The Tandroy brother,
      in a huff, claimed that pork was taboo for him. Tandroy still do not eat
      pork. Fagereng, E. (1971), *Une Famille de Dynasties Malgaches: Zafindravola,
      Maroserana, Zafibolamena, Andrevola, Zafimanely* (Oslo: Universitetsforlaget).
      However, the idea of kingship might also have African roots, from knowledge
      of the kingdom of Zimbabwe, and perhaps even of African gold. See Brown,
      M. (1995), *A History of Madagascar* (London: Damien Tunnicliffe).

94   "At length enters": The prose is surely the transcriber's, but the forest roots and
      named spirits sound authentic. For recent sorcerers' charms, see Heurtebize
      (1997), *Marriage et Deuil.*

5. I Begged My Grandmother to Tell the Governor-General

97   *Maro Taolo:* Tsiaketraky, pers. comm.; P. Tsimamandro, pers. comm.; Jean de
      Heaulme, interview Sept. 27, 1999; Madame Norosoa Rasamimanana (née
      R'abel Andrianimanana), interview Sept. 16, 1999; Chantal Dupray, interview
      Jan. 5, 2000.

98   sacrifice that dignifies death: Ramahatra, R., and Patterson, H. (1993), *Poverty
      in Madagascar* (Antananarivo: UNDP); Jean de Heaulme, interview Sept. 26,
      2000.

100   entitlement to food: Sen, A. (1981), *Poverty and Famines: An Essay on Entitle-
      ment and Deprivation* (Oxford: Clarendon Press). See also Decary, R. (1969),
      Souvenirs et Croquis de la Terre Malgache (Paris: Éditions Maritimes et d'Outre-
      Mer).

100   Cayla mobilized drafts: Ralaimihoatra, E. (1982), *Histoire de Madagascar,* 4th
      ed. (Antananarivo: Éditions de la Librairie de Madagascar).

101 French opinion swung: Martin du Gard, Maurice (1949), *La Carte Impériale: Histoire de la France Outre-Mer, 1940–1945* (Paris: Éditions André Bonne).

102 General Gallieni: Photographs of Gallieni's welcome and of the wrecked *La Perouse* are in the collection of Jean de Heaulme.

102 cruise ships: In the year 2000, five cruise ships put into Fort Dauphin, but four of them did not unload their tourists. Jean de Heaulme, pers. comm.

103 Libanona: The peninsula now holds the Centre Ecologique de Libanona, where a few lucky American undergraduates attend the School for International Training.

103 their family will not eat: Mulligan, P. (1999), "Greenwash or Blueprint? Rio Tinto in Madagascar," *IDS Bulletin* 30, no. 3 (Globalization and the Governance of the Environment): 50–57.

103 "deep muffled eruption": Harker, J. S. (1971), *Well Done, Leander* (Auckland: Collins), 108.

104 three hundred tons of food: Auphan, R.A.P., and J. Mordal (1859), *The French Navy in World War II* (Annapolis, Md.: United States Naval Institute), 203.

104 "a real privateer": Jean de Heaulme, pers. comm.

105 secure Diego Suarez: Royde-Smith, J. G. (1980), "World wars," *Encyclopaedia Britannica* 19: 942–1013; James, A.S.W.M. (1946), *The British Navies in the Second World War* (London: Longmans, Green); Churchill, W. S. (1951), *The Second World War*, vol. 4: *The Hinge of Fate* (London: Cassell); Auphan and Mordal, *French Navy in World War II*, 204; Martin du Gard, *La Carte Impériale*.

106 "The *Anthony*'s chances": James, *British Navies in the Second World War*, 153.

107 "as long as possible": Woodward, L. (1971), *British Foreign Policy in the Second World War*, vol. 2 (London: Her Majesty's Stationery Office); Martin du Gard, *La Carte Impériale*, 256.

107 "There were so many": Dr. Philibert Rakotosamimananana, pers. comm.

108 The de Guitaut family: de Guitaut, A., "Souvenirs des Guitaut à Madagascar," manuscript.

109 Chantal loved traveling: Chantal Dupray, interview Jan. 5, 2000.

110 Jean de Heaulme joined: Jean de Heaulme, interviews Sept. 15, 2000; Oct. 24, 2002.

114 turn the clock back: Ralaimihoatra, E. (1982), *Histoire de Madagascar* (Tananarive: Éditions de la Librairie de Madagascar); Emmerij, L., et al. (2001), *Ahead of the Curve* (Bloomington: Indiana University Press).

114 Robert Dama: Dama, R. (1997), "La Guerre a Anosibé-Anala," in *Témoins de l'Insurrection;* Fanony, F., and N. J. Guenier, "Antananarivo, Foi et Justice," B.P. 3832: 21–87. The Malagasy text was originally published as a pamphlet in 1967 by the Librairie Ny Nosy.

115 Maître commandeered: "Temoinage d'un Européan," Dossier 7 in Tronchon, J. (1982), *L'Insurrection Malgache de 1947: essai d'interpretation historique* (Fianarantsoa: EFA), 268–72.

115 Rabemananjara, the youngest: Declaration of Jacques Rabemananjara, Député, Sept. 27, 1947, in Tronchon, *L'Insurrection*, 284–87.

116 11,000 to 90,000 killed: Tronchon, *L'Insurrection*.

116 Patrice Ndrova: Fanony and Guenier, *Foi et Justice*, 95–97.

117 machine-gunned by French and Senegalese: There are many accounts of this massacre, since people in Moramanga knew of the initial killings in the railroad cars. The description of the shooting in the forest rests on Rakotoniaima's account; no other prisoners survived. Tronchon, *L'Insurrection,* 292–95.

118 Some still live: Maître Jean Christophe Rakotozandry, pers. comm. I thank Maître Christophe for permission to cite the list of prisoners initially condemned to death, which he prepared for his own account of the events of 1947–49. General accounts of arrests, torture, and starvation are confirmed by three survivors interviewed by Benoît Damy and one interviewed by Georges Heurtebize.

119 Prince Pierre Ramahatra: Pierre Ramahatra, interview Sept. 21, 2000.

120 Gallieni decided: Even before he arrived in Madagascar, Gallieni wrote of his intention to shoot prominent men as an example, which led to the trumped-up trial and execution of Prince Ratsimamanga and the minister of the interior, Rainandriamampandry. Gallieni is better known in Europe as the World War I hero who sent French soldiers in taxis to win the battle of the Marne.

121 Andreas, a police inspector: Several members of the Andreas family later became government ministers.

122 prominent Malagasy and Frenchmen: Pierre named them: "Zafy, Arémie; Rasaona, Edouard; Rasaname, Albert; Rabarijaouna; Dr. Raharison, Armand; Rahamatsy, Boniface. Also Dr. Giles le Meteaux, who was a French captain; Monseigneur Silva, the bishop; La Roussigny, the commander of the fort; and de Heaulme."

125 his secretary: The father of Guy Razanamasy, later mayor of Antananarivo and acting prime minister.

6. Me? I'm a Lathe Operator

127 Madame Marcou: Guy and Éliane Marcou, interview at La Monzie St. Martin, Dordogne, June 27, 2000, supplemented by interviews with Jean de Heaulme, Sept. 8 and Oct. 1, 1999.

134 Madagascar flying foxes: see Long, E. (2002), *The Feeding Ecology of* Pteropus rufus *in a Remnant Gallery Forest Surrounded by Sisal Plantations in South-East Madagascar* (Aberdeen, Scotland: University of Aberdeen).

135 Tsiaketraky: interview Sept. 23, 2000; Jean de Heaulme, interview Sept. 15, 2000.

138 Honnette: interview Sept. 1999.

141 "What courage": Chantal Dupray, interview June 27, 2000.

144 "paper bags to appear": Lalut, J. (1997), *Sont Devenus Deux Beaux Arbres à Présent* (Paris: Éditions des Écrivains Associés), 126.

144 "sometimes presented": Ibid., 129.

146 "Oh, we were young!": Jean de Heaulme, interview Sept. 15, 2000.

150 signing of the constitution: République Malgache, (1958), *Les Journées Historiques des 14–15–16 et 21 Octobre 1958* (Tananarive, République Malgache: Ser-

vice Générale de l'Information). Along with writing the constitution, the Assembly chose a seven-member Council of Government to steer the transition to independence. The French high commissioner presided, seconded by Philibert Tsiranana, soon to be Madagascar's first president. Brown, M. (1995), *A History of Madagascar* (London: Damien Tunnicliffe); Jean de Heaulme, interview, Oct. 1, 1999.

151   Rabemananajara pleaded: Rabemananajara, J. (1962), "Présence de Madagascar," in *Anthologie Africaine et Malgache,* ed. L. Hughes and C. Reygnault (Paris, Éditions Seghers), 263–66; Rabemananjara, J., "Quelques réflections sur le sous-dévelopment," ibid., 266–74. I thank Mme. Norosoa Rasamimanana for lending me this book.

151   "Beneath a bluff peasant": Brown, *History of Madagascar,* 278.

152   The genial politician: The independence parties shifted as their leaders fissioned and fused. For more detailed political history, see Brown, *A History of Madagascar.*

152   "Tomorrow you will": Ibid., 284.

7. A Very Cheap Wife

155   "To the naked feet": "Song of the Wise Children," in Kipling, R. (1940), *Rudyard Kipling's Verse, Definitive Edition* (New York: Doubleday, Doran), 89–90.

155   My letter home: Jolly, A., letter to Morris and Alison Bishop, Feb. 15, 1963. My husband remarks that my writing style hasn't changed in forty years. Of course I was trying to impress my professorial parents and to tell them that I really was all right in Madagascar.

160   In another letter home: Jolly, A., letter to Morris and Alison Bishop, Feb. 21, 1963.

160   I told my parents: Jolly, A., letter to Morris and Alison Bishop, Feb. 28, 1963.

163   Let Chantal tell it: Chantal Dupray, interview Mar. 14, 2000.

164   a girl with green eyes: Dr. Philibert Rakotosamimanana, pers. comm.

172   how colonialism attempts: Jolly, R. (1969), *Planning Education for African Development* (Nairobi: East African Publishing House).

173   conference on the environment: The conference, Malagasy Nature, World Heritage, was organized by Jean-Jacques Petter and Monique Pariente and presided over by Charles Lindbergh, then president of the World Wildlife Fund. I got into trouble by giving a paper written with Richard: "National Parks: Who Benefits and Who Pays." Lindbergh himself instructed me that of course poor people are forced to give up their land for national parks, but that should not be said in public. The African delegates, on the other hand, invited me home to stay with them.

173   book about conservation: Jolly, A. (1980), *A World Like Our Own: Man and Nature in Madagascar* (New Haven: Yale University Press).

174   hosted a whole string: In the 1970s Professor Peter Klopfer sent out Ph.D. students from Duke University Primate Center: Robert Sussmann, Norman

Budnitz, Kathryn Dainis, Lee McGeorge, Jay Russell, and Anne Mertl, joined by Alison Richard and Robert Martin from London. They found out much more about the lemurs and their forest. The density and actual ranges of the ringtail troops I had studied a dozen years earlier, however, resembled the troops Anne Mertl watched in 1975. Mertl-Millhollen, A. S., et al. (1979), "Population and Territory Stability of the *Lemur catta* at Berenty, Madagascar," *Folia Primatologica* 31: 106–22.

8. If We Hear They Hurt You, We Will Come Back with Our Spears

176 The worst night: Jean de Heaulme, interview Sept. 15, 2000.

176 Monja Jaona: Philibert Tsimamandro, pers. comm.

177 he urged the southerners: Brown, M. (1995), *A History of Madagascar* (London: Damien Tunnicliffe), 313–14.

177 Jaona Tsiminono: interview Dec. 1999.

178 bullets were water: Lahivano, pers. comm.

179 "The French not only": Brown, *History of Madagascar,* 308–9.

180 Colonel Ratsimandrava's plan: Ibid., 322–24.

184 "It is not us": Arnaud de Guitaut, letter, July 3, 1976; Aymar de Guitaut, undated letter; both courtesy of Bernard de Guitaut.

184 Jean de Heaulme told Aline: Aline de Heaulme, interview Sept. 14, 2000.

184 "Why should I go": Henry de Heaulme, pers. comm.

186 Fort Dauphin incident: Aline de Heaulme, interview Sept. 14, 2000; Monseigneur Pierre Zevaco, interview Feb. 2001.

187 two sons: Philippe de Heaulme, interview Nov. 3, 2000; Henry de Heaulme, interview Nov. 2, 2000.

188 Prison was filled: Aline de Heaulme, interview Sept. 14, 2000.

189 most poignant memory: Bénédicte de Heaulme, pers. comm. Nov. 11, 2000.

191 "There had already been": Jean de Heaulme, interview Sept. 14, 2000.

191 "Oh, no!": Alexandre Mosa, interview Sept. 27, 1999; Jean de Heaulme, interview Sept. 14, 2000.

192 "Go home": Jean de Heaulme, interview Sept. 14, 2000.

194 Aline and Bénédicte: The family's passports had been confiscated by the Malagasy government. Jean's was casually sent back by hand, by two visitors to Berenty: Norman and Janet Moore of Cambridge University, who went out to the forest to look at dragonflies. We foreign scientists knew so little of what was happening in the country that we innocently went to look at dragonflies! Norman and Janet Moore, pers. comm., Mar. 2001.

9. Our Country Is Committing Suicide

196 "Why not?": Léon Rajaobelina, interview Feb. 25, 2001; and Keith Bezanson. Léon now directs the Madagascar branch of Conservation International. He

believes in conservation. Also, conservation aid is one of the biggest economic levers in town.

200 debt payments: The Club of Paris in 2001 announced further cancellation of ninety percent of Madagascar's debts and rescheduled another tranche over twenty-three years. As with most "debt relief," this plan will take several years to actually happen. See *Revue de l'Océan Indien,* Apr. 2001.

201 Washington religious credo: The neoliberal position paper on Africa was largely drafted by Elliot Berg: World Bank (1981), *Accelerated Development in Sub-Saharan Africa: An Agenda for Action* (Washington: World Bank). One critique at the time used the word "credo" and questioned the applicability of pure neoliberal doctrine to the African situation. Allison, C., and R. Green (1983), "Stagnation and Decay in Sub-Saharan Africa: Dialogues, Dialectics and Doubts," *Institute of Development Studies Bulletin* 14: 1–10. See also George, S., and F. Sabelli (1994), *Faith and Credit: The World Bank's Secular Empire* (Boulder, Col.: Westview Press).

201 grew far worse: Per capita income in sub-Saharan Africa and Madagascar was ten percent lower in 1990 than in 1960. See United Nations Development Program (1996), *The Human Development Report 1996: Economic Growth and Human Development* (Oxford: Oxford University Press).

201 Richard went public: Jolly, R. (1985), "Adjustment with a Human Face," Barbara Ward Lecture, Society for International Development, Rome, Italy; Cornia, G. A., R. Jolly, and F. Stewart (1987), *Adjustment with a Human Face* (Oxford: Clarendon Press).

201 statistics on malnutrition: Catholic Relief Services.

202 "Our age is the first": Arnold Toynbee, quoted in Jolly, R. (2001), "The Man Behind the Vision," in *Jim Grant, UNICEF Visionary,* ed. R. Jolly (Florence, Italy: UNICEF), 64.

202 "If we can relieve": Primo Levi, quoted ibid.

203 "Monsieur J. de Heaulme": letter from Jay Russell and Lee McGeorge to Norman Budnitz and Kathryn Dainis, June 30, 1974, reprinted by permission of Kathryn Dainis and Lee McGeorge.

204 with the BBC: Jolly, A. (1983), "Tropical Time Machine," *Horizon,* BBC 2.

205 Earthwatchers loved Berenty: Long John Walker turned up in the first team. He did not just follow, he led. When the second team came, John quietly instructed newcomers. He even served as the standard measure: exactly two meters tall with his hat on. John has returned every year since. Sheila O'Connor co-led the teams while writing her Ph.D. thesis on grazing effects in forest. Her husband, Mark Pigeon, censused Berenty's one hundred species of birds. Sheila went on to head WWF's Madagascar programs, then all science policy of the U.S. WWF.

206 Rosiane H. Rasamimanana: interview May 28, 2001; Norosoa Rasamimanana, pers. comm. May 29, 2001.

211 an about-face: In the hard political years beforehand some Malagasy did continue with conservation. In 1978 the Académie Malgache, under ex-ambassador Césaire Rabenoro, invited foreign lemur-watchers for a carefully chaperoned

conference. Philippe Ravelojaona, the dean of the university's school of agron-
omy, and Guy Ramanantsoa, a forestry professor, worked with Alison Richard
of Yale and Robert Sussman of Washington University to establish a new reserve, Beza Mahafaly, that year, at the height of the xenophobia.

212 *reniala:* baobab, *Adansonia grandidieri.* That forest also contains *A. fony* and
A. za.

212 giant jumping mouse: or giant jumping rat, *Hypogeomys antanimena.* See Som-
mer, S. (1997), "Monogamy in *Hypogeomys antimena,* an Endemic Rodent of
the Deciduous Dry Forest in Western Madagascar," *Journal of Zoology* (London) 241: 301–14.

213 "committing suicide": I have wondered if the Duke was briefed from my book,
for which he wrote the preface: Jolly, A., P. Oberlé, and R. Albignac, eds.
(1984), *Madagascar: Key Environments* (Oxford: Pergamon). I quoted botanist
Rachel Rabesandratana, who exclaimed, "Our country is committing suicide!"
as she watched a forest fire. But perhaps it was just an obvious thought in the
circumstances.

214 I wrote home: A. Jolly, letter, July 8–9, 1989. I was in the group as a consultant
for the United Nations Educational, Scientific, and Cultural Organization
(UNESCO), working on plans for environmental education.

218 "The de Heaulme family has won": It was John Terborgh, a renowned Amazo-
nian ornithologist and ecologist, who suggested recognizing Berenty Reserve
with a Getty Prize.

219 *National Geographic:* Marsden, L. (1967), "Madagascar: Island at the End of the
Earth," *National Geographic* 132: 443–93; Jolly, A. (1987), "Madagascar, a World
Apart," *National Geographic* 171: 148–83; Jolly, A. (1988), "Madagascar Lemurs:
On the Edge of Survival," *National Geographic* 174: 132–61; Lanting, F. (1990),
Madagascar: A World Out of Time (New York: Aperture); Rekanoky, interview
Sept. 25, 1999.

220 the fright of her life: Chantal Dupray, interview Jan. 6, 2000.

10. SOS: Save Our South!

225 Helen Crowley: Helen is now the Madagascar representative of the Wildlife Conservation Society, 2300 Southern Blvd., Bronx, NY 10460; www.wcs
.org.

225 Wildlife Preservation Trust International: The organization, now called Wildlife Trust, is based at Lamont-Doherty Earth Observatory, 61 Rte. 9W, P.O.
Box 1000, Palisades, NY 10964; www.wpti.org.

231 Starfish: Starfish, Inc., 251 King St., Yellow Springs, OH 45387; www.starfishinc
.com.

231 Monsieur and Madame Rakotomalala: interview Sept. 14, 1999.

11. Here the Children Inherit

234 one of the poorest: Madagascar's purchasing power parity (PPP) income in 1999 was $766, which is adjusted for local prices and supposedly reflects the standard basket of goods available to an American with that income. In 1999 the per capita dollar income, a measure of the ability to buy such things as oil and gas on the world market, was $250. Madagascar's rank was 192nd and 187th, respectively, for those two measures, out of 206 countries. See World Bank (2000/2001), *World Development Report: Attacking Poverty* (New York: Oxford University Press). However, Madagascar's human development index ranked 23 points higher than its PPP income rank. See UNDP (2000), *The Human Development Report 2000: Human Rights and Human Development* (New York: Oxford University Press).

238 Tourist Front ringtails: Jolly, A., et al. (2002), "Demography of *Lemur catta* at Berenty Reserve, Madagascar: Effects of Troop Size, Habitat and Rainfall," *International Journal of Primatology* 23: 327–54.

239 "Oh, the worst": Benoît Damy, interview Oct. 1999.

241 Filomana and his wife: interview Sept. 24, 1999, and pers. comm.

242 a quarter of the acacias: Rasamimanana, H. R., et al. (2000), "Storm Damage at Berenty Reserve," *Lemur News* 5: 7–8.

245 Alexandre Mosa: interview Sept. 18, 2000.

248 always the powerhouse: Jean de Heaulme, interview on economic history with Daniel Lambert, of Quebec Madagascar Minerals, Oct. 15, 2000.

251 "You only accomplish": Jean de Heaulme, interview Oct. 12, 2000.

12. "This Is Anything But Idiot. This Is Whole"

257 Philibert Tsimamandro: His father was a chauffeur on the west coast at Morondava. In 1975, when the Morondava sisal plant closed, the father returned to Amboasary and wanted to settle in town. Philibert's aunt and uncle, conservative people who lived in a rural village, taunted him: "What will you do in Amboasary? Sell fried bread by the side of the road?" (Selling fried bread is very, very shameful to a Tandroy.) They threatened to disinherit him — ostracize him from the clan, the root of Tandroy identity — unless he came to live in the village with them. Philibert's father complied. Then Philibert left to join an older brother in town so he could go to school. The uncle and aunt were disgusted. "If you send him to school," they announced, "he will not know how to herd cattle and he will turn into a Betsileo" (a plateau tribe with more education). After the '92 famine the International Labor Organization started a school-building program. The village all turned out to meet the foreigner who was going to bring them a school and pay them with food to build it. Up drove Philibert, as ILO representative, in his Nissan four-by-four! At last his family was convinced that education could pay, though they were still a bit grudging. (Tsimamandro, pers. comm.)

261 "In the dawn": Guérin, M. (1977), *Le Defi: L'Androy et l'appel à la vie* (Fianarantsoa, Madagascar: Librairie Ambozontany), 77.
262 Sakalava weaverbirds: *Ploceus sakalava.*

Epilogue

268 under siege: This account comes from newspaper articles collected by madainfofr@yahoogroupes.fr, and from the remarkable e-mail journal of the crisis by a veteran medical missionary, Dr. Stan Quanbeck, which should be a book of its own (SALFAusa@aol.com). Hanta Rasamimanana also e-mailed accounts of life in the beleaguered capital. Frank Hawkins, of Conservation International, pointed out that in any other country this period could have been a bloodbath.

Index

ᏕᎷᏕ